Praise for *The Leftmost*

"*The Leftmost City* is a wonderful contribution to urban political theory as well as a concrete guide for how to exploit new opportunities for moving urban America forward. Without cynicism or romantic illusion, the authors use Santa Cruz to show the possibilities for community groups to exert effective local action against entrenched business interests. Thanks to their keen ethnographic eye and fast-paced narrative style, Santa Cruz becomes a laboratory for understanding how to take and hold power, and for seeing what local power can and cannot do."

> —Harvey Molotch, professor of Sociology and Metropolitan Studies,
> New York University; coauthor of *Urban Fortunes*

"*The Leftmost City* gives the reader lively prose, provocative arguments, and a fresh stream of ideas. Advocates of progressive politics will find this book a rich resource to draw on. Across the political spectrum, all will learn from the extraordinary politics of Santa Cruz, thanks to the lucid and down-to-earth instruction by authors Gendron and Domhoff."

> —Clarence N. Stone, research professor, George Washington University;
> author of *Regime Politics*

"This is a terrific book that shows how cities can chart a course between self-destruction at the hands of the 'growth at any cost' advocates while maintaining the tax base to provide social services and preserve neighborhoods. It's a lively case study of two decades of progressive government, carefully documented, reads like a novel. And along the way, Gendron and Domhoff provide a theoretical underpinning that suggests how this experience can be repeated elsewhere."

> —Pierre Clavel, professor of City and Regional Planning,
> Cornell University; author of *The Progressive City*

"*The Leftmost City* provides cogent insights on the opportunities for and persisting barriers to progressive politics at the local level. From a rigorous case study of Santa Cruz and critical analysis of urban political theory, this book offers essential reading to anyone who wants to understand and change the quality of life along with the opportunity structure in the nation's metropolitan areas."

> —Gregory D. Squires, professor of Sociology and Public Policy and
> Public Administration, George Washington University; coauthor of
> *Privileged Places: Race, Residence, and the Structure of Opportunity*

"A well-researched and richly detailed empirical case analysis, which adds an important and compelling theoretic contribution to the ongoing debate about the nature of power and governance in American cities."
—David Imbroscio, University of Louisville; coeditor of *Theories of Urban Politics*

use value - it's usefulness; purpose. SUBJECTIVE ie. cars
more qualitative than quantitative. secondary to
exchange value

exchange value - relationship to other commodities. Quantitative.
it's price.

Marx says if there is no use value to an item, it can't
have an exchange value.

THE LEFTMOST CITY

The system depends increasingly on exchange value.
Since use value is so subjective.

growth coalition is interested in EXCHANGE value
want profit

THE LEFTMOST CITY

POWER AND PROGRESSIVE POLITICS IN SANTA CRUZ

RICHARD GENDRON

DEPARTMENT OF SOCIOLOGY AND ANTHROPOLOGY
ASSUMPTION COLLEGE
WORCESTER, MA

G. WILLIAM DOMHOFF

DEPARTMENT OF SOCIOLOGY
UNIVERSITY OF CALIFORNIA
SANTA CRUZ, CA

A Member of the Perseus Books Group

Find us on the World Wide Web at www.westviewpress.com.

Westview Press books are available at special discounts for bulk
purchases in the United States by corporations, institutions, and other
organizations. For more information, please contact the Special Markets
Department at the Perseus Books Group, 2300 Chestnut Street,
Suite 200, Philadelphia, PA 19103, or call (800) 810-4145, ext. 5000,
or e-mail special.markets@perseusbooks.com.

Designed by Trish Wilkinson
Set in 10.5-point Minion

Gendron, Richard.
    The leftmost city : power and progressive politics in Santa Cruz / Richard
Gendron and G. William Domhoff.
        p.   cm.
    Includes bibliographical references and index.
    ISBN 978-0-8133-4438-6 (pbk. : alk. paper) 1. Political participation—
California—Santa Cruz. 2. Political activists—California—Santa Cruz.
3. Coalitions—California—Santa Cruz. 4. Santa Cruz (Calif.)—Politics and
government. 5. Coalitions—Case studies. 6. Progressivism (United States
politics)—Case studies. I. Domhoff, G. William. II. Title.
JS1450.S313G45 2009
320.9794'71—dc22   2008039283

10 9 8 7 6 5 4 3 2

To Ruth,
Without whose love, friendship, encouragement,
and good cheer this book could not have been written.

CONTENTS

TABLES AND MAPS

ACKNOWLEDGMENTS

A s is so often the case with books building on the myriad details that do not appear in the written record, it truly would not have been possible to write this one without the time and help of a great many people. First and foremost, we thank the several dozen local activists, elected officials, and business owners who were willing to take the time to talk to us in the early 1990s, and/or in 2007, about the political aftermath of the catastrophic earthquake that battered the downtown area in October 1989.

In addition, we are grateful to Peter Kirkup, Sally Kirkup, and Cynthia Mathews of the Downtown Neighbors Association for making available numerous documents and other personal correspondence related to this neighborhood group and the rebuilding of Santa Cruz. Ralph Meyberg of the Downtown Neighbors Association also gave us important help by providing us with archival materials on post-earthquake redevelopment efforts. Julia Anthony, a member of the board of directors of Vision Santa Cruz, the public-private partnership that rebuilt the downtown, lent us her extensive clip files on post-earthquake reconstruction.

For historical perspective and the correction of many mistakes about Santa Cruz politics, we thank several local activists and political leaders who read the entire manuscript and then endured many follow-up questions: Bruce Bratton, Denise Holbert, Gary Patton, Mike Rotkin, Andy Schiffrin, and Mardi Wormhoudt. Their careful readings and critical comments provided us with a solid reality check and brought us a better understanding of the way in which they perceived and experienced the events and decisions of which they were a vital part. The fact that they often had their own take on many of the issues we discuss helped us clarify our own arguments. In much the same way, former city planners Charles Eadie and Joe Hall read through the whole manuscript with care and provided us with new ideas, new information, and original perspectives based on their unique window on many of the conflicts. We add a further thanks to Joe for giving a revised version of the manuscript a careful reading and patiently answering many additional questions about planning problems in Santa Cruz.

We are grateful to Stanley Stevens, a map librarian at the University of California, Santa Cruz, for sharing his detailed knowledge of nineteenth-century Santa Cruz history with us and providing us with many invaluable documents. Stan not only answered dozens of questions but greatly improved our chapter on the early history of Santa Cruz through his editorial suggestions, saving us from several mistakes. He also provided a very careful proofreading of the entire manuscript. Our thanks to local historian Sandy Lydon, now retired from Cabrillo Community College, for answering several of our questions, and to Rick Hamman, author of *Central Coast Railroads*, for his many helpful comments on the chapter on Santa Cruz history. Rick added new information and also corrected many mistakes. Peter Spofford, one of the pioneer students on the University of California, Santa Cruz, campus in 1965, now retired from a career as a county administrator, helped us understand several important points about the delivery of social services in the Santa Cruz area.

For very helpful comments on the origins of the Community Studies Program at the University of California, Santa Cruz, and the role its students played in the controversy in 1969 over the widening of the coastal north-south highway that runs through Santa Cruz, we thank William H. Friedland, the sociologist who founded the program. For systematic information on the political attitudes of University of California students from the 1970s to 2004, we thank Julian L. Fernald, director of Institutional Research at the University of California, Santa Cruz, and Gregg E. Thomson, director of Student Research at the University of California, Berkeley. Bert Muhly, a former county planner and elected city official, provided maps, documents, and invaluable insights on planning and politics in the 1960s and 1970s. For their perspectives on neighborhood politics in the 1970s, we thank Sally DiGirolamo, Carole DePalma, and Shelly Hatch. For fresh insights and the correction of factual errors concerning the battle over putting a pharmacy and sundries store on the main commercial street on the west side of Santa Cruz, we thank Sally Arnold, Bruce Bratton, Geoffrey Dunn, Don Lane, and George Ow Jr. We add an extra thanks to Geoffrey for allowing us to draw on his encyclopedic knowledge of Santa Cruz and its history and for several important editorial suggestions.

For a careful reading of the first version of the manuscript and many valuable comments from their vantage point as urban sociologists, we are indebted to John Gilderbloom and Harvey Molotch. We also thank Molotch for his reading of the final version of the manuscript and for helping us to realize that our findings could be useful to those who want to think about alternative futures for American cities. We are equally indebted to Pierre Clavel, who has written extensively on power and planning in progressive cities, for comments based on his career as a professor in the Department of City and Regional Planning at Cornell University. We also benefited from suggestions by John Isbister, a former economics professor at the University of California, Santa Cruz, now the dean of social sciences at Laurentian University in Ontario, who was also a tireless Santa Cruz activist of the 1970s and 1980s.

We tip our hats to our sociology colleague and friend Craig Reinarman for many conversations in which he shared his extensive knowledge of Santa Cruz politics, and we remember with fondness another of our sociology colleagues, the late John Kitsuse, for the many times he raised important questions that brought us to think of some issues in new ways. For several important editorial suggestions and a constant reminder to tell the story in a clear and readable way, we thank Joel Domhoff, who spends much of his time helping students at the University of California, Santa Cruz, with their writing, and Lizzy Kate Gray, a graduate of UC Santa Cruz who spends much of her time studying sociology.

We thank our research assistant, Adam Schneider, for the excellent tables and superlative maps included in the book, and our editor, Alex Masulis, who made the publishing process fast, easy, and painless.

The first author would like to acknowledge the love and encouragement of his son, Jonah Gendron, who still lives on the "Left Coast" and makes occasional trips back to his old stamping grounds on the Santa Cruz campus and on Pacific Avenue. The second author would like to make the same acknowledgment for the same reasons to his children, Lynne, Lori, William P., and Joel, who help in many different ways to make Santa Cruz a better place to live and raise children.

We dedicate this book to Ruth Thibodeau. Her love and support over many years made it possible for the first author to complete his graduate studies and undertake the extensive research for this book. And her continuing love, dedication, and profound patience also made it possible to complete this project. Quite simply, this book could never have been written without her. The second author adds his thanks to Ruth for urging us to write this book and for the days in the late 1980s when they became friends through conversations about their many common academic interests and then co-taught a course in the early 1990s at the University of California, Santa Cruz, while she was finishing her PhD in social psychology.

1

~~~~~~

THE LEFTMOST
CITY IN AMERICA

Santa Cruz, California, a picturesque city of fifty-eight thousand people on the Pacific coast seventy-five miles south of San Francisco, is not paradise by any stretch of the imagination, but it's an attractive and easy place to live compared with many American cities. Nestled on a ten-mile strip of coastal shelf land between the heavily forested Santa Cruz mountains to the north and the shorelines of the beautiful Monterey Bay to the south, the city has breathtaking vistas from both its hillsides and its beaches. It also has a live-and-let-live ambience and a tolerance for personal idiosyncrasies. As the bumper stickers say, "Keep Santa Cruz weird."

The city enjoys an invigorating climate characterized by moderate temperatures year-round, with average high temperatures in the mid seventies throughout the summer months and in the low sixties through the winter. Rainfall averages thirty-two inches per year, with most of it coming in late fall, winter, and early spring, leaving many months of the year free of precipitation. The wind can be chilly at night and the fog a bit depressing when it hangs on late into the day for a week or two, but most days are sunny and clear.

Because of its beachfront setting, Santa Cruz started to be a tourist destination only a few years after California became a state in 1850, and it has long been known for its laid-back atmosphere and the honky-tonk amusement park and arcade on its beach and boardwalk, complete with an old-fashioned roller coaster—the Giant Dipper—that dates back to 1924. It's also renowned

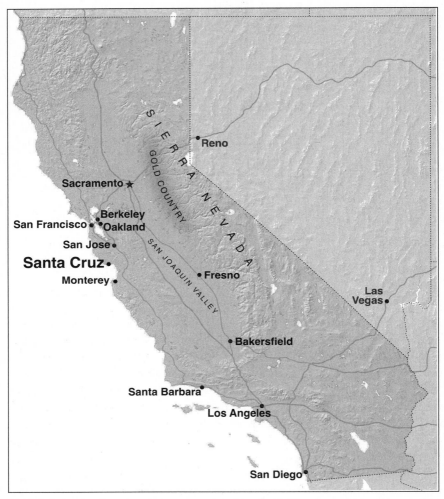

MAP 1.1 Santa Cruz in relation to major cities in California and Nevada, and to the Gold Rush country that influenced its early growth

as a great place to surf or watch surfing contests, earning it a mention in the Beach Boys' 1963 classic, "Surfin' USA." It became a college town in 1965 with the opening of a new campus of the University of California, and in the 1980s it became a bedroom community for the fabled Silicon Valley on the other side of the mountains—a thirty-five- to fifty-five-minute commute, depending on traffic and weather, over a four-lane divided highway with plenty of twists and blind curves.

If that's all there was to it, Santa Cruz would be just an enjoyable and mildly unusual urban setting, hardly worthy of any attention by social scientists interested in understanding power and politics at the urban level. But right below the surface of this seemingly placid coastal city lie nearly forty years of major political conflict and a highly atypical set of power arrangements. The once-ascendant business community lost on every major expansion project it proposed after 1968, whether the issue was widening highways, building a convention center, expanding the downtown, or constructing new housing on open spaces. Just as rare and surprising for any city of over twenty-five thousand people, business leaders long ago lost their majority on the city council as well. Instead, the council has been controlled since 1981 by an unlikely "progressive" majority—a confederation of socialist-feminists, social-welfare liberals, neighborhood activists, and environmentalists—that has put Santa Cruz further to the left for a longer period of time than any other city in the country, bar none, since at least the heyday of the New Deal.

The control of Santa Cruz city government by progressives makes the city a good place for comparing four theories of urban power developed in the 1970s. These theories were responding to an acrimonious debate triggered in the 1950s, when two iconoclastic sociologists, Floyd Hunter (1953) and C. Wright Mills (1956, Chapter 2), asserted on the basis of their research that a relatively small business elite—overlapping pyramids of corporate and real estate power in Hunter's case, the local upper class of "Main Street" business owners in Mills's scenario—was the dominant element in most cities. This claim flew in the face of the prevailing wisdom that no single group controls city governments, even though some groups do have more power than others. According to the reigning "pluralist" view of the time, elected government officials are responsive to many and varied organized constituencies, no one group dominates across a range of issues, and there are shifting coalitions from issue to issue. As the most prominent pluralist critic of Hunter and Mills put it, city politics is characterized by "dispersed inequalities" (Dahl 1961, 15). However, as dozens of studies subsequently showed, business interests usually are the ascendant force in city politics (Domhoff 1983, Chapter 7; Dreier, Mollenkopf, and Swanstrom 2004).

The fact that the organized business community regularly prevails in most cities makes Santa Cruz one of those highly atypical or deviant cases that can be revealing in two slightly different ways for studying urban power structures. First, deviant cases can eliminate some theories from consideration if the theories cannot explain unexpected events. Second, if the anomalous case introduces new factors into the equation that have not been considered by the best remaining theory or theories, then it provides the opportunity to extend and deepen those theories. We think our study is useful in both these ways.

Beyond its atypical power structure, there is a second reason why Santa Cruz is a valuable case for those who want to understand urban power structures. Eight years after the progressives took control of the city council, they faced an unprecedented challenge when the main business district was almost completely destroyed by a large earthquake that struck the San Francisco Bay Area on October 17, 1989. The quake's epicenter was just ten miles from Santa Cruz. Three people were killed in the downtown area, and nearly one half of the downtown buildings had to be torn down, with many others suffering damage that required major repairs. Stunned city residents huddled in grief as they saw the entire downtown core being fenced off. Familiar landmarks lay in a tangled heap of brick, cement, cracked beams, and broken glass. Some people talked in animated fashion as they gripped the wire fences in the days and weeks after the quake struck, others just stood and stared, and a few wiped tears from their eyes as they tried to comprehend the extent of the destruction.

The downtown businesses that didn't go bankrupt or move elsewhere had to manage for up to three years in large tent-like pavilions that were hastily erected on city parking lots just outside the cordoned area. The earthquake not only heavily damaged the downtown, making an arduous rebuilding process necessary. As accidents, scandals, and unexpected disasters often do, the quake also put power issues on the table once again, providing an opportunity to examine key elements in the power equation that are rarely accessible to outsider observers (Molotch 1970; Molotch and Lester 2004; Molotch 2004). Since no one knew that a disaster was about to occur, no one could be ready with prepared scripts and press releases. Nor could there be any prior negotiations or backroom deals. Everyone had to scramble, including the progressive leaders, and it is that scramble we describe in our fifth and sixth chapters.

Specifically, the earthquake handed the disheartened business leaders what some of them saw as a golden opportunity to regain their political ascendancy by showing how necessary they are to economic prosperity. Landowners and real estate developers in particular were invigorated with renewed hope as they negotiated with elected city officials about rebuilding the downtown. For the progressives, however, the disaster was fraught with political danger. They needed to rebuild the downtown in order to have the tax revenues to continue their ambitious social programs, but they feared and distrusted the downtown land and business owners after almost two decades of bitter political warfare. Cooperation was necessary, but as one progressive political leader told us, "There was great suspicion and paranoia about what the agendas of the various sides were." In the end, the progressives, to the surprise of many local political analysts, maintained control of city government and gained even more political power by winning elections in 1990 and 1992 that increased their majority on the seven-person city council from 5–2 to 6–1.

   The complete ascendancy of the progressive forces provides a third reason why a study of politics in Santa Cruz is highly useful, not only for theory building but for understanding the dilemmas of local progressive politics in the United States as well. That's because the progressives began to fight openly among themselves over proposed development projects, which may provide a window into why the opponents of business interests in other cities are so seldom able to succeed. Some members of the coalition, the ones we call social-welfare liberals and socialist-feminists, wanted to increase the tax base so the city could provide still more social services and affordable housing, which of course would require further intensification of land use and maybe even some new development projects on open space. But other members of the coalition, those whose primary concern was the protection of neighborhoods and the environment, wanted to keep everything as it was, which meant they wanted little or no growth. Despite these differences, which property owners and storeowners tried to exploit, the progressives remained in power and in 1994 took over the remaining pro-growth seat on the city council. Although the two wings within the progressive coalition were still doing battle with each other as of 2008 over just about every new proposed business expansion or housing development, they have never had to worry about a challenge from the business community.

   As this brief overview of Santa Cruz politics implies, there are several central research questions that this book will attempt to answer. First, how was it possible for a strongly entrenched local power structure, rooted in real estate and downtown businesses, to be defeated by a coalition led by socialist-feminists, social-welfare liberals, neighborhood activists, and environmentalists? Or, to pose the same question from the other side of the battle line in a way that may have strategic implications for future urban progressives, how could a progressive coalition block major developments and then win control of the city government? Second, how were the progressives able to retain their political power during the rebuilding process while negotiating with business leaders who were out to defeat them politically? This is a question that may have strategic implications for urban progressives who win power in the future. Third, does an understanding of the divisions within the progressive coalition in Santa Cruz hold lessons for those who want to understand why local progressives elsewhere, who played an important role in many city governments in the 1970s and 1980s, were unable to consolidate their power or create a nationwide progressive coalition?

   We attempt to answer these three main questions by using participant observation, in-depth interviews, and archival materials to construct a detailed account of the rise, decline, rebirth, and eventual demise of the business-based Santa Cruz power structure. Shortly after the earthquake, the first author spent many hours walking the perimeter of the fenced-off downtown area, observing people's interactions and talking informally with local residents and storeowners. As the rebuilding debates began in early 1990, he also attended approximately twenty-five meetings of the city council and other public hearings on the rebuilding of the downtown. From the summer of 1992 through the summer of 1993, he conducted formal, semi-structured interviews with twenty-three of the thirty-six members of the board appointed by the city council to plan for the new downtown, which included several former and current city council members. He also interviewed four progressive activists and the city manager. The interviews, which ranged in duration from thirty minutes to over three hours, were taped and transcribed (Gendron 1998). Many years later, in 2007, the second author interviewed several key activists and city staff members from the 1980s and 1990s, as well as present and former elected officials.

This interview-based research was checked and supplemented through a careful concurrent reading and clipping of local newspapers and magazines for the years 1989 to 1993 and 2005 to 2007. Finally, the relevant aspects of the history of the city were reconstructed from newspaper archives, books, and research reports reaching back to the 1840s, many of them in Special Collections in the McHenry Library at the University of California, Santa Cruz.[1]

FOUR THEORIES OF URBAN POWER

As we stated earlier, we use our findings to reconsider the major theories of urban power that developed in the 1970s in reaction to the heated argument started by Hunter (1953) and Mills (1956). We begin with a thorough account of the theory that will serve as our main starting point, *growth coalition theory*, and then turn to briefer accounts of three competing theories—*Marxist urban theory, public choice theory*, and *regime theory*. Although the four theories have some points in common, it is the differences that we will stress here. In the final chapter we present a critical assessment of the three

1. Since we have relied extensively on newspaper accounts for some types of information, including many that have no named authors, we have decided not to list them by the hundreds in the reference section unless a reporter wrote a signed article that went beyond straight reportage, or "guest columnists," often local political figures, authored an opinion article. Instead, we simply refer in the text to the name of the newspaper (e.g., *Sentinel, Surf, Independent*), the date of the article, and the page or pages on which it appears.

competing theories and then suggest changes in growth coalition theory based on our findings. We also use the final chapter to discuss the key issues that face activists who want to create progressive urban coalitions—or a nationwide progressive coalition—in the future.

Growth Coalition Theory

Growth coalition theory was first proposed in an attempt to connect traditional urban sociology's interest in markets, land use, and neighborhoods with the focus on power and hierarchy in the community power structure literature generated by the work of Hunter and Mills (Molotch 1976, 309). According to growth coalition theory, local power structures are coalitions of land-based interests and associated businesses that profit from the increasingly intensive use of land, not simply undifferentiated groups of "business leaders," as they were for Hunter, Mills, and their pluralist critics. Instead, at the core of local power structures is a set of real estate owners who try to increase the value of the land by attracting more businesses, government agencies, educational institutions, nonprofit organizations, residents, and tourists to their area. They come to believe that working together benefits all of them, although usually just enough individualists and contrarians among them cause the majority to create a united front and form an organization that can present its positions to government and try to take control of it.

Starting from the level of individual ownership of pieces of land and the formation of organizations to represent their interests, a growth coalition arises that develops an in-group feeling among its members, even though they sometimes fight among themselves over the sites for new investments or disagree on various issues not related to growth (Logan and Molotch 1987). This in-group sense is reinforced and elevated to an "us-against-them" stance by the fact that the pro-growth real estate interests and their allies—public utilities, mortgage bankers, storeowners, and newspaper publishers—soon attract a set of staunch opponents, who are most often neighborhood leaders and environmentalists. Sometimes aiding this opposition group are socialist-feminists and social-welfare liberals who have chosen to agitate at the local level for class-oriented social change or for social justice for women and people of color.

In economic terms, the "place entrepreneurs" at the center of the growth coalitions are trying to maximize "rents" from land and buildings, a concept that includes payments to developers, mortgage lenders, title companies, real estate agents, and other firms necessary to the maintenance and sale of properties. Although rents are of course a type of "profit," the goal of the growth coalition is nonetheless somewhat different from the goal of other capitalists, who produce commodities and services for sale in the marketplace. This difference leads to a complex relationship between what are at bottom two segments of an overall ownership class, a relationship which can include tension and antagonism as well as cooperation and mutual support against common opponents. In particular, industrial and service corporations can relocate if they think local wages, taxes, or business regulations are becoming too onerous for them, which can have a devastating impact on a local growth coalition. Moreover, corporate capital's ability to move from locale to locale contributes to a constant competition among cities for new capital investments, creating tensions among growth coalitions as well as between individual growth coalitions and corporations. Place entrepreneurs in rival cities also compete for new university campuses and cultural institutions, which can be as important for land values as business investments.

Growth coalitions have a well-crafted set of rationales to justify their actions to the general public. Most of all, this ideology is based on the idea that growth is about jobs, not about profits. Thanks in part to their image as responsible citizens who just want to help everyone by creating jobs, local growth coalitions sometimes include useful junior partners, most notably the building trade unions, which are often highly visible on the side of the growth coalition in battles against neighborhood groups and environmentalists. Beyond the emphasis on jobs, which unites real estate interests and construction unions, there is another ideological glue that makes the growth coalition a powerful force in shaping local economic development: the dominant belief in "value-free development" (Logan and Molotch 1987, 32–33). It just "makes sense" that land should be put to its "highest and best use." It is only natural to put the most valuable building possible on a piece of land, even if it means uprooting existing neighborhoods, an unquestioned doctrine in urban economics, planning, and architecture until the last quarter of the twentieth century.

Despite the use of a discourse about job creation and value-free development, local power structures often face considerable opposition when their expansionary projects affect neighborhoods through the introduction of commercial buildings, high rises, new highways, increased traffic, industrial pollution, noise, and other noxious factors. They incur the wrath of local residents who want to protect an established way of life that satisfies both material and psychological "use values," which include a sense of safety and security, access to an informal support network of like-minded neighbors, the assurance of good playmates for children, and the pleasure of living in an area that expresses one's status or ethnicity. As Logan and Molotch argue, "a shared interest in overlapping use values (identity, security, and so on) in a single area is a useful way to define neighborhood" (1987, 108). Even in a fast-paced and wired world, where many people find "community" in networks of friends who transcend any one geographical area, neighborhoods are imbued with deep sentiments and inspire strong attachments. "From the point of view of residents," say Logan and Molotch, "the creation and defense of use values of neighborhood is the central urban question" (1987, 99). Neighborhoods therefore frequently organize to fight new growth or any other intrusions into their way of life.

The concept of neighborhood use values is more encompassing than it may seem at first glance because it includes most of what are now called "environmental issues" within urban and suburban areas, such as struggles over redevelopment proposals, the placement of power plants, and resistance to the siting of toxic waste facilities. Just as the long-standing battle over health and safety issues in the workplace, a class-based issue, is now talked about in terms of "environmental safety" or the "workplace environment," so too it makes political sense to encompass neighborhood use values under terms such as "urban environmentalism" and "environmental justice" (e.g., Szasz 1994; Warner and Molotch 2000). This rhetorical strategy enfolds the environmentalists' original concern with forest and river conservation, wildlife preservation, open space, and air quality into a larger use-value coalition, as the case of Santa Cruz will make abundantly clear. Members of this use-value coalition agree that they are brought together by concerns with the quality of life, not profits.

Although most Americans tend to have very positive associations with concepts such as "sentiments" and "identity," the deep attachment to neighborhood does not mean neighborhood resistance to change is inherently progressive. To the contrary, it sometimes involves racial, religious, or ethnic exclusion. For example, racial covenants were quickly built into mortgages in reaction to the influx of Jewish immigrants from Eastern Europe starting in the 1880s and the northward migration of African Americans after World War I; in addition, the neighborhood groups formed in cities all over the country in the 1950s usually tried to keep out African Americans, who were migrating from the rural South in even greater numbers after World War II in search of freedom and opportunity (Gotham 2002). Later, new neighborhood groups were created in an attempt to "manage integration," which meant implementing a set of strategies to keep neighborhoods from becoming completely black by offering neighborhood amenities to the remaining white families, such as better schools, crime prevention measures, new recreational facilities, community centers, and tenant referral services (Molotch 1972).

In abstract terms, the growth coalition's pursuit of "exchange values" (land values and rents) and the neighborhood's attempts to preserve use values are inherently opposed. In addition, this conflict is the main axis around which power struggles unfold at the local level, providing the dynamic core of growth coalition theory. Landowners and developers can compromise on some growth issues, and neighborhood residents want their homes to retain their resale value, and even to rise in value, which means they are concerned about exchange values as well as use values. But the primary goal for the growth coalition remains a constant increase in rents, while the main concern for most neighborhood residents remains their "quality of life," which is in any case an essential factor in maintaining the exchange value of their homes. There are conflicts within urban areas over class-oriented and social justice issues, and there can be unusual temporary coalitions on specific development proposals, as we will see in the case of Santa Cruz, but conflicts over the exchange and use values of land are what animate the most central and enduring political struggles in any city.

In most instances, growth coalitions win out over people who are protesting intrusions into their neighborhoods because the residents grow tired of the battle or are eventually mollified by the developers with stop signs, street barriers, or parks. Those who can afford to do so move to suburbs that are primarily focused on neighborhood use values. Growth coalitions also win out because it is difficult to organize neighborhoods in general to fight a city-wide battle. People tend to focus on their own neighborhoods, as the well-known phenomenon of NIMBYism ("not in my backyard") demonstrates, and they have trouble overcoming differences arising from varying income levels and racial identifications. Moreover, it is usually not in the interest of one neighborhood organization to rally to another's cause. This is especially the case when the issue at hand is stopping an unwanted land use, because the neighborhoods that come to the aid of the first residential area might end up with the negative development in their own backyards. Nevertheless, victories for the growth coalition in battles with neighborhoods are by no means guaranteed, as Santa Cruz and several earlier cases show (Capek and Gilderbloom 1992; Clavel 1986).

The ability of growth coalitions to dominate city governments gradually increased throughout the twentieth century because of changes that pro-growth urban policy experts made in local electoral rules and governmental structures to ward off challengers. This process began as early as 1894, when leaders of growth coalitions from twenty-one cities in thirteen states met as the National Conference for Good City Government. There they formulated plans to deal with the new problems they faced as a result of rapid urbanization and the influx of immigrants into the cities as the country industrialized. In particular, they worried about the rise of ethnically based political machines, usually affiliated with the Democratic Party, but they soon grew concerned about the Socialist Party after it was founded in 1901. At their high point in 1912, the Socialists elected twelve hundred members in 340 cities across the country, including seventy-nine mayors in twenty-four different states (Weinstein 1967, 83–118).

The National Conference for Good City Government led to the formation of a permanent National Municipal League, which honed the general ideology and formulated the specific policies for local growth coalitions. Its urban policy experts claimed that the electoral changes they pulled together as a model city charter, including city-wide nonpartisan elections and the council-manager form of government, would make government both more democratic and more efficient, but their proposals had the effect of centralizing decision making, removing more governmental functions from electoral control, and decreasing the percentage of blue-collar workers and Socialists elected to city councils. Although the reformers were not immediately successful in the face of determined opposition from Democrats and Socialists, they made progress after 1912 because of the backlash against the large gains by Socialists between 1908 and 1912 and then capitalized on the fear and patriotism created by World War I to brand their opponents as unpatriotic.

By 1919, leaders in the National Municipal League and related organizations had been able to implement their model charter in 130 cities nationwide, and by 1965 over half of all cities between twenty-five thousand and two hundred fifty thousand in population were functioning under council-manager government, including Santa Cruz (Goodall 1968, 60–61; Hays 1964; Schiesl 1977; Weinstein 1962). A large-scale survey conducted in 1991 revealed that 59 percent of American cities use citywide elections and 75 percent have nonpartisan elections, once again including Santa Cruz, a clear indication of the lasting impact of the growth coalitions' efforts to reshape local government (Renner and DeSantis 1994). At the same time as these electoral changes were being implemented, an urban policy-planning network—funded by a handful of large corporation-related foundations—was created to provide facts, figures, and staffing for city governments, as well as advice on drafting legislation and creating administrative structures (Brownlow 1958; Domhoff 1978, Chapter 5; Roberts 1994; Stewart 1950).

As shown by this brief overview of how growth coalitions have dealt with challenges by changing the structure of local government and creating a nongovernmental policy-planning network, growth coalition theory starts with the idea that growth coalitions need power over both local government and neighborhoods if they are to realize their goals (Molotch 1976, 312). It is therefore not surprising that leaders of the growth coalition are major participants in local government (Logan and Molotch 1987; Molotch 1988). Neighborhoods, on the other hand, need power over government if they are to prevail in their desire to stop encroachments by growth coalitions that impinge upon residents' use values. That is, both growth coalitions and neighborhoods have deep-seated preferences that they try to maximize whenever possible, with little room for compromise.

Depending on the outcome of the clashes between growth coalitions and use-value coalitions, very different types of power structures can emerge at the local level, starting with complete dominance by growth coalitions, which was the norm in most American cities in the twentieth century. Despite all the changes in electoral rules and governmental structures, however, cities can have more liberal growth coalitions, which means there is a somewhat greater sharing of power because of the success of neighborhood-based activists and their allies (DeLeon 1992; Dreier, Mollenkopf, and Swanstrom 2004; Swanstrom 1985). In some cities even environmentalists and neighborhood activists have a major influence on government, as in the case of Santa Barbara (Warner and Molotch 2000, 30–36), or socialist-feminists, neighborhood activists, and environmentalists create a lasting coalition that becomes the dominant influence on city government, as the case of Santa Cruz attests. In fact, as long as a city can raise the revenues to provide urban services, whether by increasing taxes on wealthy residents, creating an attractive central business district that becomes a cash cow through sales taxes, or forcing developers to provide set-asides and linkages, it can function without doing the bidding of landowners and developers.

Marxist Urban Theory

decisions made @ large, powerful, international corporations is what makes really makers; what makes a difference

Several variants of a neo-Marxist structural theory arrived on the scene about the same time as growth coalition theory to argue that the earlier debate between pluralists such as Dahl and "elite theorists" such as Hunter and Mills over the concept of power had overlooked what Marxists see as the most crucial issue of all when it comes to cities: the structure of the national capitalist political economy constrains local politics, making the matter of "who governs" in the city of secondary importance. Private property, market forces, and local government's dependence on private capital provide a built-in structural advantage to those who pursue profits over and against the use-value interests of others, meaning that workers and neighborhood residents are at a distinct disadvantage when it comes to the exercise of power. As Altshuler and Luberoff (2003, 63) put it in their overview of Marxist theory, local governments must fulfill three needs of the capitalist class—economic expansion, social control of the working class, and the "reproduction" of the social and economic institutions necessary to maintain the system (cf. Castells 1977, 1978).

In theorizing about capital in relation to local government, Marxists focus on the flow of capital investments from the "primary circuit" of capital, meaning investments in productive capacity, to the "secondary circuit," meaning real estate investments (Harvey 1973, 1985). When there is a surplus of investment in the primary circuit, and a consequent decrease in profits to be derived from further investment in productive capacity, investment capital shifts to real estate. When Marxist theory turns to a discussion of conflict in the city, it describes the two opposing forces this way: preserving "the exchange values of past capitalist investments" versus having to destroy "the value of these investments in order to open up fresh room for accumulation" (Harvey 1981, 113). That is, old structures, including housing, have to be torn down to make way for bigger and more profitable structures, as codified in the "highest and best use" doctrine. For Marxist theory, then, the main conflicts are between fractions of capital and between capital and labor, rather than between a growth coalition on the one hand and neighborhoods on the other.

Although some Marxist theorists have discussed the conflict between exchange values and neighborhood use values (Lefebvre 1970; Harvey 1973, 1982), their general tendency has been to view all conflicts between growth coalitions and neighborhoods as an expression of class conflict that has been displaced from the "sphere of production" into "collective consumption" struggles (Castells 1977; Cox 1981). The conflicts between growth coalitions and neighborhoods are said to be "mere reflections of the underlying tensions between capital and labor," as in the following summary by David Harvey, perhaps the leading Marxist urban theorist of the past thirty years:

> Conflicts in the living space are, we can conclude, mere reflections of the underlying tensions between capital and labor. Appropriators and the construction faction mediate the forms of conflict—they stand between capital and labor and thereby shield the real source of tension from view. The surface appearance of conflicts around the built environment—the struggles against the landlord or against urban renewal—conceals a hidden essence that is nothing more than the struggle between capital and labor. (Harvey 1976, 289)

Although there are class conflicts within urban areas, Marxist theory leaves little or no room for an independent role for the local growth coalition or local government officials because the key issues are rooted in the nature of the national economy. Nor is there much room for actions by local residents that are not class-based.

Public Choice Theory (aka Pluralism) consumers get to decide in the end

Building on ideas put forward by the Chicago School of free-market economists, the public choice theory of urban politics begins at an individualistic level with the assumption that "the consumer-voter may be viewed as picking that community which best satisfies his preference pattern for public goods" (Tiebout 1956, 424). More exactly, the consumer-voter (which is the theory's conception of a citizen at the local level) tends to seek the best tax-to-services ratio, as do local businesses when they search for the most profitable city in which to locate. Individuals and businesses thereby end up trying to maximize their self-interest within a market of city locations in which city officials are also forced to compete if they want their cities to thrive and if they want to retain their elected positions. The result is strong competition among cities, just as there is in growth coalition theory, but for different reasons (Peterson 1981).

Within this context, public choice theory suggests that there are three main types of governmental policies at the local level: economic development, redistributive, and allocational. The competition among cities for residents and capital investment means that economic development polices are naturally the province of business leaders, with government officials in a weak and subordinate position. Yet the key factor is not that these business elites are powerful or have the capacity to cause others to do their bidding. Instead, cities have a "unitary interest" in pursuing pro-development policies because such policies fulfill the rational self-interest of everyone involved (Peterson 1981). Business elites are empowered by the people to carry out collective goals, so there is little or no conflict at the local level over growth issues.

Redistributive policies, meaning types of social spending that aid low-income individuals or disadvantaged groups, are in effect swept off the local political agenda by elected officials because they are viewed by potential investors as driving up the costs of doing business through progressive tax policies. In addition, the cost of such programs would cut into funds available for tax incentives to attract business. Therefore, according to public choice theory, redistributive policies should be formulated and implemented at the national—not the local—level (Peterson 1981).

Allocational policies concern the placement of facilities—both desired ones, such as new schools and parks, and noxious ones, such as homeless shelters, waste sites, and low-income housing projects. It is in this realm that local

"nothing conspiratorial happening in corporations.
Voting evens everything out."

political conflict occurs, in the sense of arguing and bargaining over who receives or gets stuck with what. Fundamentally, this conflict is among neighborhoods, not between growth coalitions and neighborhoods.

In general, then, the city's need for revenue in an overall economic system of intercity competition constrains urban politics to the point at which "political variables no longer become relevant to the analysis" (Peterson 1981, 12). In fact, political variables are "pointless" in explaining city policies (Peterson 1981, 147). It is policy preferences that shape politics, not vice versa. As already noted, economic development issues are so fundamental that there usually is no widespread or serious conflict over them. Although there is conflict over allocational policies, which can have important effects on the quality of life and residential property values in specific neighborhoods, this policy area is seen as secondary at best. In a fundamental sense, this theory acknowledges no "power actors" except for consumers and voters, who realize their individual preferences through markets and voting booths.

Regime Theory

group that in control. itself is the group can be arbitrary.

Reflecting the focus in political science on government and what makes it tick, as compared to the concern with general societal power in sociology, regime theory begins with the assumption that local governments in the United States do not have the capacity to govern without entering into stable public-private coalitions with one or more interest groups or social classes. Because businesses have the power to affect economic prosperity, and hence the stability of the government, through their exclusive right to make or withhold capital investments in a system of private property, they have a "systemic power" that makes them very attractive coalition partners for government officials (e.g., Elkin 1985; 1987; Stone 1989). Nevertheless, regimes based on coalitions with other private interests, including neighborhoods, are possible for government officials when citizen groups are well organized and there is high voter turnout (Stone 1993). Most generally, then, regimes are "simply the informal arrangements through which a community is governed" (Stone 2005b, 250).

Because of the presumed need for stable public-private coalitions if anything is to be accomplished at the local level, the primary emphasis in regime theory is on "power to," also called "collective power," which is based on cooperation among individuals and groups. Collective power is seen as more important than "power over," also called "distributive power," which focuses on the inherent conflicts between groups or classes that are seeking dominance over each other, as foregrounded in growth coalition theory and Marxist theory. Regime theory's emphasis on collective power, however, does not mean that all partners in a local regime have equal resources, only that power "is something created by bringing cooperating actors together, not as equal claimants, but often as unequal contributors to a shared set of purposes" (Stone 1993, 8).

This focus on collective power leads to the formulation of a "social production model" in which the issue is not domination and subordination, as it is for growth coalition theory and Marxist theory, but a capacity to act and accomplish goals (Stone 1989, 227–229). This model is contrasted with a "social control" model, which stresses distributive power and conflict in understanding urban politics. Since the costs of enforcing compliance become enormous for any group trying to dominate a large number of people on a wide range of issues, proponents of regime theory argue that social control models are based on the idea that consent and consciousness can be manipulated, an idea that they find untenable (Stone 2006, 25). In addition, according to regime theory, operating from a social control model leads progressive activists, with their concern for greater equality and participation, to overemphasize resistance as a strategy and to shortsightedly attempt to undermine the legitimacy of the established power group.

Regime theory assumes that the preferences of each competing group, because of its need for interdependence and cooperation, are less fixed and less closely tied to the group's position in the social structure than do other theories of urban power. Instead, strongly held initial preferences can evolve "through experience and therefore are informed by available opportunities" (Stone 1993, 8). It follows that the key task of governance involves bringing contending groups together so that new preferences can arise based on what is practical, feasible, and achievable.

Because there are likely to be initial differences in preferences, which leads to a potential for misunderstandings and breakdowns, regimes do not form easily and automatically. In fact, the potential partners in the coalition often have to "educate one another about the nature of their interdependence" (Stone 1993, 14). Regimes only gradually develop an "agenda," that is, a set of goals they want to accomplish. For this reason, regime theory stresses that a successful electoral coalition is not necessarily or usually a sound basis for a governing coalition; an electoral coalition may well be temporary and have very few resources to offer elected officials (Stone 1993, 2005a).

The similarities and differences among the four theories on four key issues are summarized in Table 1.1. These four issues will be commented upon throughout our discussion of the Santa Cruz case and then focused on more directly in the final chapter, when we critically evaluate the usefulness of the competing theories in explaining our findings. We have placed growth coalition theory next to regime theory in the first two columns of Table 1.1 to show that they differ completely on the importance they give to distributive power and fixed preferences, as shown in the top two rows, while agreeing that local power actors and local politics matter greatly, as shown in the bottom two rows. The table also shows that growth coalition theory and Marxist theory agree as to the primacy of distributive power and fixed preferences, but disagree about the efficacy of local power actors and the potential independence of local government from domination by economic elites. As for Marxist theory and regime theory, they are at odds on all four issues. When it comes to a comparison of Marxist theory and public choice theory, however, the seeming similarities are somewhat deceptive because Marxist theory begins with the importance of classes and distributive power, whereas public choice theory focuses on the individual level and sees power almost entirely in terms of cooperation and coordination.

[handwritten: meets needs of their own coalition]   *[handwritten: meets of needs of vast majority]*

TABLE 1.1
Key Issues in Four Theories of Urban Power

	Growth coalition theory	Regime theory	Marxist theory	Public choice theory
"Power over" is primary?	yes	no	yes	no
Fixed preferences?	yes	no	yes	yes
Local power actors matter?	yes	yes	no	no
Local government potentially independent?	yes	yes	no	no

[handwritten: Key Ideas — real estate, land-owners local; no special quality of land-owners; use value thinkers; capitalist class as a whole; maximize profit; voting everyout; meet everyone's needs]

ORGANIZATION OF THE BOOK

[handwritten: opponents?]

To see what the city of Santa Cruz has to tell us about competing theories and future progressive strategies, the next five chapters go into considerable detail about the rise and fall of its growth coalition. In Chapter 2 we give an overview of the crucial moments in the history of the downtown growth coalition from its inception in the late 1840s to the emergence of Santa Cruz as a Middle American tourist destination between 1880 and 1940. We then chronicle the city's considerable decline during World War II, when the war effort and gas rationing combined to slow growth to a trickle. The chapter reveals the many ingenious ways in which the growth coalition took a very active role in bringing investment to the city, sometimes working with one or another set of San Francisco capitalists, while never overlooking an opportunity to obtain help from the state and national governments as well. During most of this time span, the Santa Cruz growth coalition faced little or no opposition from within the city, but in 1911 it did change the structure of local government to ward off unexpected challenges from the local chapter of the Socialist Party. This is the kind of evidence for the independent power of private business interests that public choice theory and regime theory tend to ignore. The chapter also allows us to demonstrate, contrary to Marxist theory and public choice theory, that local business leaders have the autonomy—and can take the initiative—to induce growth that benefits their property holdings.

In Chapter 3 we describe how the lagging growth coalition of the 1940s projected a new future for the city as part of a nationwide effort to assure postwar prosperity, an effort coordinated by the national-level Committee for Economic Development, a newly minted leadership group of moderate conservatives within the corporate community. This cooperative arrangement shows that national-level capitalists do not dictate to local growth coalitions, and that the two segments of the business class in America often work together. As part of this process, we once again show how local growth coalitions can change the form of government when need be, a fact that is not given sufficient attention by either public choice theory or regime theory. In this chapter we also reveal that the growth coalition's successes turned out to contain the seeds of its own undoing. We show how its leaders worked night and day for nearly three years to win the competition for a new campus of the University of California, which they saw as the ideal complement to their summer-oriented tourist economy and as a basis for generating new knowledge-based local industries. Then we explain how the university instead became a competing power base, with its faculty, staff, and students providing the previously outgunned neighborhoods with the added money, expertise, and leadership to tip the scales in a more liberal direction.

The chapter next shows how the campus became a Trojan horse after 1971 as a result of the unanticipated Twenty-sixth Amendment to the Constitution, which granted voting privileges to eighteen-year-olds and made an already activist student body into an overwhelmingly progressive voting bloc, large enough to swing elections in a pro-neighborhood, pro-environment direction when it could be mobilized. At the same time, we also reveal that the cagey leaders of the growth coalition did everything they could to neutralize or discourage student voting. We also explain how and why anti-war, feminist, and other social justice activists from the 1960s and early 1970s gradually abandoned their anti-electoral stance and joined with neighborhood and environmental activists to take over the city council in 1981. We argue that the makeup of the progressive coalition refutes the Marxist claim that class struggle is the main axis of local politics. Moreover, the high level of sustained local conflict over growth from the late 1960s onward casts doubt on the key assumption of public choice theory: that growth policies are not controversial.

In Chapter 4 we discuss the successes and failures of the progressives in their first eight years in power, which add up to success on neighborhood and local social service issues, but failure in implementing any of the small steps toward socialism envisioned by the socialist-feminists, who played a leading role in creating the coalition. We also outline the electoral strategies the progressive coalition used to maintain its majority despite intense efforts to unseat it by real estate interests inside and outside the city. Contrary to public choice theory, this chapter once again shows that there is constant conflict over growth issues, even after voters have spoken against growth-inducing programs, and that redistributive policies that aid previously marginalized groups can be implemented at the local level. In addition, the chapter raises questions about regime theory because it shows it is possible for a neighborhood-based electoral coalition to function extremely well as a governing coalition without having to share power with the growth coalition, despite the systemic power of business in a capitalist economy.

In Chapter 5, we describe the behind-the-scenes power struggles over rebuilding the downtown after the earthquake. This chapter allows us to examine several key issues concerning the interplay among national economic conditions, national business organizations, downtown landowners, progressive city officials, and neighborhood and environmental activists. We note that leaders within the growth coalition reached out to allies outside the city, as both growth coalition theory and Marxist theory would expect, and especially to experts on creating commercially successful downtowns. We also see that the progressive political leaders tried to deal with divisions within their ranks over how much of the downtown area, if any, should be turned into plazas and other public spaces. Most of all, we observe that the progressives reluctantly agreed to a public-private partnership proposed by the growth coalition, but then made sure that it did not last very long and did not have the impact the ever-hopeful growth coalition envisioned for it. Contrary to regime theory, the chapter shows that both the growth coalition and the progressives had fixed and antagonistic preferences and that the two groups were only able to cooperate on a few shared issues once the major goals of the growth coalition had been put aside. At the same time, this continuing conflict over growth casts further doubt on the main claims of public choice theory.

In Chapter 6 we discuss the political dynamics of the city after the rebuilding was finally underway, showing that the growth entrepreneurs were still vanquished politically even while they prospered economically more than they ever had before. The progressives, on the other hand, had difficulty formulating their own plans because they were divided over key issues. We explain this conflict as one between class-oriented policies aimed at increasing social benefits for low-income people, which were advocated by both socialist-feminists and social-welfare liberals, and the concerns of neighborhood activists and environmentalists. When progressives on the city council from the class-oriented camp voted to approve two new commercial development projects, despite strong opposition from pro-neighborhood forces, they widened the rifts that had emerged within progressive ranks. The conflicts generated by these two development proposals are not directly relevant to assessing Marxist, public choice, or regime theories of urban power, but they do allow us to enrich growth coalition theory by exposing the nature of the divisions that often lead to the defeats suffered by the progressive opponents of growth coalitions in other cities.

As part of our account of these two post-quake conflicts in Chapter 6, we show that there can be temporary alliances between segments of the two rival coalitions. In making this point, we focus in particular on the support that socialist-feminists and social-welfare liberals received from leaders in the growth coalition because of their common interest in the intensification of land use, albeit for very different reasons. But we also note that neighborhood-oriented activists made common cause with downtown storeowners to oppose one of the two commercial development projects alluded to above. We also show how the temporary alliance between class-oriented progressives and the growth coalition resurfaced in 2005 in a failed attempt to expand a beachfront hotel. Even with all the tensions within the progressive coalition, however, the neighborhood base was not neglected, and the progressives continued to win elections. In fact, we show that neighborhood use values always proved to be the most important factor in the progressive coalition, which is strong support for growth coalition theory and a difficult point for the other three theories to incorporate.

In Chapter 7 we draw out the theoretical implications of our findings in more detail by comparing and contrasting the four theories of urban power on the four dimensions summarized in Table 1.1. We argue that the clash between pro-growth landowners and storeowners seeking exchange values and neighborhoods defending their use values is indeed the primary dynamic that animates urban politics in the United States, as growth coalition theory suggests. But we then suggest that further layers of complexity have to be added to the theory.

In the concluding section of Chapter 7, we briefly consider the problems that face future progressive activists. Based on the outcome of battles inside the progressive coalitions in Santa Cruz and other cities, we claim that neighborhood use values will set the limits on how far local progressive activists can go until such time as they can formulate a nationwide political strategy that might convince local residents to transcend their neighborhood-based perspective and come to agree with progressive values and programs on environmentalist and class-based issues. In effect, this reformulation would involve nothing less than an incorporation of local use-value politics into a national-level politics of a redistributive nature, such as government health insurance and other social benefits that are often included under the concept of a "social wage" for employees. But class-based issues concerning wages, hours, working conditions, and social benefits are not necessarily compatible with use-value politics, which is one reason why it has proven so difficult in the past for local progressives to forge a national coalition.

The problems progressives face in navigating the passage between class-based and use-value issues are demonstrated throughout our study of Santa Cruz by the compromises the class-oriented socialist-feminists and social-welfare liberals had to make in order to keep the progressive coalition in power. Based on our case study of Santa Cruz and our reading of the literature on progressive city governments, we conclude that in certain rare circumstances neighborhood and environmentally based progressive coalitions can put strong limits on local growth coalitions, or even displace them, but we also suggest the reasons why it is even rarer for progressives to take their local triumphs beyond their use-value limits.

For readers who want to know more about the history of Santa Cruz and some of the colorful personalities involved in the power struggles we chronicle, or to view photographs of the beach and boardwalk, the old Victorians, the old downtown, and the devastation caused by the 1989 earthquake, we provide a website at Leftmostcity.com, which also includes links to several local websites.

2

~~~~~~

THE RISE AND DECLINE
OF THE SANTA CRUZ
GROWTH COALITION

THE BIRTH OF A GROWTH COALITION

That Rhetoric Though

The foundation for the Santa Cruz growth coalition was created in early February 1848 by Elihu Anthony, a thirty-year-old blacksmith from Indiana and one of the first Euro-American entrepreneurs to reach the area after the United States took California away from Mexico. Anthony bought approximately fifteen acres of vacant government land a few hundred feet from the swift-flowing San Lorenzo River, paying a mere $15.62 for this prime land, including $3.62 for the filing fee and deed. He quickly built a small foundry, a merchandise store, and a hotel that attracted other new arrivals who were looking for a place to settle and work. He next subdivided half of the remaining land into twenty-one lots, which he sold over the next few years to merchandisers, hotel managers, and saloonkeepers for an average price of $100. The return on his investment, a whopping 13,334 percent, was about as good as any real estate developer before or since could ever hope for, and the new growth coalition was off to a roaring start.

Only 294 people lived on the many thousands of acres of terraces and rolling hills surrounding the river basin, 56 of them newly arrived from other parts of the United States and northern Europe. Nevertheless, Anthony had little choice about where he could buy land because most of that seemingly empty land still officially belonged to a handful of families who had been given thousands of acres in land grants just a few years earlier, mostly between 1822 and 1845, by the Spanish and Mexican governments (Reader 1998, 13). These *Californios,* as they had come to call themselves, made their living as largely self-sufficient cattle ranchers who also bartered with each other and traded hides and tallow with the sailing ships that arrived at very irregular intervals.

Still, Anthony probably could have purchased land on the bluff just above the river basin, now the predominantly residential West Side of the city, where there were only a few buildings left over from the Mexican era, along with the remnants of the struggling Mission Santa Cruz, which had been in decline ever since the Mexican government ended support for it in 1834. But the government land by the river was much cheaper and, perhaps even more important, its location gave Anthony law-enshrined "appropriative water rights" to all the free river water he needed for his foundry and the other businesses he hoped to attract to his site. He therefore made a decision that left the downtown vulnerable to destructive floods from virtually the day the area was settled until the river was channeled by the Army Corps of Engineers in the 1950s. The decision also put the downtown at the mercy of an even more devastating force of nature, earthquakes, because the soil in a floodplain quickly liquefies when the ground starts to shake, destroying the foundations of buildings in an instant. Anthony's choice of locations thus supports the new adage, "there is no such thing as a natural disaster" (Hartman and Squires 2006).

The small land boom from which Anthony benefited so handsomely was made possible by the accidental discovery of gold in January 1848 in the foothills of the Sierra Nevada Mountains, 150 miles to the northeast of Santa Cruz, at the time a four-day trip across two mountain ranges (Bean and Rawls 1983; Hutchinson 1972). The ensuing Gold Rush transformed Santa Cruz by enticing two hundred thousand people into the state over the next four years, all of whom needed food, clothing, and shelter, thereby creating a demand for the raw materials that could be extracted and the foodstuffs that could be grown in the Santa Cruz area. Gold miners also needed pick axes and other tools, so one of the first things Anthony did in his new foundry was to make ninety axes and send them to gold country on a mule pack, realizing a very large profit in the process. By 1849 he had built the first wharf for transporting foodstuffs to San Francisco, a day or two to the north by sailing ship.

In the short run, the first effect of the Gold Rush on Santa Cruz was to decrease its population by several dozen people because many recent arrivals quickly headed northward in the hopes of striking it rich. By 1850, however, the population for the county as a whole was nearing a thousand, well above pre–Gold Rush levels. At that point the fledgling town of Santa Cruz won the right to be the county seat, an enormous advantage over its potential rivals— the even smaller settlements in Soquel, five miles to the south, and Watsonville, twenty-five miles to the southeast. For one thing, serving as a county seat meant the infusion of state money. For another, it brought clear economic benefits for local newspapers, which were paid by the government to print legal documents and notices of public hearings; this kind of revenue was certainly a factor in encouraging an enterprising journalist to leave the established city of Monterey, forty-three miles to the south of Santa Cruz, on the other side of the bay, to start the Santa Cruz *Sentinel* in 1856.[1]

Most of all, securing the county government for Santa Cruz meant that communication and contact between local business leaders and political officeholders would be facilitated, a fact well understood by the original power structure of the city, with Anthony and other downtown landowners and store owners exercising governmental power as members of the Board of Supervisors for the county.

The river and heavily forested mountainsides gave Santa Cruz a number of natural assets that made it possible for Anthony and his early colleagues in the central business district to attract capitalists and workers to the area. For starters, the river currents were ideal for powering lumber and paper mills, which provided a major boost to a timber industry that was profitable first and foremost because of its giant redwood trees, renowned for their beauty, durability, and resistance to decay and insects. In combination with an ample supply of madrone and alder trees, which provided a good base for making explosives, the river also brought a manufacturer of blasting powder and gunpowder to an area in the mountains a few miles northeast of the city.

Then, too, the abundance of bark from tanbark oaks—a cheap source of the tannic acid necessary for tanning hides—led to a large tanning industry; by 1870, ten tanneries, making use of hides from Mission Santa Cruz and the few remaining cattle ranches, supplied half the saddle leather produced in the state. Finally, the limestone in the hills and mountains behind Santa Cruz became valuable through its role in making plaster and mortar, which were used

---

1. Although there have been other newspapers in Santa Cruz at various times in its history, the *Sentinel* has been the principal "newspaper of record" for the city ever since it began publication. It is therefore an important source of information on the viewpoints and tensions within the growth coalition and often the only source available for the reconstruction of key political conflicts.

in the construction of stone or brick structures. By 1880 several limestone quarries were supplying more than half of the lime used for construction in the fast-growing cities of San Francisco, Oakland, San Jose, and Sacramento (Fehliman 1947; Hinman 1976; Perry 2007).

Although Anthony and several of the men who purchased land from him in the downtown area remained at the heart of the growth coalition well into the 1870s, often entering into joint ventures, the story of the Santa Cruz growth coalition during its first fifty years is best told through the career and activities of one of its youngest members, a twenty-two-year-old German immigrant, Frederick Hihn (pronounced "Heen"). In a career typical of many early California pioneers, Hihn left his native land in his teens, having been trained in merchandising, and sailed around the tip of South America to California to take advantage of the Gold Rush. He spent two years selling candy in the mining area and running a hotel in Sacramento, fifty miles from the major gold mines, and another year managing his own drugstore in San Francisco, which he lost when much of the young city burned to the ground in 1851. He arrived in Santa Cruz that same year and built a general merchandise store on a lot purchased from Anthony. By the time Hihn died in 1913, he had amassed a fortune of $50.2 million at today's prices, making him far and away the richest resident in the Santa Cruz area. To put his fortune in perspective, the wealthiest family in the year Hihn died—that of John D. Rockefeller Sr. and his descendants—was worth nearly four hundred times as much, about $20 billion in current dollars, but Hihn was nonetheless among the truly wealthy of that era. In the late 1880s he still owned nearly thirteen thousand acres, after selling several thousand acres in the 1870s, and paid 25 percent of the taxes collected by the city of Santa Cruz.

As Hihn's business prospered, he joined Anthony in building what became the county court house and helped organize what was soon the major bank. He set about amassing as much land as he could, starting with commercial lots in the downtown core and then land for residential construction within a few blocks of his store. Hihn acquired additional land by giving credit to the cash-poor *Californios,* who used the deeds for their land as backing. When they fell behind in their payments, as they often did, especially during an unusually bad recession in 1853, they had to give him part of their vast holdings to pay off their debts, or auction off some of their land, which Hihn and his associates purchased. He also served on the county board of supervisors and in the state legislature.

With the local population growing at a good pace, there was need for a stable supply of drinking water, which Anthony and Hihn provided in 1856 by purchasing land on the rolling hills of the upper West Side that contained a natural spring. They then piped the water to the downtown area through hollowed redwood trunks from trees on Hihn's mountain lands. Within a few years, their company was supplying all the water for the northern half of the county. In 1858, to encourage visitors and potential investors, Hihn and two partners built the first wagon road directly over the mountains, saving a day or two of travel to other cities in Northern California and making it possible to have regular stagecoach service to San Jose.

By the late 1850s Hihn was already a well-to-do man, one of the two or three largest taxpayers in the county, but he became even wealthier in the 1860s as one of those who profited from the growing pressure by restless settlers to strip the *Californios* of the rest of their land. This land hunger led to legal battles, physical conflicts between owners and squatters, and the lynching of "dozens of Spanish-speaking men" in the region between Santa Cruz and Monterey in the 1850s and 1860s (Lydon 1998, 10). When an adjudicatory Land Commission set up by the federal government finally made its most crucial decisions about the validity of the *Californios'* land titles in 1863, many of which were denied, Hihn was able to buy 15,464 acres a few miles southeast of the city, stretching from the bay to the wooded mountainsides. This timberland soon supplied the lumber for building the houses in downtown Santa Cruz that he constructed for new arrivals, as well as for shipments to other cities. To ship his timber to San Francisco, Hihn constructed a four-hundred-yard wharf where a large creek flowed into the bay.

Because of the nearby extractive industries, ranches, and farms, Santa Cruz had a prosperous central business district by 1866, the year it was incorporated as a town, with forty-seven sundry stores, twenty-seven saloons, several brothels just off the main street, three hotels, and two livery stables (Reader 1998, 17). The need for the kind of equipment used in the extractive industries, such as engines, boilers, and pumps, meant new business for Anthony's foundry and several other foundries and repair shops, creating a small industrial base in the city as well. In addition, Santa Cruz was becoming known as a tourist resort. The *Sentinel* provided a perfect characterization of what this tourism looked like in 1862, a characterization that was to hold ever after despite the best efforts of the tourist industry to create an upscale image: "It is not a fashionable watering place, but rather, a desirable place for quiet sensible people escaping from the heat of the interior," the newspaper reported. "It is for those who desire to live without ostentation or extravagance" (Lydon and Swift 1978, 12).

As tourism developed, Hihn gained a piece of that business, too, when one of the farmers leasing land from him had the idea of developing a simple campground on some of the beachfront land Hihn had recently purchased, not far from his wharf. Hihn called it Camp Capitola, a name chosen in honor of the growth coalition's vain attempt the previous year to tempt the state's leaders to move the capital from the unpleasant city of Sacramento—too hot in the summer, too cold and foggy in the winter, often infested with mosquitoes—to the Soquel–Santa Cruz area.

It is no wonder, then, that the decade from 1860 to 1870 recorded the fastest population growth the city ever experienced, from 950 to 2,561, a 170 percent increase. However, the future was by no means assured for Hihn and the rest of the growth coalition. They knew they might lose out if they did not find ways to attract or build the railroad lines that were becoming a life and death matter for cities everywhere in the United States. The pressures began to mount in 1869, when the intercontinental railroad was completed and the powerful Southern Pacific Railroad started to plan for a rail line from San Francisco to Los Angeles.

THE RAILROAD WARS

Hihn and the many smaller landowners in and around Santa Cruz needed a railroad to transport timber and limestone from their mountain landholdings, and they wanted a railroad with connections to San Francisco and San Jose to bring in tourists from inland cities. Serving as the leading member of the county's Railroad Commission, which led him to have frequent conversations with representatives of the Southern Pacific, Hihn believed that its owners were firm in their plan to run their San Francisco to Los Angeles line along the coast and through Santa Cruz, which would all but guarantee the future growth of the city. Instead, the growth coalition suddenly faced a major threat to its interests in 1870, when the Southern Pacific unexpectedly decided to bypass Santa Cruz by building on the San Jose side of the mountains, where much of the land was still government owned, making it possible to take advantage of federal land grants to acquire right-of-way (Bean and Rawls 1983, 178). Even worse, the new route took advantage of a wide pass in the mountains twenty miles south of Santa Cruz to turn westward to a depot and freight yard near archrival Watsonville, raising the possibility that the center of population growth, and even the county seat, would shift to that city (Hinman 1976, 15).

Hihn immediately fought back by bringing together a large consortium of investors, mostly local, to build a railroad from Santa Cruz to the area near Watsonville where the Southern Pacific planned its new station. Although the investors read like a who's who of the local growth coalition at the time, half of the money came from Hihn and another successful German immigrant, Claus Spreckels, a San Francisco capitalist who was on his way to making a

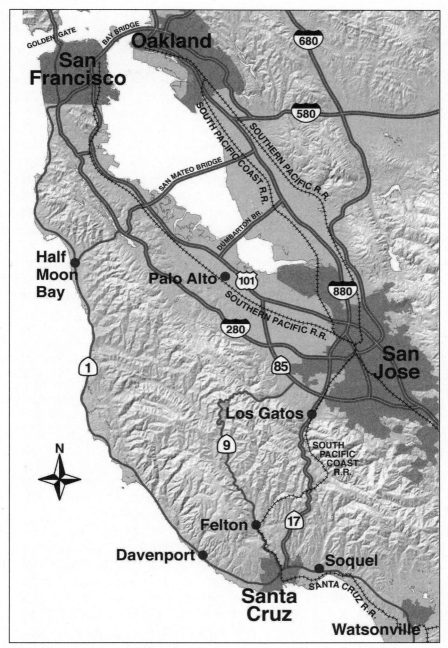

MAP 2.1 Santa Cruz in relation to the Bay Area, including the major highways of today and the railroad lines that were important in the late nineteenth and early twentieth centuries

huge fortune in sugar refining, with a large mill forty miles southeast of Santa Cruz and another in Hawaii. He also owned 2,300 acres overlooking the bay fifteen miles southeast of Santa Cruz, an ideal spot for a tourist hotel, which gave him more than a passing interest in the railroad project. Moreover, Hihn's plan had financial support from the county government because the voters had agreed by a wide margin to tax themselves to support the railroad.

Despite their considerable private wealth and the county subsidy, Hihn and his associates did not in fact have enough capital to build a standard-sized railroad. They therefore had to take a chance on a smaller and less costly narrow-gauge railroad (with rails only 36 inches apart, instead of the standard 54.5 inches), which was adequate for the smaller payloads on short-haul routes. The more important issue was the placement of the route to enhance the interests of key owners. To the annoyance and bitterness of competing landowners, Hihn first of all purposely bypassed Soquel and placed a depot closer to the bay, so it could more easily service Camp Capitola, thereby making his land all the more valuable. Soquel never recovered from this decision, ending whatever chance it once had of overtaking Santa Cruz as the most important city in the county, while Camp Capitola became a major tourist destination over the next fifty years as well as an attractive site for summer homes (Lydon and Swift 1978, 24). Hihn also located the tracks so that there would be a stop right in front of the resort that his partner, Spreckels, was in the process of building.

When the first train on the new Santa Cruz Railroad finally made its journey from Watsonville to Santa Cruz in May 1876, the *Sentinel* editor poetically heralded this triumph for the local growth coalition: "At last our enterprising young city is in full connection with the rest of mankind. At last she is free from the rule of the sleepy stage coach" (*Sentinel*, May 13, 1876, 3). More exactly, Santa Cruz was now within five hours of the growing San Francisco and Oakland markets, which made the county's timber, farming, and fishing industries more profitable, and its resort areas more accessible, an ideal synergy from the point of view of Hihn and other local landowners.

While all this maneuvering and construction were going on south of Santa Cruz, Hihn caught a lucky break when two prominent San Francisco capitalists decided to build another railroad, the South Pacific Coast, through the mountains north of the city to compete with the Southern Pacific, using one of the routes Hihn had helped to survey several years earlier. The new venture was once again a narrow-gauge rail line, and therefore easier and less expensive to build through a mountainous region. Originating from the Oakland side of the San Francisco Bay, the eighty-mile railroad required eight tunnels—two of them a mile long—which were built by six hundred low-wage Chinese workers, thirty-seven of whom lost their lives in the process (Lydon 1985).

As a result of the new railroads and increased market access, Santa Cruz grew at a fast pace during the 1870s, once the economic downturn caused by the nationwide financial crisis of 1873 had ended. The city even added to its industrial base by producing train parts and passenger cars for its narrow-gauge railroads (MacGregor 2003, Chapter 6). It seemed likely that the good times would continue for decades when the South Pacific Coast opened in 1881, just in time to give the Southern Pacific a run for its money. The South Pacific Coast had a slightly faster and far more scenic route, but the competition was nonetheless very even, with both lines bringing two thousand passengers to Santa Cruz on July 4, 1884, for example. The South Pacific Coast also carried lumber, limestone, gunpowder, and dynamite from the San Lorenzo Valley to San Jose and Oakland, another ideal synergy for the Santa Cruz growth coalition.

But once again the growth coalition had to make sudden adjustments because the Southern Pacific decided to compete for a larger share of the tourist trade by building a spur to the picturesque city of Monterey, which retained its charm and mystique from its days as the Spanish capital of California. Then the Southern Pacific's land subsidiary purchased a six-thousand-acre tract just east of that city and built the Del Monte Hotel and the 17-Mile Drive, now familiar to many Americans because the Pebble Beach Classic and other golf tournaments are held there. In those early days, however, the main attractions were the scenic views, such as a Chinese fishing village that could be observed from the large horse-drawn passenger car that traveled back and forth along the 17-Mile Drive, and imported buffalo and other animals that were put out to graze. Monterey became a destination for the wealthy, forcing the Santa Cruz tourist industry to settle for its niche as a pleasant place for sensible and unostentatious people.

Although Hihn and his associates were glad to have the South Pacific Coast coming into downtown Santa Cruz, it was the beginning of the end for their own little railroad to Watsonville. When a major flood badly damaged their bridge over the San Lorenzo River in 1881, Hihn bought up the shares held by his partners and sold the unprofitable railroad to the Southern Pacific, which promptly repaired the trestle and widened the track, making it possible for the Southern Pacific to benefit from Santa Cruz tourism (Olin 1967). When the two main owners of the South Pacific Coast began to quarrel in 1887, the Southern Pacific was able to purchase their railroad, too, removing a thorn in its side and consolidating its grip on freight and passenger service in Santa Cruz County (Hamman 1980/2002). Supplementing the efforts of the local growth coalition's Santa Cruz Development Association, the Southern Pacific now promoted the city as part of its broader marketing efforts to attract visitors and potential residents to California from all parts of the country. (Because of government land grants, the company had 11.5 million acres to develop in California and nearly 11 million more in Nevada, Utah, and Oregon.)

TENSIONS IN THE GROWTH COALITION

By the late 1890s, just when the growth coalition seemed to have engineered an ideal balance between industry and tourism, with a big assist from San Francisco capitalists, the city slowly began to lose its industrial base. The redwoods and other prime timber had been projected to last for two hundred years, but they lasted less than sixty, turning into housing, telephone poles, railroad ties, and fences much faster than anticipated. The increasing scarcity of tanbark oaks, combined with a decline in cattle raising in the area, led to a shrinkage of the tanning industry to one company by 1900. As for the limestone industry, it reached its peak production in 1904 and gradually declined because the construction industry, spurred by the massive damage to buildings in San Francisco during the 1906 earthquake, began to use stronger and longer-lasting cement and concrete materials (Perry 2007).

Technological advances in harnessing steam and electric power also meant industrial decline for Santa Cruz because sawmills and paper mills were no longer dependent upon river currents. Now they could move to larger cities, where demand was higher and there were larger labor pools. The blasting powder and gunpowder company was by then owned by the DuPont Corporation; with the madrone and alder trees depleted and with no need for water mills, it moved its operations to a plant north of Oakland in 1914. The railroads were now fully constructed, and the Southern Pacific had no need for local equipment makers and repair shops, so the foundries declined or disappeared as well. In 1881, Santa Cruz County was second only to San Francisco County in industrial production, but by 1900 it was already down to fourteenth in the list of fifty-eight counties, and by 1910 it was eighteenth.

Although the city and its land values continued to grow in the early twentieth century despite its industrial decline, disagreements developed within the growth coalition between those who thought the city should try to attract new industries and those who thought it wiser to focus almost exclusively on tourism. This disagreement was expressed very graphically by A. A. Taylor, the editor of the Santa Cruz *Surf*, who said, "There has always been an irrepressible conflict in Santa Cruz between factories and frivolities. The New England mill village with a payroll was one ideal and the gaieties of Atlantic City the other ideal" (Barber 1982, 13).

The conflict within the growth coalition was also reflected in editorials appearing in the two main newspapers of the era, the Republican-oriented *Sentinel*, which championed both industrial development and tourism, and the

Democrat-oriented *Surf,* which supported the "right kind of industry" to some extent but was more sensitive to preserving the environment to keep the area attractive for tourism. Perhaps overstating their differences somewhat to create drama and sell newspapers, the editors of the two newspapers engaged in a running editorial feud throughout the first two decades of the twentieth century. Taylor of the *Surf* touted the "Yankee" value of diligence. In his view, the city should seek to create a steady, solid plan for economic growth based on the development of manufacturing and trade, but without despoiling the natural environment and thus jeopardizing tourism. Economic prosperity should be built on "industry" in two senses of the term, the creation of a manufacturing base and the development of a value orientation rooted in the Calvinist ethic of discipline and hard work. He contrasted this sober, steady development—with its normative emphasis on developing a citizenry with the proper moral values—with the freewheeling, big-dreaming boosterism advocated by the *Sentinel.* He linked the *Sentinel's* perspective to the efforts by Santa Cruz tourist moguls to develop and promote a "wide open city," where liquor flowed, dice rolled, and much money could be made satisfying these diversions and "vices," and with a willingness to accept potentially noxious industries that would undermine the natural amenities of clean air and water.

The stark contrasts between these rival views of development arose most dramatically in 1903, when a San Francisco capitalist, labeled "the cement king" in the press, proposed to invest $1 million in a cement plant on the upper West Side, just below the Cowell Ranch and less than a mile from the downtown. Santa Cruz was an ideal location for the new venture because it had plenty of lime rock in the foothills and easy ocean transport less than two miles away. But obtaining lime rock would mean loud noise from frequent dynamite explosions and a large amount of dust from turning the rocks into powder. Nevertheless, at least some members of the city council seemed favorably disposed at first, and the *Sentinel* editor lobbied for the project for the jobs it would bring, along with likely federal subsidies for expanding the harbor. Meanwhile, the editor of the *Surf* and other citizens joined together to create protest meetings that included damaging testimony from people who lived near a similar plant in a city north of San Francisco. The cement king withdrew his proposal and soon thereafter built the plant in a rural area ten miles north of the city, where it filled the air with dust clouds and covered houses with dust well into the 1960s (Orlando 1994).

Although the argument over how best to create growth in Santa Cruz was to continue for decades, the beach-oriented crowd was in the ascendancy as the twentieth century began. This is best demonstrated by the fact that two of the five members of the city council were directors of both the recreational/bathing facilities on the beach—featuring a casino and arcade games—and the bank that financed them. A third council member, the principal of the high school, was a director of the same bank, creating a triple interlock between the bank and the council, and a fourth council member owned a lumber business that supplied building materials for the construction of the tourist-serving amenities. The fifth council member was a local grocer.

The point man for the main beach tourist attraction, Fred Swanton, is the third person, after Anthony and Hihn, who exemplified the general development of the Santa Cruz growth coalition. Born in Brooklyn in 1862, he came to Santa Cruz as a young boy, where his father later built the first three-story hotel and included him as a business partner. He went on to make and lose fortunes in two ambitious ventures—the first hydroelectric plant in the West and the first commercial telephone system in the state of California—before turning his attention to transforming the beach area into a nationally known seaside resort (Barber 1982, 12; Olin 1967). Starting in 1903 with the acquisition of bathhouses from an early pioneer of the Santa Cruz tourism industry, he soon created the Santa Cruz Beach, Cottage and Tent City Corporation in order to add small overnight dwellings to his holdings. Two years later he expanded into rides and a pinball arcade (Schirmer 1987). Taking advantage of connections with people he knew from his previous business ventures, he was able to entice many notable people to vacation in Santa Cruz, including the president of the United States, Teddy Roosevelt, whose highly publicized visit in 1903 proved to be a boon to the tourist industry. In the summer of 1906 the California Republicans held their state convention in Swanton's beachfront facilities.

Swanton also had the support of capitalists and corporations from outside the city, notably the Southern Pacific, which provided him with special booster trains that he personally rode to every city within several hundred miles, featuring brass bands and other forms of hoopla and honky-tonk (Barber 1982, 12). Always ready to boast about the importance of his outside contacts, Swanton claimed that only $70,000 of the estimated $7.3 million invested in his beach accommodations and attractions came from local investors, with the lion's share from San Francisco capitalists whose wealth derived from railroads and utilities (Olin 1967, 34). When his recently constructed pavilions and boardwalk burned to the ground in 1906, it was San Francisco capitalists who paid for the construction of the ornate new buildings that are still the main assets of the now locally owned Seaside Company.

CHALLENGES TO THE GROWTH COALITION

As Santa Cruz boomed ahead on railroad excursion tourism, the population increased from 5,659 in 1900 to 11,146 in 1910, a near doubling. It was the highest rate of increase since the 1860s and has yet to be exceeded. The success of the local growth boosters not only increased profits and population but generated a self-conscious local working class and expanded the electorate as well, leading to political conflict of a kind never seen before in a city that had been dominated by the several hundred voters in and around the growth coalition. Indeed, it included some of the class conflict at the heart of Marxist theory.

To the consternation of the owner-editors of both the *Sentinel* and the *Surf,* the growth coalition was opposed in 1904 by a Union Labor ticket put forward by the Santa Cruz Labor Union and Improvement Club, which included small shop owners and artisans as well as what today would be called blue-collar workers. Despite their disagreements over growth strategies, the two newspapers were in complete agreement in their opposition to this ticket, arguing that the Union Labor ticket represented the unwarranted intrusion of the "labor element" into politics. The *Surf* editor allowed that labor unions have "a place, a very important and essential one." Then he added, "But that place is not in politics." Unions were a special interest that would undermine the common good. They should be "minding their own business" when it came to politics (*Surf,* April 12, 1904, 4).

To make their point that business interests dominated the city at the expense of workers, supporters of the Union Labor ticket raised questions about the interlocks between Swanton's beach enterprises and the city council. This critique quickly drew a heated response from the *Sentinel* editor, who turned the allegation of undue business influence into a virtue by claiming that cooperation between the private and public spheres resulted in the betterment of the entire city. He ended with an exhortation: "Citizens should think well of this, and what has been accomplished during the term of the present Mayor and Common Council, and VOTE for those men who have given Santa Cruz a successful administration and a Boom of Progress to Our City" (*Sentinel,* April 11, 1904, 8). Happily for the growth coalition and the pro-growth newspapers, all of the incumbent council members and the mayor were reelected by comfortable margins (*Sentinel,* April 12, 1904, 1).

The interlock issue resurfaced in 1906, this time through a reform ticket put forward by the faction within the growth coalition that wanted to encourage industry as well as tourism. Organizing themselves as a Good Government League, with connections to the emerging urban policy-planning network that was briefly mentioned in Chapter 1, the Santa Cruz reformers wanted local government to be run more like a business by taking the "politics" out of city administration (e.g., Schiesl 1977). Although their platform did not represent a challenge to dominance by the growth coalition, they wanted the city to grow by attracting businesses and permanent residents "imbued with the highest ideals of personal character and responsive to the appeals and duties of the purest citizenship" (*Sentinel*, March 28, 1906, 1). According to a statement in the *Sentinel* by the local chapter of the nationwide Socialist Party, which would soon mount a challenge of its own, the 1906 municipal election was strictly an intra-class conflict between "two factions of the privileged class":

> From the Socialist standpoint, the present fight is merely a conflict between two factions of the privileged class, in which workers have no concern . . . Analyzing the situation according to the law of economic determinism, we find two factions of small capitalists arrayed against each other. One wants a "wide open" town which will attract pleasure seekers with the disposition and the wherewithal to have a good time. The followers of this faction own the means whereby the desires of this class are gratified. The other faction wants a moral and temperate town, which will attract wealthy home seekers. The following of this party is composed of real estate owners and others who would benefit by the development of a home town. (*Sentinel*, April 5, 1906, 4)

In the weeks immediately preceding the elections, both daily newspapers repeatedly urged citizens to turn out in droves to reject the Good Government candidates and support the incumbent officeholders, but the challengers nonetheless won the mayoralty and two council seats, thus securing majority control of city government and showing that newspapers are not the primary factor in determining voter preferences.

To achieve its goal of a vice-free city with a more efficient form of municipal government, the Good Government League next pushed for a revision of the city charter. This effort began with the election in August 1906 of a commission of fifteen "freeholders," a term that originally referred to people who owned real property but by then tended to mean a registered voter. They were charged with rewriting the charter that had been in place since 1876. The advertised hallmark of the new charter was an increase in the number of wards from four to seven, a surprise in an era when most charter revisions replaced ward voting with at-large elections. But the more critical change in the long run was the decision to move local elections from even to odd years, based on the rationale that local issues should be kept distinct from the state and national elections held in even years. Actually, this reform had the effect of reducing voter turnout in most cities because there was less interest in local elections without the pull of statewide and national elections (Alford and Lee 1968). The new charter passed by a margin of five to one in a special election in January 1907 (Wright and Gundersgaard 1976, 18).

The city elections of 1907 and 1909 were uneventful in terms of under-standing dominance by the growth coalition in Santa Cruz. But the Socialist Party, which had been enjoying increasing success in city and county elections in many different parts of the country, caused some stir in the November 1910 Santa Cruz County elections, even though it lost, because candidates drawn from its local chapter received more votes than the local newspapers expected (*Sentinel*, November 16, 1910, 1). Moreover, the local vote for Socialist candi-dates running for statewide offices in that same election was even higher, an ominous sign in the eyes of the *Sentinel*. The local Socialists were further em-boldened by a Socialist's election to the House of Representatives from a con-gressional district in Milwaukee in 1910, and by the fact that Milwaukee Socialists gained control of municipal government in the same year and worked to clean up neighborhoods and nearby factories by building new san-itation systems and taking ownership of the water and utility companies. (The Socialists lost control of the city council within an election or two, but they did elect a Socialist mayor in 1916 who stayed in office until 1940 [Wisconsin Historical Society 2007; Weinstein 1967]). Both successes were interpreted by Santa Cruz socialist leaders as harbingers of future electoral success at a large rally held at the People's Hall, owned by a local Socialist (*Sentinel*, November 23, 1910, 1).

Although the Santa Cruz Socialists had not won anything yet, city leaders decided it was time to draw more fully on the policy suggestions developed in the urban policy-planning network by changing the electoral rules before the next city election. The general package of reforms by this time included: (1) *at-large elections* to replace district elections, which made it more difficult for neighborhood leaders, whether Democrats, Socialists, or ethnic and racial mi-norities, to hold their seats on city councils because they did not have the money and name recognition to win citywide elections; (2) *nonpartisan elec-tions* to eliminate party competition, which made it necessary for candidates to increase their name recognition because lower-income voters could no longer rely on labels like "Democrat" or "Socialist" to identity those candi-dates with whom they sympathized; (3) *off-year elections* to replace elections that coincided with state and national elections, which reduced voter turnout and obscured the policy connections between local and national levels; and (4) either the *commission* or *council-manager* form of government to elimi-nate strong mayors, both of which lead to city councils that set general poli-cies carried out by trained professionals.

Leaders in the Santa Cruz growth coalition once again started with the elec-tion of a commission of fifteen freeholders, ten of whom were members of the chamber of commerce (nine of those ten had served on the 1906 charter revision commission). To help ensure that their views would be insulated from challenges by the public as the charter revision proceeded, the freeholders instituted strict rules limiting public participation at their meetings (Wright and Gundersgaard 1976, 19). Billing its work as a quest to find an even more efficient form of government, the freeholder group recommended a commission form of government "to do business by business methods without so much red tape" (Sentinel, November 30, 1910, 8, as cited in Wright and Gundersgaard, 1976, 19). For the most part, this added up to a reduction in the size of the council from seven members and a mayor to four members and a mayor, which was also advertised as a way to reduce endless arguments at council meetings.

However, red tape was the least of the issues in terms of actual political power. The two crucial elements in the new charter were rule changes that made it much more difficult for average citizens to mount electoral challenges to the growth coalition. First, council members would be elected by all voters in the city rather than from separate wards. Second, a majority vote was now required for election, which meant there would be run-off elections if they were needed; this change provided a backstop in case a pro-union or Socialist candidate obtained a plurality in the preliminary election because two or more growth coalition candidates split the pro-business vote. These changes, when combined with the off-year elections created in 1907, meant that the Santa Cruz growth coalition had advocated three of the main reforms that reduce voter turnout and make it easier for growth coalitions to control local government (Alford and Lee 1968).

The new charter passed by a two-to-one margin in early February 1911, setting the stage for the regular elections three months later. Reflecting voting patterns throughout the country, the Socialist candidate for mayor outpolled six other mayoral hopefuls in the preliminary election, winning 28 percent of the total vote, and the four Socialist candidates for commissioner also made it into the run-off election two weeks later. The possibility that Socialists might govern the city, although unlikely to have a large impact, at least immediately, nonetheless brought about instant unity within the growth coalition. The rival factions quickly put aside their differences and organized themselves into the Citizens Charter Party to endorse a local physician in the run-off for mayor, along with the four non-Socialist candidates for the council. The new party set up headquarters in a large hotel in the heart of the downtown, holding frequent campaign rallies at which its candidates could talk with passersby and petitions could be circulated endorsing their candidacy. In addition, the daily newspapers ran a barrage of anti-Socialist editorials and ads, and bolstered this attack by reprinting a number of articles from other newspapers that condemned Socialists and socialism. The *Sentinel* editor, who was also a director of the bank that helped finance Swanton's beach enterprise, was one of the non-Socialist candidates, making his editorial attacks on the Socialists even more self-serving.

The large front-page headline in the *Sentinel* on election day warned of "political insurrection," but the Socialist candidate for mayor, who ironically worked as a printer for none other than the *Sentinel,* increased his vote total from 536 in the primary to 874 in the run-off, so the all-out attack on him by his employer did not scare away his voting base and may have enlarged it (*Sentinel,* May 16, 1911, 1). He nevertheless fell short of victory, gaining just 44 percent of the total vote cast. One of the Socialist candidates did win a seat as a commissioner, but the election of two local businessmen and the *Sentinel* editor insured continued political leadership by the growth coalition. It would be another sixty-two years before candidates from one or another faction of the growth coalition would face a serious challenge from anyone outside their ranks.

FINANCIAL TROUBLES FOR THE BEACH CROWD

Having met the overblown threat posed by the local Socialist Party, the Santa Cruz power structure looked ahead with eager anticipation to a period of continuing growth for the local economy. But shortly after the elections of 1911, there were signs that all might not proceed as planned, when Swanton's next effort to expand his tourist enterprises ran into local opposition. The source of the problem was a petition circulated in early 1912 that protested his plans to widen and extend two major commercial thoroughfares just north of the city's central business district in order to provide shorter travel times between his recently completed, three-hundred-room luxury beach hotel and a golf course under construction just north of the downtown. The core of the opposition consisted of small property owners in the assessment district who didn't think it was right that they should pay an additional tax to support Swanton's project. But Swanton believed that they were backed by important downtown businessmen who were afraid of losing customers to the beach area (*Sentinel,* January 12, 1912, 3).

Moreover, it turned out that Swanton was in financial trouble as a result of overspending, mismanagement, and a depressed national economy that was causing problems for businesses everywhere. He was hoping that the road improvements and the new golf course would save the day for him, but time ran out. His vaunted beach enterprise unexpectedly closed later in the year (Barber 1982, 12). The local landowners and merchants who took temporary control had to limp along on the low budget they could provide until Swanton was able to sell the property in 1915 to a group of investors, several of them from San Francisco, led by the owner of a company that contracted with the city to provide it with gas for heating and lighting (Beal and Beal 2003). But the combination of problems at the beach, the economic depression, and war in 1917 spelled trouble for the growth coalition as a whole. For the first and only time in its history, the city declined slightly in population in the second decade of the twentieth century, even though the new cement plant north of the city was doing a booming business and significant amounts of lumber were still being shipped.

Nevertheless, Santa Cruz tourism blossomed once again as part of the good times called the Roaring Twenties, despite constant bickering between the rival factions in the growth coalition. The conflict led the *Sentinel* editor to lament the absence of a "common foe that the principals in our civic battles will admit is worthy of their combined efforts" (*Sentinel,* May 8, 1923, 3). Although the railroads continued to bring most of the tourists, now tourism was bolstered by improvements in the new highway between San Jose and Santa Cruz, first built between 1912 and 1915, and then fully paved in 1921 and widened in 1923. Tourists had begun to turn to the automobile for weekend trips and longer vacations (Lydon and Swift 1978, 76). In fact, tourism prospered as never before, with Swanton—now venerated as a pioneer citizen, promoter, and booster—returning to the limelight as the leader of a fleet of convertibles that toured inland cities to call attention to the wonders of Santa Cruz (Barber 1982, 13; Olin 1967). After Swanton started a Miss California contest in 1924, the city began to market itself as the "Atlantic City of the Pacific."

Based on his new acclaim as a booster, Swanton transformed himself into a politician and won the race for mayor in 1927, giving him an even bigger platform from which to advertise the city. "The election of Fred W. Swanton," said one overly optimistic San Francisco capitalist, "virtually brings about a 25 percent property valuation increase overnight" (Santa Cruz *News,* May 4, 1927, 1). Despite the continuing prosperity of the next two years, however, Swanton's swashbuckling pro-tourism style once again came under fire from more staid members of the growth coalition, many of them located in the downtown core. They drew upon the classic language of Progressive Era reformers to describe his tenure as one marked by "maladministration," "one-man dictatorship," and "bossism," all of which were earlier said to be impossible with the form of government adopted in 1911 (Santa Cruz *News,* May 2, 1929, 1). The result was a serious challenge to Swanton's mayoralty in the 1929 election by a well-known lawyer and judge, Donald Younger, who also happened to be one of Hihn's grandsons.

Younger and his many supporters in the downtown business community focused on Swanton's alleged failure to run the city in a "business-like" manner, arguing that his celebrated entrepreneurial style did not serve the needs of the city. But they were also rankled by his ties to San Francisco promoters who favored tourism, which Younger saw as the central point of contention: "If elected as the city's chief executive, I would operate the mayor's office independently of any person or faction and I would not as mayor be controlled nor influenced by any San Francisco capitalist carpet-bagging promoters" (Santa Cruz *News,* July 5, 1929, 5).

The pro-Younger forces also claimed that the investments Swanton brought to Santa Cruz had not benefited ordinary citizens, but newspaper coverage of the campaign suggests that their chief concern was for the economic well-being of downtown business interests. In response to a question during a public campaign appearance about whether Swanton's reputation as a promoter of investment in the downtown area was deserved or not, Younger replied that virtually none of the new buildings there had been realized through any efforts by Swanton. The message was clear: Swanton's "city building" overlooked the needs of the downtown. The long-simmering tension within the growth coalition between downtown business interests and Swanton's "Beach Crowd" was the key issue in this election.

Despite Younger's well-organized challenge, the attempt to unseat Swanton by turning his reputation for wheeling and dealing into a liability backfired: Swanton emerged as the clear winner, with 55 percent of the vote (*Sentinel,* May 8, 1929, 1). The fact that he was admired for his style and his success in promoting tourism proved to be decisive with the voters. But for all Swanton's goodwill tours, connections, and electoral success, his personal fortunes could not escape the impact of the major depression that hit the United States a few months after his reelection. With $57,000 in debts and a salary of only $100 a month from the city, he declared bankruptcy in 1930. But even personal bankruptcy had no effect on his continuing popularity: he went on to be reelected in 1931 and 1933.

As the Great Depression enveloped the nation, both factions of the growth coalition recognized that they would need to rely on tourism more than ever. They therefore worked together in 1934 to convince the Roosevelt administration to improve and widen Highway 17 once again, this time as a Works Progress Administration project (Wills 1981, 16). The improvements cut driving time from San Jose to one hour, half of what it had been before. The growth coalition also drew on the tourist industry's long-standing focus on inexpensive entertainment for a mass market, keeping a vacation in Santa Cruz within the reach of average Californians despite the tough times. The coalition was further saved by a new low-cost Suntan Special excursion train that the Southern Pacific instituted in 1927 as a way to make use of its commuter passenger cars on Sundays and holidays. Leaving in the early morning from San Francisco, with stops in Palo Alto and San Jose, the packed trains had a festive atmosphere as they snaked through the curves and tunnels of the Santa Cruz Mountains. They arrived at the beach and boardwalk just before noon to be greeted by a big brass band, and then left the city at five PM, with many happy customers catching a nap on the way home. As many as five thousand to seven thousand people enjoyed this sightseeing and sunbathing trip each Sunday during the Depression years, arriving in up to seven different trains (Hamman 1980/2002, 257–258).

In January 1939, reacting to signs that the worst of the Depression might be over, the growth coalition began yet another campaign to diversify the local economy. Calling themselves the Santa Cruz Advertising Council, several mainstays of the chamber of commerce underwrote research in an attempt to come up with new ideas to promote growth. Soon thereafter a fifteen-part series on growth opportunities appeared in the *Sentinel*, with the usual hopes expressed in the headline of the first article: "Year-Round Stability Is Aim of Santa Cruz." The series acknowledged the centrality of tourism to the local economy, but once again argued that other industries were needed for Santa Cruz to continue to grow after it gained fewer than six thousand new citizens between 1920 and 1940. As part of a special series it ran in 2006 to commemorate 150 years of publication, the *Sentinel* reprinted a 1983 reminiscence written by Gordon "Scotchy" Sinclair, the longtime managing editor of the newspaper. Recalling those pre–World War II years of slow population growth and a moribund economy, Sinclair stated, "Employment was poor." As he continued to reminisce, he added, "It picked up a little in the summertime as the visitors were beginning to come back, but after Labor Day, you didn't exactly see too many people if you took a stroll down Pacific Avenue" (*Sentinel*, September 17, 2006, 1 [originally published February 16, 1983, 1]).

And then the Santa Cruz Advertising Council's warning about relying too heavily on the tourist industry finally proved to be all too accurate for an unexpected reason: World War II. Unlike the 1930s, when the residents of the hot inland valleys still could afford to come to the beach via train or car for a weekend respite, or a week of outdoor camping, the war years were a near disaster for tourism. The domestic use of the automobile was curtailed by strict rationing of vital commodities, especially gas and tires, and the Southern Pacific's Suntan Specials were halted in 1941 because railroad equipment was needed for the war effort. Wartime restrictions on the supply of newsprint, necessary for tourist advertising, also hurt.

Even worse, the city began to lose its prominent position in the California tourist industry in the postwar era because other areas in the state—particularly in the growing southern region around Los Angeles—were becoming competing tourist destinations, featuring newly constructed accommodations and facilities. The Seaside Company's amusement park, with its aging facilities beginning to show signs of wear, was at a competitive disadvantage (Olin 1967). Although the Santa Cruz population increased by 30 percent between 1940 and 1950, from seventeen thousand to twenty-two thousand, mostly after the war ended, that figure lagged considerably behind the 48 percent county growth rate and even farther behind the 53.3 percent increase in the state population. It also included a growing number of middle-income retirees, who didn't make for a dynamic economy.

Since World War II marked the end of an era for Santa Cruz, we can pause in our history of the local growth coalition to take stock of the years between 1848 and 1945 from a theoretical perspective. Looking back, we can see that the leaders of the coalition demonstrated plenty of independence and ingenuity in trying to make the city attractive to outside investors, something that is not emphasized in Marxist theory. They also reshaped local government during the Progressive Era in the face of a nascent working-class challenge of the kind that Marxist theory predicted would happen, although the challenge was on a far smaller scale. In any event, the restructuring of the local government by the leaders within the growth coalition helped to ensure that they would remain in complete charge of it, a very frequent occurrence throughout the United States in the first half of the twentieth century and one overlooked by regime theory when it takes the weakness of American government as a given.

Nevertheless, despite all their efforts to generate growth, the land-based entrepreneurs lost out in their competition with other cities for both capital investments and tourist dollars, a possibility that is an inherent part of growth coalition theory. Although they had shown initiative and the ability to shape local government, as growth coalition theory would expect, they had nonetheless failed. It was once again time to search for a new growth strategy.

a combination of growth theories since SC is so different

3

〜〜〜〜〜〜〜〜〜〜〜〜〜〜〜〜〜〜〜〜〜〜〜〜〜〜〜〜〜〜〜〜〜〜

THE REBIRTH AND DEFEAT OF THE SANTA CRUZ GROWTH COALITION

The Santa Cruz growth coalition's concern about its postwar economic future was far from an isolated phenomenon during the 1940s. Leaders in both the national corporate community and city growth coalitions feared that the economy would experience a downturn after the war ended, plunging the United States back into depression. To ward off this possibility, national-level policy groups, most notably the Committee for Economic Development (CED), actively advocated a growth agenda that emphasized the importance of establishing local planning groups to guide economic development (Collins 1981; Schriftgiesser 1960). As the organization's leaders repeatedly said to more conservative business executives, they thought it was better to instigate the right kind of planning rather than having the wrong kind—i.e., ambitious New Deal programs—forced upon them (Eakins 1966, 1969).

In keeping with this call for planning, highly visible California members of the CED made a luncheon visit to Santa Cruz in August 1945 to explain their overall mission to local leaders, who had just formed a local CED chapter. The roster of speakers included a commercial vice president from General Electric, who worked out of San Francisco; a general sales manager from Pacific Gas and Electric, the main utility company in Northern California; and a representative from the California Farm Bureau, which spoke for the powerful agricultural industry in the state (*Sentinel,* August 16, 1945, 5). Not surprisingly, the main point each speaker addressed was the need for economic development planning, to be accomplished in a cooperative endeavor between the CED and local chambers of commerce.

THE GROWTH COALITION'S THREE-PART PLAN

The plan that soon emerged for Santa Cruz included three new possibilities. First, the city would build a small airport that could be used by both tourists and new local businesses. To that end, the city purchased a large tract of land along the coast in the northwestern corner of the city. Second, the city would seek federal monies for the construction of a yacht harbor, which was seen as essential for attracting a higher class of tourist to the area (*Sentinel,* August 25, 1947, 1). Third, and most important, the planners announced that they would seek a community college or four-year college as the ideal way to develop a year-round economy without causing any damage to the clean environment essential to the tourist industry.

Buoyed by news from the area's congressman that the city had a good chance of receiving federal funds for highway construction and other infrastructure projects, including the airport, chamber officials and other prominent businessmen in the local CED chapter launched a campaign to rally the growth coalition and the citizenry behind their program of economic development (*Sentinel,* August 30, 1945, 5). This concerted effort was necessary because even with money from the federal government, local CED leaders recognized that the city would still need to raise taxes to finance needed infrastructure improvements, which might prove to be politically problematic.

To head off any potential opposition from local voters, including the highly vocal ultraconservatives in the small-business sector, the local CED leaders and their close allies organized a somewhat broader group—called Progressive Associates—to orchestrate a plan to bring more efficiency and economy into municipal government. As the name suggests, Progressive Associates invoked the classic Progressive Era principle of making government run like a business. The best method of achieving this ambition was now considered to be the adoption of the council-manager form of municipal government, long championed by the National Municipal League and other organizations in the urban policy-planning network. The 1911 business-led move for charter reform, focusing as it did on eliminating any challenges from Socialists and labor union members, had not included this particular reform. Now it made sense to a new generation of leaders in a different set of circumstances that called for new planning mechanisms and procedures, carried out by purportedly value-neutral administrators.

Under the new plan, the council would be enlarged to seven members elected at large in off-year, nonpartisan elections. The mayor would be selected by the council from among its members, not elected by the voters, thereby reducing the position to largely ceremonial duties when it came to setting policies. The administration of the city would be carried out by a professional city manager who would follow the guidelines set out by council decisions, thereby ensuring that any new tax hikes would be used sensibly. In other words, the Santa Cruz growth coalition was now prepared to adopt the full program that had been formulated by the National Municipal League during the Progressive Era.

With the Progressive Associate's program for charter revision underway, one of the city council members returned from a regional governmental meeting in September 1946 to formally advise his elected colleagues to consider instituting the council-manager form of government. Political legitimation in hand, the chamber and the local CED chapter, once again in concert with the Progressive Associates, began an extensive advertising campaign in the local press in January 1947 to urge adoption of the council-manager structure. At its annual meeting a few weeks later, the chamber membership voted to request that the political leadership of the city call for a special election to select a group of freeholders to rewrite the city charter.

As might be expected by now, ten of the fifteen people elected as freeholders were either chamber members or chamber-oriented people who had been formally endorsed by another closely related business organization, the Merchants Association. Even with that strong majority, the chamber continued to monitor the freeholders' deliberations closely, imploring them to propose the new system. The freeholder group formally recommended that the city adopt the council-manager plan in September, and three months later the city council announced a special election for March 1948 to vote on the issue. With no organized opposition and strong support from the *Sentinel,* the charter was approved by a five-to-two margin. Now that the government was reshaped to its liking, the growth coalition could set its sights on realizing the substantive elements of its plan.

In May 1947, nearly a year before the special election, the Progressive Associates had already selected twelve people to be on the board of trustees for the proposed college, but now their earlier college plans became more focused. They envisioned the college as a four-year institution specializing in business administration and public relations, which would help to create a labor force for the industries they hoped to attract as part of their larger growth plans. Although this four-year college was at the top of the agenda, they knew it would take more time to develop, so most of their efforts were devoted to securing state and federal monies for highway improvements, the airport, and the yacht harbor.

Eight years later, however, they had very little to show for their efforts. The airport did not prove to be financially feasible, leading to the sale of most of the land that had been set aside for it with the city realizing a small profit in the process. The yacht harbor was still in the planning phase and did not finally open until 1964. And no four-year college had been interested in locating in Santa Cruz, leading to scaled-back plans for a community college, which finally began accepting students in 1959 after leaders from Santa Cruz and Watsonville ended their wrangling and agreed to locate it in the center of the county, halfway between the two cities (Jones 2000a).

In 1955, with most of its development plans thwarted or delayed, the growth coalition was hit with the most devastating natural disaster ever to befall the city up to that point, a record-setting flood that left the downtown and nearby neighborhoods under water for many days, destroying most of the buildings immediately adjacent to the river. However, the flood turned out to be a golden opportunity to expand the downtown because just one year earlier the first Republican Congress since 1930 had enacted amendments in the Housing Act of 1949 that made it easier to use federal housing funds for downtown renewal (Domhoff 2005b). Fearing an economic slowdown and responding to intense lobbying by the urban policy-planning network, the Eisenhower administration and Congress provided generous funding for the new urban renewal program, making it possible for every city with a halfway reasonable plan to obtain money (Sanders 1987).

Alerted to this potential bonanza, the Santa Cruz City Council quickly set up a new Redevelopment Agency and drew expansive boundaries for a redevelopment area on both sides of the river. The ensuing federal money made it possible to buy out small landowners and remove all their buildings, including the few remaining buildings in the old Chinatown on the downtown side of the river. The result of this ten-year effort was a new shopping center a block from the main downtown street, along with a large new county building, a Holiday Inn, and a new condominium development on the other side of the river. To make sure that the new infrastructure would be secure, the Army Corps of Engineers now built levees that had been authorized back in the 1930s but never constructed. They were guaranteed to insulate the city from future flooding, although the river came perilously close to overflowing into the downtown in 1982. In the process, however, the Corps destroyed the scenic river by removing its curves, turning it into little more than a drainage ditch. Over the next thirty years the river gradually slowed to a trickle during the summer months, as the city's reservoir and new development projects in the San Lorenzo Valley drew off most of the water before it reached the downtown area.

FROM TOURIST MECCA TO UNIVERSITY TOWN

Even with the funds for urban renewal, the future did not look good for Santa Cruz until the Board of Regents, the governing body for the University of California, announced in October 1957 that it intended to expand the six-campus university system by adding three new campuses—one near San Diego, one near Los Angeles, and one seventy-five to a hundred miles south of the San Francisco Bay Area in the Central Coast region. Well aware that there were several potential sites in Santa Cruz County, which had many thousands of underutilized acres, growth coalition leaders throughout the county realized they had an excellent chance to win the competition for the Central Coast campus and finally reenergize their seasonal economy. After preliminary analyses by two or three members of the growth coalition who were alumni of the University of California, Berkeley, working in coordination with an architectural planner hired by the university as a consultant, it was decided that six hundred acres from the old Cowell limestone and ranch lands, in conjunction with four hundred undeveloped acres just below the ranch, would be an ideal site to present to the Board of Regents. This possibility seemed all the more attractive because the Cowell Ranch had not been used for more than cattle and horses for decades, leaving it relatively untouched and easy to develop. None of the founder's five children had any children themselves, so their fortune, including the ranch, was in the process of being transferred to a new foundation, the Cowell Foundation, which would be run by former Cowell lawyers and financial advisors in San Francisco.

Led once again by the Chamber of Commerce—and most notably, the managing editor of the *Sentinel,* Gordon "Scotchy" Sinclair, along with Harold Hyde, an owner-executive for a local department store—the growth coalition then orchestrated a three-year-effort to attract the new campus to Santa Cruz (Hyde and Jarrell 2002; McFadden 1981). The Santa Cruz leaders met with university administrators numerous times, made detailed presentations to the Board of Regents, replete with promises of every possible accommodation the regents might wish from the city, and lobbied state and country elected officials. Their offer, however, was not impressive enough to sway the regents from making a preliminary decision in December 1959 in favor of a site south of San Jose, which had the advantage of proximity to the newly emerging electronics industry in what soon came to be known as the "Silicon Valley."

Undaunted, the Santa Cruz boosters persevered in their efforts by drawing once again on their connections as graduates of the Berkeley campus to convince the regents to reopen the question and entertain a revised proposal. Now all the land would be on the old Cowell Ranch, so the regents would not have to deal with several different landowners. Furthermore, the price was lowered to a very attractive $1,000 per acre, about $250 per acre below the assessed value of the property, which would make it possible for the university to buy twenty-three hundred acres instead of the thousand originally planned. In addition, the Cowell Foundation in effect promised to return $975,000 of the purchase price through a grant to build the first cluster of dorms, dining facilities, administrative offices, and faculty offices, which would be named Cowell College (Johnson 1994, 11; Jones 2000c). The city and county offered $2 million in infrastructural improvements.

The Santa Cruz growth coalition also had the good fortune to have two local Republican representatives at the state level, one in the Assembly, one in the Senate, who were part of the local growth coalition and on key committees in the legislature. These two elected officials in effect made it clear to the regents, through personal visits and newspaper interviews, that they would be extremely disappointed if university officials chose the San Jose location, where land was much more expensive. They also stressed that the San Jose area already had a state college, San Jose State, which was part of the rival state college system that vied with the University of California system for state monies (Hyde and Jarrell 2002; Jones 2000c).

At this point the Santa Cruz growth coalition was aided by the fact that on closer inspection the site south of San Jose began to look less attractive because the university would have to initiate condemnation procedures against a Catholic novitiate to secure part of the necessary land. The growing problems with smog in the area were also stressed by critics of the San Jose location. When the pluses of a Santa Cruz location and the strong stands by the Santa Cruz representatives in the state legislature were stacked up against the problems that might develop if the San Jose location were chosen, the scales began to tip in Santa Cruz's favor.

The more attractive offer from the Cowell Foundation may not have been a completely altruistic one. In the long run its acceptance would vastly increase the foundation's wealth because it also owned nearly half of the land abutting the proposed campus site. Thanks to the appreciation in assessed valuation that the foundation's remaining land was likely to enjoy after the campus was constructed, its trustees knew their offer to the university would provide the foundation with new revenues for future grantmaking. With the campus planned for 27,500 students by 1990, the city was projected to experience a five-fold population increase in the same time period, from 25,000 in 1960 to 125,000 in 1990, which would mean that the foundation's land would be ideal for housing for faculty and staff. The original growth projections also envisioned the development of 150 acres of foundation property near the campus as commercial, office, and industrial space (Johnson 1994, 11).

The close cooperation between local business interests and political officials that characterized the successful effort to entice the university to Santa Cruz continued after the regents' final decision was announced in December 1960. Within a week, city and county officials met with representatives from the university to set a timetable for construction of the campus and access roads for an opening in September 1965. In what turned out ten years later to be a fateful political decision that undermined the local power structure, the city council agreed to put those parts of the vast campus that were to be developed in the first twenty years inside the city limits to make it easier to provide water and utilities services.

About the same time, county supervisors and Chamber of Commerce directors convened a meeting to develop a strategy for attracting industries to Santa Cruz that might be interested in locating near a research university. It was decided that Chamber staff would begin surveying different university communities "for information relative to industrial development which took place in conjunction with the location of a major campus" (*Sentinel*, March 24, 1961, 1). Two years later, as actual construction began, the founding chancellor of the new campus asked Harold Hyde, the local department store executive mentioned above, to become his chief business and financial officer, further cementing the ties between town and gown (Hyde and Jarrell 2002).

The energetic planning for the arrival of the new university campus took place in the context of yet another general planning initiative by city leaders that had begun while the location for the campus was still uncertain. This effort was called the Santa Cruz of Tomorrow Citizen's Committee, and its goals were expansive. The downtown subcommittee laid out plans for an expansion of the downtown that would remove most of the old residential structures from the streets just off the main commercial strip—houses that dated back to the nineteenth century, including the stately Victorians that had been built by Hihn and other wealthy elites. They would be replaced with commercial buildings, apartment buildings, and tourist motels. At the same time, the beach area subcommittee argued for the expansion of tourism through the development of a new hotel and convention complex. It would be located on thirty-seven acres of fallow coastal farm land along West Cliff Drive, a scenic two-lane city road that winds along the low cliffs overlooking the Monterey Bay on the west side of the city, about a mile from the boardwalk and two miles from the downtown. The site lies directly across the road from one of the city's most beautiful bay vistas and hallowed surfing areas, where visitors can park their cars and watch the seals on Seal Rock and the surfers in Steamer Lane.

To provide automobile access to all these improvements with the greatest possible ease, the traffic subcommittee said it was necessary to build or expand several state-financed highways that would speed traffic to both the downtown and the beach area, neither of which was easy to reach at the time because there were no direct routes. Based on this aggregation of plans, city leaders applied to the federal government's Housing and Home Finance Agency for an urban redevelopment grant that could be used to hire a city and regional planning firm in San Francisco to suggest a detailed general plan that would incorporate the university into the growth coalition's ambitious expansion plans.

By 1963 the consultants presented both a *General Plan for Future Development* and a *Downtown Santa Cruz Sketch Plan*. They concurred with the general tenor of the Santa Cruz of Tomorrow Committee's vision of the future and suggested sites for the "new and desirable industry" that would be attracted by the campus (Williams and Mocine 1963b, ii). They warned against "invasion by modern competitive shopping centers" that might steal the department stores considered essential to downtown prosperity (Williams and Mocine 1963a, 1). This recommendation was a veiled reference to plans already on the drawing boards for a regional shopping center—later to be named the Capitola Mall—on hundreds of acres of open farmland in the middle of the county, just a few miles south of Santa Cruz, and not far from Hihn's now quaint tourist area.

To set the stage for the dramatic changes that were deemed necessary, including a doubling of the size of the downtown from 85 to 170 acres, the reports documented a downtown area "beset with problems of traffic congestion, outmoded buildings and obsolescent land use" (Williams and Mocine 1963a, 1). There would be a need for new and larger buildings, especially for the department stores, and the center of the shopping district would be focused on malls, walkways, and plazas, with limited automobile traffic. As in the Santa Cruz of Tomorrow report, the housing just off the commercial area would be replaced by a combination of new retail space, motels, and apartment buildings. In order to accomplish these ambitious goals, the report concluded it would be necessary to float municipal bonds and to make use of the wide range of federal subsidy programs that fall under the rubric of urban renewal (Williams and Mocine 1963b, 39). In fact, urban renewal offered "the only means to cope with the most deteriorated downtown blocks in Santa Cruz," with the city's one-third share of the cost being paid for with municipal improvements such as parking structures (Williams and Mocine 1963a, 14).

Turning to the beach area, the reports first recommended a widening of the fishing wharf so that it could hold more restaurants and shops. They then spelled out the economic justifications for the new hotel and convention center on Lighthouse Field, dubbed "the Court of the Seven Seas" on the map enfolded into the plan booklet. The consultants went one step further than the

Santa Cruz of Tomorrow Committee by saying that all the single family hous-ing on West Cliff between Lighthouse Field and the current beach/motel area would "give away gradually to apartments and hotels," which added up to a major expansion of the tourist area (Williams and Mocine 1963a, 23). Several streets in the hill area just behind the beach, a tangle of small hotels and old summer cottages, would become part of an urban renewal area that would lead to bigger motels.

Since the expansions of both the downtown and the beach might lead to even more traffic congestion, the plan called for an elaborate set of short ur-ban freeways, collectively called "the Beach Loop." These new freeways would encircle the downtown area, with exits for the beach area. This new freeway loop would be supplemented by an inner loop of existing streets, starting with the extension of one of the two main streets to the beach area by means of a new bridge. This extension then would go through a low-income neighbor-hood near the boardwalk—Beach Flats—and end up in a giant parking lot. As for the other main route to the beach, Chestnut Street, which is the anchor of the residential neighborhood near the downtown, it would be widened into a four- or six-lane expressway and extended to the beach area.

In all, the new freeway plan as finally put forward in 1969 would displace over four hundred houses, two churches, and a school, most of them near the downtown (*City on a Hill Press,* October 5, 1969, 1–2; *City on a Hill Press,* Oc-tober 17, 1969, 1). As far as leaders in the growth coalition were concerned, a more efficient circulation of traffic was essential because it meant a more effi-cient circulation of capital—more time for shopping is more money for landowners. In particular, the new convention center and related facilities planned for Lighthouse Field would be much more lucrative with the Beach Loop. Not surprisingly, then, all aspects of the new general plan were greeted with enthusiasm by the spokespersons for the growth coalition, and at that point they met with little or no opposition from the general citizenry. The plan was adopted by the city council with minor changes in 1964, and the city's planning department and the Redevelopment Agency were instructed to take the necessary steps to implement it.

UC SANTA CRUZ TRANSFORMS THE CITY

In the first of many unanticipated outcomes, however, the university did not prove to be a draw for industrial development. Instead, it was focused on a classical liberal arts education within a cluster of small colleges of six hundred to eight hundred students, on the model of Oxford and Cambridge, but with a core of common natural science, social science, and humanities buildings in the center of the campus, along with a large campus-wide library. The idea was to combine the best of a small liberal arts education with the upper-division, research-oriented classes that a large-scale university has to offer. This plan was the pet project of the president of the university system at the time, industrial relations expert Clark Kerr, and the founding chancellor of the Santa Cruz campus, Dean McHenry, a political scientist who had been friends with Kerr since the 1930s, when both were enthusiastic supporters of the New Deal.

Because of the focus on a classical liberal arts undergraduate education, and with no plans for an engineering school for several years to come, most traditional businesses did not think the campus had much to offer them. Instead, it became a magnet for the kind of liberal-minded people who run bookstores, music/record stores, art galleries, head shops, and student-oriented cafes, bistros, and bars. Still, the arrival of the university did help to revitalize what had come to be a run-down beach and retirement town, with several empty storefronts in the central business district. Swallowing their disappointment, city officials greeted the first contingent of 650 eager and well-scrubbed "pioneer" students, as they were called, with joy in September 1965. This initial cohort included approximately 500 first-year students and 150 junior transfers. City leaders and the *Sentinel* also showered attention on the faculty, many of whom were not much older than the students.

The student body was unique in many ways. Because of the emphasis on the liberal arts, with no applied or technical programs, and no athletic scholarships (or even any collegiate teams), the students tended to be searchers and seekers who did not yet have focused educational or career plans. Because the campus was so small, the admissions office could be selective, leading to a student body that had more students from the highest few percent of their graduating high school classes than the larger University of California campuses. The early adoption of a pass/fail grading system, along with detailed written evaluations of the students' performance in each class, added to the campus's appeal to many idealistic students of that era. The complete absence of fraternities and sororities, which were actively discouraged in order to make the small colleges the center of student life, also contributed to a unique collegiate atmosphere, at least for a public university of any size.

The students arrived with positive attitudes toward authority figures and were primarily concerned with educational issues, not politics, but all that began to change from almost the moment the first quarter began. The army had sent 3,500 combat troops into Vietnam in the spring of 1965, hardly enough to make most students sit up and take notice, but there were 175,000 more there by the end of that year, and 350,000 by mid-1966, with the level reaching over 500,000 in the next few years. This huge build-up was accompanied by a massive air war against North Vietnam that began in March 1965, soon destroying its meager industrial infrastructure—25,000 sorties in 1965, 79,000 in 1966, and 108,000 in 1967 (Hess 1998, 87–89). It was not long before few bridges remained standing, the roads were pulverized, and people were being napalmed, all of which was graphically portrayed on television for everyone to see, including the Santa Cruz students.

By the end of the first year, the nicely dressed and well-mannered students had become longhaired, scruffy, militant, and strongly opposed to the Vietnam War. The possibility of being drafted, the fate of loved ones who were sent to Vietnam, and the seeming futility of the war became burning issues over the next few years. So did continuing concerns with civil rights, the environment, feminism, and the plight of low-paid farm laborers, leading some of the most politically committed students to work in César Chávez's long struggle to create the United Farm Workers through the use of strategic nonviolence and boycotts.

The founding of a unique liberal arts campus at this particular moment in history, we argue, led to the institutionalization of a politically liberal and activist student culture that probably would not have developed otherwise. By placing emphasis on the activist culture that developed at UC Santa Cruz, we are not overlooking the fact that there was major leftist activism at universities all over the country in the late 1960s and early 1970s. During the two or three years before the highly visible and militant Students for a Democratic Society imploded and splintered into rival Maoist factions in the summer of 1969, its leadership was widely admired and followed by a significant minority of college students of that era, temporarily eclipsing the usual hegemony of student government leaders, fraternities and sororities, and athletic teams. Nevertheless, our point is that this leadership role was not sustained on very many campuses, and, even more important, that it rarely became part of local electoral movements in the way it did in Santa Cruz. The coincidence of a new campus of highly liberal students in an institutional framework that did not feature sports and a fraternity/sorority system made UC Santa Cruz unique for the next twenty to twenty-five years.

This claim is supported by the findings on the political attitudes of incoming college freshmen in 1970 by the Higher Education Research Institute at UCLA. In that survey, 41.0 percent of the first-year students at 536 American universities considered themselves to be "liberal" or "far left," whereas the figure was 82.7 percent for Santa Cruz. Santa Cruz was not only twice the national norm but higher on the liberal-left percent than the best-known "radical" campus of the time, the University of California, Berkeley. In 1972, the first year for which we could obtain these numbers for UC Berkeley, 56.5 percent of its first-year students considered themselves liberal or left, compared to a much higher figure of 80.4 percent at UC Santa Cruz for the same year. Furthermore, the almost complete absence of a similar activist student political culture at the very different campuses opened at UC Irvine and UC San Diego—far more traditional in most ways, more focused on graduate programs and natural sciences and information sciences—in the same year as UC Santa Cruz began to admit students shows that the leftism of Santa Cruz students was not simply a function of UC Santa Cruz having a new and small student body.

The ongoing surveys by the Higher Education Research Institute also show that these differences were maintained over the decades even though there was a gradual decline in student liberalism at Santa Cruz from 1972 to 1982, as there was at other colleges and universities, with the figure reaching a low of 49.4 percent at Santa Cruz in 1982. By 2004, however, it had crept up to 60.4 percent, still the highest figure of all University of California campuses by six percentage points, and still double the nationwide average for all first-year students in public universities, 29.1 percent. Table 3.1 shows these trends and continuing differences for selected years for UC Santa Cruz, UC Berkeley, the nationwide sample of public universities, and a subset of "select" public universities first reported in 1980.

To provide further perspective on the continuing liberal atmosphere at UC Santa Cruz, even in an era in which the students are far less likely to vote or take any interest in local politics, Table 3.2 presents the percentage of liberals and leftists in the first-year class for the eight undergraduate campuses of the University of California in 2004, along with the national norms for all public universities in the sample and the select public universities. This table suggests that UC Santa Cruz continues to attract the most liberal first-year students in the University of California system, even though they are less activist than they were before 1978. It is our claim that for many years these liberal and leftist students reinforced and sustained the original activist student culture that developed on the campus in the 1960s, which in turn may have had an impact on many of those students who left for college with more moderate or less formed political views.

In claiming that an activist student culture developed at UC Santa Cruz, we are not saying that all students, or even very many of them, were activists. But research on social movements suggests that only a handful of activists are needed to ignite social change because they have the time and motivation to learn how to strategize, organize, and take the kind of actions that galvanize others into joining them (Flacks 1988, 2005). In the case of Santa Cruz, this nationally oriented activism was eventually to have major consequences for the local growth coalition: the activists were able to mobilize the liberal student body as a key part of a pro-neighborhood and environmentalist voting bloc.

TABLE 3.1

UC Santa Cruz Students' Political Attitudes: Trend Data

	1972	1974	1978	1982	1990	1996	2002
Santa Cruz	80.4%	77.2%	63.7%	49.4%	58.2%	61.5%	58.1%
Berkeley	56.5%	49.1%	37.7%	32.9%	42.9%	NA	45.2%
Select public	NA	NA	NA	24.0%	32.1%	32.7%	32.6%
All public	39.5%	33.9%	28.0%	N.A.	28.3%	26.1%	27.7%

This table shows the percentage of incoming students who describe themselves as "liberal" or "far left" at public universities, select public universities, UC Berkeley, and UC Santa Cruz for selected years between 1972 and 2002.

Source: Cooperative Institutional Research Program Freshman Survey, Higher Education Research Institute, University of California, Los Angeles

TABLE 3.2

UC Santa Cruz Students' Political Attitudes: 2004

All public	Select public	Santa Cruz	Berkeley	UCLA
29.7%	35.4%	60.4%	54.3%	48.3%
Santa Barbara	**Davis**	**San Diego**	**Irvine**	**Riverside**
48.0%	45.7%	44.2%	37.6%	35.7%

This table shows the percentage of first-year students who described themselves as either "liberal" or "far left" at public universities, select public universities, and the eight undergraduate campuses of the University of California in 2004.

Source: Cooperative Institutional Research Program Freshman Survey, Higher Education Research Institute, University of California, Los Angeles; UC Undergraduate Experiences Survey, Office of Student Research, University of California, Berkeley

SPRUCING UP THE DOWNTOWN

Downtown business owners and city officials took their first step toward implementing the new general plan in March 1967, with the formation of a Mall Committee to turn the main downtown commercial avenue—Pacific Avenue—into a "semi-pedestrian mall," a type of mall that allows for some automobile traffic while giving priority to pedestrians and shoppers. Although shopping-oriented malls and semi-malls were coming into vogue at the time, the Pacific Garden Mall was created with the added idea that it should be a cultural core as well as a marketing area in order to draw more potential customers into the downtown. The landscape architects therefore laid out a plan whereby a single sinuous traffic lane—much narrower than the existing street—snaked along just about the entire length of the old Pacific Avenue as a way to limit traffic speed and allow for wider sidewalks. The plan also called for the planting of trees and shrubs, along with the installation of benches and fountains (*Sentinel,* April 14, 1967, 17). By the next year 70 percent of downtown property owners had signed on, well above the 60 percent minimum required for approval.

Opened in 1969, during the heyday of the hippies and the counterculture, the new mall soon exuded far more "culture" than the growth coalition had anticipated: it became the site of a vibrant but unconventional amalgam of local residents, tourists, students, hippies, street musicians, panhandlers, elderly bench sitters, and downtown merchants. While storeowners who catered to students and the youthful counterculture lauded all of this as a revival of the central business district, others began to complain that the design of the mall was conducive to the congregation of persons who disrupted commerce. In fact, an anti-loitering law was soon being considered by the city council, although nothing came of it. From the perspective of growth coalition theory, the use-value amenities of the downtown mall were thought by some landowners and merchants to be interfering with, not augmenting, the more central issue of exchange values. It is a conflict that continues to the present day.

Despite the qualms over hippies and panhandlers, downtown real estate values rose markedly, and new construction activity was brisk. The assessed value of total taxable property in Santa Cruz County, which had increased by 45.4 percent between 1960 and 1965, leaped ahead by 164 percent over the next ten years, far more than the increase for the state as a whole (California Institute of County Government 1966–1969, 1973, 1976–1977). Retail sales rose by 72.7 percent between 1967 and 1972, faster than the 46.0 percent rate for California as a whole (U.S. Bureau of the Census 1977). Overall, Santa Cruz became one of the fastest-growing counties in the state, much of it attributable at the time to the city and the university (McFadden 1981, 40).

THE FIRST DEFEAT FOR THE GROWTH COALITION

The plans for a major commercial and tourism development at Lighthouse Field first came to the attention of the newly arrived faculty, staff, and students at UC Santa Cruz through a brief news item in the *Sentinel* on October

16, 1968, which mentioned the possible construction of a $20 million hotel and convention complex—along with related commercial developments, such as retail shops, a theater, and restaurants. Public relations support for the project was spearheaded by the local chamber of commerce through its Convention and Visitors Bureau. This effort was augmented by the Overall Economic Development Plan Commission, created in 1966 as an extension of the Santa Cruz County Advertising Committee, the major growth-booster organization since 1939.

Playing its usual role as growth statesman, the *Sentinel* strongly endorsed the project on its editorial pages two days later, asserting that a "convention center and a major tourist attraction such as proposed by the Lighthouse Park Development Company is in the best interests of the Santa Cruz area" (*Sentinel*, October 18, 1968, 19). The newspaper editorial addressed the complex contractual negotiations facing the city, county, and private developers, but did not seem to foresee the possibility that the convention project might be opposed by environmentalists and organized residents of the neighborhood adjacent to the proposed development site.

In order to realize this ambitious development plan, city leaders first had to show the state government that they had the support to move ahead with the expansive highway plans called for in the 1964 general plan. This would first of all entail the widening of the historic two-lane coastal highway, Route 1, which connects Santa Cruz to San Francisco in the north and Monterey in the south, into a six- or eight-lane freeway, perhaps depressed below street level, with exits at three or four major cross streets. This highway, named "Mission Street" once it enters the city, is also a significant commercial area for West Side residents, with restaurants, grocery stores, drugstores, dry cleaners, and specialty shops for household needs.

The widening of Route 1/Mission Street was seen as an essential first step in the overall transportation plan by all members of the growth coalition for two reasons. First, it would put the several thousand acres of ranch and farm lands on the coast northwest of the city limits within a few minutes of the downtown and the university, making that land ripe for annexation and an ideal location for major housing developments whose residents would be able to shop in the downtown with relative ease. Developers projected that as many as forty thousand people might be living on these open lands within the next twenty to thirty years. Second, a wider highway would make for easier beach and boardwalk access for tourists by means of the adjoining six-lane Beach Loop described in the 1964 general plan. As already explained, carrying out this plan would lead to major residential demolitions, especially in the neighborhoods near the downtown commercial strip.

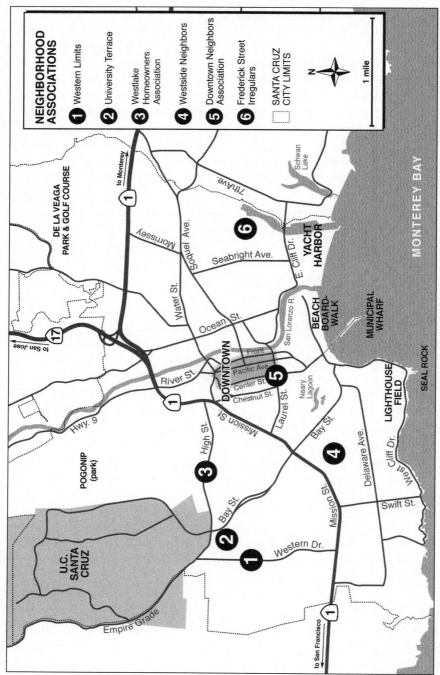

MAP 3.1 Santa Cruz and its vicinity, along with the locations of the major neighborhood groups that played a role in the progressive takeover

Although the managing editor of the *Sentinel*, Scotchy Sinclair, served on the regional advisory board of the state's highway commission, and had considerable influence, the exact location of the new highways was not a done deal. Nor was it certain that the new highways would be built any time soon because there was fierce competition among cities for the highways they all wanted to facilitate expansion. Furthermore, state highway engineers had drawn several slightly different plans for the routing of the north-south coastal road. Most of the alternatives were close to the old highway, but one of them bypassed the downtown and instead angled up near the university entrance, cutting through the neighborhoods favored by faculty members, local professionals, and business leaders. The alternative near the university, called the "edge-of-town" alternative, had the unintended consequence of arousing everyone into action against that option, but especially the university administrators and the residents in University Terrace, recently developed just about the time the university opened, and residents of Westlake, one of the most expensive neighborhoods within the city limits.

The edge-of-town alternative even upset the downtown land- and storeowners because it would make it far easier for residents of two solidly middle-class neighborhoods near the university to shop in the slowly emerging Capitola Mall, putting it within five or six minutes of them. Given the unanimous organized opposition to this option by the local growth coalition, the university, and the two neighborhoods near the university, it seemed unlikely that it would be chosen by the highway commission, but its critics felt they had to remain vigilant throughout the selection process. (As one side effect of this option, the newly formed Westlake Homeowners Association was able to halt plans for a small shopping center between the university's main entrance and the Westlake neighborhood, with the land remaining vacant for two decades before housing was built on it.)

As for the more traditional route along or near Mission Street, it pitted virtually every neighborhood in the city against the growth coalition. The pro-highway forces called themselves "progressives," people who were trying to move the city forward by creating new jobs and new housing for future Santa Cruzans. With the help of the *Sentinel*, the growth coalition tried to characterize the neighborhood defenders and environmentalists as mere "traditionalists" with narrow, selfish interests, but it was a label they refused to accept.

[handwritten margin note: traditionalists win]

Although there had always been some liberals and potential neighborhood activists in what was an overwhelmingly conservative city, many of the anti-highway activists were not simply concerned citizens of long standing but also members of the new university community, both its faculty and its staff, along with their spouses. These campus-based activists had the singular advantage of being independent of local business owners for their livelihood; their pay-checks came from the university system's Office of the President in Berkeley, courtesy of the state legislature and the taxpayers of California. Many of them had secure jobs because of tenure, as well as flexible work hours that allowed them to participate in politics. And they felt no deference toward local business leaders because they tended to look to nationally oriented status hierarchies re-lated to their academic discipline for their social identities.

Faculty and staff members and their spouses were used to speaking in pub-lic and arguing, and they had not left behind the congested freeways of major cities to see highways built through their new neighborhoods. Some of them had gravitated to the old Victorians near the downtown, which they had been able to purchase at reasonable prices because most of the local well-to-do had long ago moved into newer suburban-type housing in the Westlake area. There was also an unexpected X factor in the equation: the faculty and staff families who defended neighborhoods soon realized they had potential allies in the many students living in and around their neighborhoods, where five or six students might be sharing a house. As the campus newspaper reported, these students, and student activists on campus, were invited to attend public hearings to oppose a finalized freeway plan (*City on a Hill Press,* October 5, 1969, 1).

The prospect of a widened Mission Street and Beach Loop also generated a powerful use-value alliance between those neighborhoods that would feel the heaviest impact and local environmentalists concerned with preserving open land just a few miles north of the city. (The open land included coastlands among the most beautiful in the United States, with beaches, rocky shorelines, and jagged mountain cliffs in close proximity.) This alliance was made all the more potent because the local environmentalists, some of whom were once again linked to the university in one way or another, also had connections with environmentalists throughout the state who adamantly opposed the de-velopment of the scenic ocean-front ranch and farm lands on the narrow coastal shelf between the ocean and the mountains.

In addition, the neighborhood and environmental activists had the help of an especially activist core of university faculty and students in a new—and unique—undergraduate department, Community Studies, created in 1969 to allow its majors to focus their attention on local communities. With its special emphasis on the social circumstances and cultures of low-income or margin-alized people, it was a potential ally of any beleaguered neighborhood. Three years later, a second new interdisciplinary department, Environmental Stud-ies, quickly became actively involved in analyzing and publicizing the long-term negative impacts of many hastily drawn development projects, with its faculty and students often testifying before government agencies.

Community Studies not only focused on the community level but also emphasized internships and field studies, forms of participant learning that had slowly gained acceptance within universities over the decades as a way to learn through practical experience and at the same time earn academic credit. The pressing demand for "relevance" by college students across the country in the 1960s hastened this acceptance. In the case of field studies within the Community Studies major, they had added legitimacy: six months of full-time field study with an underserved community or organization are required for graduation. This intensive field study is preceded by standard academic courses that prepare students for their fieldwork and then is followed by courses in which the students have to analyze what they learned and relate it to ongoing theoretical debates in the social sciences. Most important, perhaps, the Community Studies major gives students the right to pick their field site. It was the first fully funded university program of its kind in an American university, and it had few imitators thereafter (Friedland and Rotkin 2003). Most of the field study programs that mushroomed at other universities in the late 1960s and 1970s depended on "soft money" (funding that has to be renewed each year) and faculty volunteers, and almost all of them were gone by the early 1980s.

The fact that Community Study students, not faculty, chose the field site made it possible for some of them to become active participants in the political activities taking place in Santa Cruz, despite protests about their presence from the downtown business community and elected officials. The protests were brushed aside, however reluctantly, by university administrators. Although most students chose sites outside of Santa Cruz, including many foreign countries, the program nonetheless provided tens of thousands of hours of organizing and staff support for the efforts of a wide range of activist and nonprofit groups in Santa Cruz, nonelectoral and electoral, for the next twenty-one years. Between 1969 and 1990, over one thousand students did field studies in Santa Cruz County, mostly in nonprofit service organizations, but many in political and advocacy groups. Dozens of these students went on to become leaders in activist groups throughout the country. For example, one helped found Hospice; another became head of Janitors for Justice, a union in Los Angeles and San Francisco; and another became a major organizer for the American Federation of State, County and Municipal Employees. Two became city managers in Northern California cities, another served as the mayor of San Jose from 1999 to 2006, and two became mayors of Santa Cruz (Friedland and Rotkin 2003).

In the specific case of the freeway controversy, Community Studies faculty and students had an impact on the decision not to build a freeway. They conducted a survey of citizen attitudes shortly after a tumultuous local hearing

held by the California Highway Commission in late September, just as the fall
quarter was about to begin. At least two thousand residents, including two
hundred university students, crowded into the Civic Auditorium located across
from the city hall for what turned out to be the beginning of a new era of local
protest and activism. In addition to environmentalists and neighborhood activists, a large contingent of organized senior citizens—urged on by a leftist social worker, who later became the dean of the School of Social Work at San Jose
State University, and an ultraconservative John Birch Society member on the
city council—protested the fact they would be displaced from their low-
income housing. Although most people in attendance opposed the freeway, six
of the seven city council members testified in favor of it. At the end of the hearing the highway commissioners explained that they were unsure as to what to
do in the face of the disagreement between the majority on the city council and
the many citizens who were present. They therefore decided to wait another
thirty days before making a decision and stressed that any communications
they received within that time period would become part of the record and
taken into account as part of the decision-making process.

Among those in attendance, mostly to gain a sense of Santa Cruz politics,
was the newly arrived founder of Community Studies, Bill Friedland, who
had already developed a somewhat similar program at Cornell. Sensing an
opportunity to show the usefulness of student-based research in a community, he was in immediate touch with several colleagues, including a statistics
professor, and convinced them they should join him in organizing a public
opinion survey to determine where the community actually stood on the freeway issue. The next day they put up posters announcing a course on community attitudes that would teach students every aspect of survey research and
allow them to do the whole project themselves. Twenty-eight students signed
up, meeting every day to design the survey, pilot test it, carry out the interviews, and analyze the results. A final report was delivered to the San Francisco office of the highway commission twenty-eight days later, based on
interviews with a carefully drawn sample of 940 people from across the city.

To everyone's surprise, and especially the pro-highway members of the city
council, who had confidently claimed they knew what their constituents
wanted, the majority of local citizens either rejected any changes in the present
highway system or wanted the decision postponed. When asked to rank four
choices—(1) a new route paralleling the existing Route 1; (2) a new route that
would literally take out the main entrance to the campus; (3) postpone a decision for further study; and (4) no new freeways—only 10.6 percent supported
the route favored by the city council's majority as their first or second choice.
The route that went through the university's entrance was the first or second
choice of 59.4 percent, to the further consternation of university administra-

tors; 45.9 percent favored postponing any decision; and 40.9 percent gave no new freeways as their first or second choice (Community Studies Proseminar 1969, 6). There were no differences by age or area of residence. Attesting to the level of concern over the potential negative impacts of the freeway proposals, 94.1 percent of the respondents had heard about the controversy, and 27.3 percent had taken part in three or more activities against the freeway (e.g., signed a petition, attended a meeting, written a letter, joined an organization) (Community Studies Proseminar 1969, 11).

Once these results were widely publicized in local newspapers, including the *Sentinel,* many leaders within the growth coalition criticized the survey as a veiled attempt by left-leaning university members to influence local political issues. When Friedland was asked about the purpose of the course and the survey, he replied, "This is a research activity." While the statement is accurate, the survey did provide information useful to opponents of the growth coalition that would not have been available if the university had not been located in the city (*City on a Hill Press,* October 17, 1969, 1).

In the end, the state highway officials did not have the stomach to widen Mission Street or build a new freeway in the face of widespread public opposition and in an era of direct action in a city with a highly politicized student culture. The efforts by the neighborhood-environmentalist-student coalition were so successful that Mission Street remained virtually unchanged for the next thirty years, when a consensus developed that a four-lane road with left turn bays was essential and permissible in order to deal with the huge increase in traffic. Just as critical from a neighborhood point of view, the plan for a new Beach Loop freeway also was abandoned. Nevertheless, the widening of Chestnut Street and its extension to the beach area remained a live option in the minds of real estate developers, the owners of businesses along the boardwalk, and the city manager for many years to come.

As would be expected by growth coalition theory, neighborhood activism gradually died down after the decision by the highway commission, but neighborhood and environmental leaders had learned that they could have success on issues of concern to them, particularly if they worked with students. In the process, the university in effect became a rival power base to the downtown growth coalition. It provided neighborhood and environmental leaders with expertise, financial support, and numerous student volunteers, many of them receiving university credit for their efforts through Community Studies or Environmental Studies. It thereby added the extra push that neighborhood leaders and environmentalists needed to prevail on growth issues.

This does not mean, however, that all members of the university community supported the gradually coalescing opponents of the growth coalition. Most high-level administrators, many with close ties to the chamber of commerce and including the founding chancellor, looked upon the new turn of events with dismay. They had neither desired nor anticipated the activism that emerged. Moreover, the university administration itself was viewed as part of the growth coalition by some faculty and many students because it had its own growth agenda, which would have a major impact on downtown infrastructure and the availability of housing over the coming decades. To make matters more uncertain and tense, the state constitution exempts the University of California's growth plans from any control by local government as long as they relate to the university's educational mission, making the Santa Cruz campus a wild card for city planners and neighborhood activists alike. Although the original plan for the Santa Cruz campus envisioned rapid growth throughout the 1970s and 1980s, that goal came to be opposed by most city residents and many faculty and students. When the pressures on the university administration were combined with a lower than expected number of new college students in California by the early 1970s, the growth goals for the campus were lowered from 27,500 to 7,500 for the year 1990. The net result was much slower growth in the 1970s, creeping from 3,713 in 1970 to 6,364 in 1980, which meant that the university did not become a target of concern again until the 1980s.

SAVING THE NORTH COAST
AND LIGHTHOUSE FIELD

Although the growth coalition's preferred first step, the widening of highways, had been stopped, that did not mean an end to the efforts to implement the next steps in the 1964 general plan. City leaders well understood that they could build new developments first and then hope that the subsequent traffic congestion would lead to pressures for the necessary highways. In fact, the idea for housing for as many as forty thousand people on two ranches on the north coast, the 950-acre Scaroni Ranch and the 2,200-acre Wilder Ranch, had already resurfaced during the 1969 highway controversy when outside development companies bought the two ranches. In 1970 local activists were attending hearings to protest the construction of twenty-two hundred houses on the Scaroni Ranch, and in 1972 the developers who had purchased the Wilder Ranch told the city they planned to build nine thousand to ten thousand houses on the property over the next thirty years. About the same time, plans for moving ahead with the hotel and convention center on Lighthouse Field were announced.

The opponents of the two plans, many of whom had worked together on earlier efforts, including a successful effort to stop a California utility company from building a nuclear plant a little north of the Wilder and Scaroni ranches, formed two overlapping organizations with the common purpose of blocking both the north coast and the Lighthouse Field developments, retaining all the land as open space. Operation Wilder was formed by six local environmental activists, including a biology professor at the community college and two current or former staff members at UC Santa Cruz, along with pro-environment lawyers. It quickly revealed the approach it would take by raising money to hire an organizer trained by Saul Alinsky to develop highly visible and confrontational tactics. The Save Lighthouse Point Association also had the support of environmentalists, but even more it had a strong base in the neighborhoods along West Cliff Drive that would be most affected by a major development in their front yards. Both organizations had the backing of two statewide environmentalist organizations, the Sierra Club and Save the Coast.

The new battles would be much tougher than the one over the freeways because immediate and major financial gains were at stake for the landowners and the downtown commercial sector. This fact was signaled very early in the game when the would-be developers of the Wilder Ranch sued several named leaders in Operation Wilder for the incredible sum of $121 million on the basis of the organization's first press release. A suit for $10,000 would have scared him, one of the founders of Operation Wilder told us in 2007, but the thought of $121 million—that's $604.8 million in 2007 dollars—was so unbelievable that he and his fellow defendants almost laughed out loud. It was an early example of a SLAPP, a lawsuit meant to stun activists into silence (Pring and Canan 1996). Operation Wilder was not silenced, but its leaders did have to spend time and energy fighting the lawsuit over the next several years with the help of numerous lawyers who donated their services. The suit was dismissed in 1974, the same year that the development plan was defeated.

Despite all the financial and legal power that the growth coalition could throw into these crucial confrontations, there was the possibility that money and corporate lawyers could be neutralized by a new weapon that had unexpectedly emerged for the challengers, the ballot box.

THE NEW ELECTORAL COALITION

Although the pro-neighborhood and environmentalist forces had been able to halt highway expansion, there was no thought that they could contest local elections and "capture the state," as some Marxist insurgents of the time dramatically put it. Council elections in 1969 and 1971 were still completely dominated by the chamber of commerce candidates. In 1971, even with the ferment over widening the highway and annexing thousands of acres on the north coast, four centrist and conservative candidates, all reliably pro-growth, won easily.

Shortly after the 1971 council elections, however, the power equation changed dramatically. The campus was transformed from a liberal magnet and rival power base into a Trojan horse by the passage of the Twenty-sixth Amendment to the U.S. Constitution, which granted the right to vote to eighteen-year-olds. The change from wards to citywide elections in 1911 and the annexation of the main portions of the campus in 1961 now made it possible for bloc voting by university students to shape the outcome of future local elections if they could be mobilized. This possibility was quickly demonstrated in the 1972 presidential elections, when campus activists registered 96 percent of the students by stressing the antiwar presidential campaign by Democrat George McGovern and the uphill Congressional race by a liberal Mexican-American Democrat, who eventually lost by a narrow margin to the incumbent ultraconservative Republican, a lawyer for agribusiness interests in Watsonville.

But it was not simply presidential and congressional politics that energized the students to register and vote. They were also well aware of the growth coalition's attempt to limit their influence on local politics through a ballot initiative to change the date of the city elections. The initiative would move local elections from the second Tuesday of April to early October, a date that just happened to be only a week or two after students return for the fall quarter on the atypical UC Santa Cruz academic calendar. Growth coalition leaders insisted that the change was not meant to disenfranchise students, claiming that this new schedule would be less disruptive of the budgeting decisions that needed to be made in the spring.

The growth coalition's argument was challenged by student and downtown activists through an ad hoc organization called Citizens for New Directions, which worked to focus the students' attention on the fact that the old guard and conservatives were opposed to their exercising their new voting rights at the local level. But rather than arguing solely on general principles against the change in the date of the elections, or solely on the basis of fairness, spokespersons for the group stressed that changing the election date meant a lengthening of the incumbent council's term of office at a time when the annexation of the ranch and farm land on the north coast, as well as the development of a convention center complex at Lighthouse Field, might come up for a vote. Since the majority on the city council had already expressed its general support for these projects, the group warned the students that the extra six months could be enough to win approval for these blockbuster projects without citizens being able to express their preferences. The importance of this point was underscored by the campus Lutheran minister, who was also an antiwar activist and a member of Citizens for New Directions: "And the most important thing to realize is that there are a number of important decisions that are going to be made during the six months from April to October of next year—the Lighthouse Point Convention Center and the Wilder Ranch development, for example—that the people may not want the present Council to decide without the election in April" (*City on a Hill Press,* September 21, 1972, 5).

Faced with these opportunities and threats, virtually all of the registered students turned out to vote in 1972, with 94 percent voting in favor of McGovern, a percentage that put even the most formidable urban Democratic machines of the past to shame. They also supported the congressional challenger and rejected the growth coalition's disenfranchisement gambit by about the same margins, thereby helping to defeat the change in the date of local elections by a citywide margin of 61 percent to 39 percent. Now the growth coalition would have to find new ways to deal with the fact that the university's students, almost all of whom originally came from outside Santa Cruz County, would make up from 10 to 13 percent of the electorate over the next nine years.

It did not take long for the neighborhood, environmental, and student activists, along with their friends who had labored during the previous three years to create a wide range of social service organizations, to realize they now had the potential to win a majority of the seats on the city council. They would thereby have an even better chance of derailing the developments they opposed, and in the process the social-services activists could allocate more funds to the programs they favored. This new electoral project was created in good part by leaders in Operation Wilder, the Save Lighthouse Point Association, and the University Services Agency, a nonprofit corporation that had supported a wide range of community-oriented service, nutrition, and ecology organizations on and off the campus. The coalition soon came to be known as the Bicentennial Committee, a name chosen to provide an association with the nation's upcoming bicentennial celebration in 1976, which might short-circuit any claims that their goals were anything but patriotic.

The new project began with a series of informal—and by all accounts, chaotic and disorganized—meetings to decide exactly how to proceed in the 1973 local elections. After general discussions, which included a wide range of activists, the coalition decided to develop a slate of three candidates who would be chosen based on interviews with all those interested in running. In the end, the three who ran were not quite the same three who seemed to be emerging from the process, or so all three of the final slate members later believed, but they did have the best nonuniversity connections and the strongest determination to run. For most activists, the main point was that there were only three of them, which meant that the emerging coalition's votes would not be diluted by a long list of headstrong candidates.

The first of the three, Virginia Sharp, was an environmentalist who had been active in the Sierra Club and Save Lighthouse Point Association as well as an effort to preserve a historic downtown building. She was probably favored by activists, she later reflected, because her low-key style made her seem benign.

The second, Sally DiGirolamo, was a real estate salesperson and, most important, a key leader in an East Side neighborhood group, the Frederick Street Irregulars. The group organized the previous year to oppose a proposal for two sixteen-story high-rise apartments at the dead end of two quiet single-home residential streets that were at the heart of the Frederick Street neighborhood. From the point of view of developers, the site was especially attractive because it was on a wooded hillside that overlooked the Santa Cruz Harbor. From the point of view of campus activists, faculty and students alike, DiGirolamo was an ideal person to oppose this and other developments because she was a native Santa Cruzan from the usually underrepresented East Side of the city, who might have legitimacy with voters based on her familiarity with the real estate industry. She also had a ready wit and the ability to relate to everyone.

The third member of the Bicentennial Committee's slate, Bert Muhly, was a one-time county planning director who had spent much of the 1960s trying to heighten concern about unplanned growth in unincorporated parts of the county through organizing neighborhood discussion groups focused on the need for growth controls and planning. Frustrated by the inadequate planning and pell-mell growth at the county level, he had resigned his position in 1970 with a fiery speech, broadcast over the local radio station, about the dominance of county politics by shortsighted real estate interests who were destroying the local environment (Glickman 1979). He then went on to teach courses in environmental studies at both San Jose State University and UC Santa Cruz (*City on a Hill Press,* April 5, 1973, 15).

Although the three candidates ran separate campaigns, they were linked in the minds of voters by the flyers passed out by activist groups, by slate endorsements in local alternative newspapers and the campus newspaper, and by a shared perspective on key land-use issues such as Wilder Ranch and Lighthouse Field (*City on a Hill Press,* February 8, 1973, 8).

Moderate conservatives within the growth coalition favored low-key rhetorical approaches in addressing local voters after the failed attempt to change the date of the elections in 1972. They did so in part because two of their candidates—one an incumbent running for reelection and a manager at a local plant of a large industrial company, the other the current chair of the city planning commission—might be able to appeal to university employees and students. But the third member of the pro-growth slate, Maynard Manson, a real estate owner serving on the school board, to which he was elected as a crusader against sex education in the schools, decided to play on the tensions between the university and the city in making his first bid for a city council seat. (He will figure again in our story in the 1990s.) Rejecting a moderate approach that might win some student votes, he polarized the election for all concerned by constantly referring to the electoral success of a left-wing political coalition in Berkeley, which in 1971 won three of four open seats on the nine-person city council. After warning that such an outcome would be a calamity for Santa Cruz, he ended every campaign advertisement with the claim that he was running to keep Santa Cruz from becoming "Berkeley-by-the-Sea" (e.g., *Sentinel*, April 4 1973, 2). The three insurgent candidates were more than happy to respond by raising the frightening possibility of "San Jose-by-the-Sea," with its smog, traffic, and cheek-by-jowl housing (*Sentinel*, April 6, 1973, 4).

The three challengers were not the only bearers of the pro-environment message. Organized environmental lobbying groups from outside the city, and especially the once-staid Sierra Club, which was becoming more radical by the week, underwrote large-space political advertisements in the local press, imploring citizens to vote in the upcoming election. In the case of the campus newspaper, their advertisement in large capital letters suggested a crisis: "ENVIRONMENTAL ISSUES ARE ON THE LINE . . . THIS CITY ELECTION IS CRUCIAL. THE GROWTH-IS-GOOD VOTERS WILL TURN OUT IN FORCE. SANTA CRUZ NEEDS YOUR VOTE" (*City on a Hill Press*, April 5, 1973, 15).

The environmentalists were emboldened to make this strong pitch in part by a recent decision issued by the Supreme Court of California that environmental impact reviews were necessary for new private development projects as well as public ones. They were also aided mightily by voter approval of a stringent new coastal protection law in November 1972. This state ballot initiative, the Coastal Zone Conservation Act, imposed strict regulations on development within a thousand yards of the coastline in order to ensure conservation of natural resources. In retrospect, it seems clear that the passage of the Coastal Zone Conservation Act was the death knell for the project at Lighthouse Field, but it is a testimony to the determination of the growth coalition that its leaders insisted on moving ahead with the project.

The challengers had one other thing going for them thanks to a legally mandated letter that the local Redevelopment Agency had recently sent to many downtown and beach area residents. The letter informed them in formal and legalistic language that they might be displaced from their homes as part of a planning process that was in a very formative stage. Since any steps toward removing houses included testimony and reports from a citizen's advisory committee made up of people who lived in the redevelopment area, the door was opened for organizing the downtown and beach neighborhoods through appointments to the advisory committee or attendance at its numerous meetings and hearings. Those active on or around the advisory committee included several young renters—some students, some not—who enjoyed the low rents, private backyards, and relaxed street scene just a block or two from the Pacific Garden Mall. This neighborhood ferment was fully exploited by the three members of the Bicentennial Committee's slate. More generally, the mailings by the Redevelopment Agency aided in the creation of the Downtown Neighbors Association in 1974, which dedicated itself from that time forth to the preservation of downtown neighborhoods.

Operating in a crisis atmosphere that helped energize campus voters, the Bicentennial slate won all three open positions on the city council by a large margin. It had overwhelming support on the campus, where voter turnout was exceptionally high: 74 percent of the eligible student voters cast ballots, and they gave Sharp 98 percent, Muhly 96 percent, and DiGirolamo 91 percent of their votes. Only Muhly, however, because of his highly visible efforts over a thirteen-year period on behalf of slow growth, had sufficient electoral support throughout the city to ensure victory if the on-campus student vote is subtracted from the final tallies (*City on a Hill Press*, April 12, 1973, 1). It was a clear indication that the student vote now mattered just as much as the growth coalition feared it would.[1]

VICTORY ON THE NORTH COAST AND LIGHTHOUSE FIELD

The 1973 city council elections were the beginning of the end for housing developments on the two large ranches on the north coast. Although both properties were owned by outside developers, they had hired members of the local growth coalition to be in charge of property development for them (Glickman 1979). Putting local figures in charge was hardly of any use to the developers, however, because Operation Wilder and other activist groups brought

---

1. Our focus on campus precincts understates the importance of the student vote because many upper-division students lived off campus and at least some of them registered at their downtown addresses. Since it proved impossible for us to make an estimate of how many students were voting in off-campus precincts, our assessment of the impact of the student vote is a conservative one.

local residents and students to public meetings of the city planning commission, the city council, and the county board of supervisors, where they pointed out the problems of coastal development and expressed doubts about any alleged benefits. The city council, even without a pro-neighborhood and environmentalist majority, delayed the annexation needed by the developers in order for them to take their next steps. Shortly thereafter, in 1974, the disheartened landowners used their connections to the conservative Republican governor, Ronald Reagan, to arrange a quick sale of the land to the state government, which turned it into a state park.

The battle over Lighthouse Field proved to be much more protracted and convoluted, even though the development was well within the thousand-foot jurisdiction given to the new Coastal Commission by the 1972 initiative. The opponents were further bolstered by the fact that the county board of supervisors as well as the city council had a vote on the convention center component of the project because both the city and the county were involved in the application to the federal government for the needed economic development funds. This fact was good news for the activists because several hastily conceived growth projects in unincorporated parts of the county had created a backlash among county residents who had moved to the sparsely populated areas to escape rapid development not be a part of it. These county battles were fought in the name of environmentalism, but they were also neighborhood use-value movements led by local residents opposed to new housing projects and new malls that would encroach on their semirural way of life. The result was the election of two environmentalists to the five-member board of supervisors, who were likely votes against the Lighthouse Field project, along with the election of a moderate supervisor, who might be tempted to join the two environmentalists in expressing concerns about a convention center near Lighthouse Point (Glickman 1979).

The final ingredient for a successful resistance strategy by the Lighthouse Field activists had been provided by the city election results. Now the neighborhood and environmental activists knew that they could put together an electoral majority for an initiative rejecting the new convention center. Soon thereafter, in 1974, 68 percent of the city electorate endorsed just such an initiative, which prohibited city participation in the project, making the project impossible as originally planned. Somewhat surprising to the anti-development activists, part of this large majority was due to the efforts of a few highly visible ultraconservatives, who opposed the convention center because of the federal government's financial support for it.

Within this new context, even a city planning commission appointed by progrowth council members voted 5–2 against the convention center. Nonetheless, the city council approved it with a 4–3 vote in front of three thousand critics in the Civic Auditorium in early 1975, claiming that the initiative prohibiting city participation was merely advisory. Finally, after many tense moments and citizen outcry, a vote by the Coastal Commission put an end to the project a few months later (Rotkin 1991, 341). As a result of these efforts, Lighthouse Field became a state beach and park in 1977, but not without a great deal of resistance by the landowners and the majority on the city council. The new park was hailed by activists as a victory for environmental protection and the use-value interests of the people of California, not just for the residents of Santa Cruz.

The state paid $7.1 million for the land at Lighthouse Field, the equivalent of $24.4 million in 2007 dollars. But the effort turned out to be in good part a neighborhood protection plan. Once victory was assured, the neighborhood at the core of the Save Lighthouse Point Association began to insist that this former farmland should be preserved as open space, even opposing recreational uses such as soccer and baseball fields or grassy areas with picnic benches. After years of argument, they wore down the city government, leaving the thirty-seven acres with only a few parking spaces along West Cliff, a few picnic benches, and a few dirt paths surrounded by high weeds. The field is not of any use to most people except as a dog run, but it does provide the buffer zone the neighborhoods wanted. This outcome is the first clear example of how severely the liberals and environmentalists in Santa Cruz were limited by neighborhood use values that are not necessarily liberal or environmentalist.

The battle over the hotel and convention center had one other long-term impact of benefit to the insurgent forces. In 1974 it catapulted the young lawyer hired by the Save Lighthouse Point Association, Gary Patton, a former antiwar activist who had not previously spent much time on environmental issues, to a seat on the county board of supervisors from the district that includes most of the city and a few adjacent areas north of the city. A recent graduate of Stanford Law School after doing his undergraduate work at the same university and a year of study at Union Theological Seminary in New York, Patton won handily in most precincts and by the remarkable margin of 1,815 to 17 on the campus, which is 99.2 percent of the student vote (Jones 2000b, 47). His victory, along with the wins by two environmentalists in districts outside the city limits in 1972, demonstrated that slow-growth and anti-growth proponents, whether environmentalists or neighborhood activists, now had an even stronger position at the county level. This in turn meant that Patton could be of assistance in many ways to the opponents of the growth coalition within the city limits. Although control of the five-person county board seesawed back and forth in the second half of the 1970s for reasons we explain below, Patton's own seat was never seriously challenged again, and activists were able to win permanent control of the county government in 1981.

The enormity of their successes between 1969 and 1975 was not lost on the informal network of local activists. In the space of five or six years, they had blocked the widening of the major highway through the city, kept the proposed Beach Loop from destroying several hundred houses in downtown neighborhoods, stopped housing developments that would have led to a major population increase on the north coast, and kept Lighthouse Field from becoming a hotel and convention complex. These victories gave activists the hope that they could accomplish many of their goals by working through government channels. Santa Cruz seemed poised to enter a whole new era of local politics.

THE COALITION FALTERS,
BUT NEIGHBORHOODS ADVANCE

As so often happens with neighborhood-based politics, the defeat of growth-coalition projects that threatened local residents' way of life turned the 1975 city council elections into a relatively low-key matter. However, no one predicted this sudden decline in activism and student involvement when the Bicentennial Committee began to put together a slate of four candidates. To make matters more difficult, Sharp had resigned midway in her first term for personal reasons and had been replaced by the majority with a supporter of the growth coalition, so the insurgents would have to win two of the four open seats to take control of the council.

The committee's troubles started when it decided to adopt a more formal selection procedure because the group had grown from a relative handful, which had made consensus-seeking procedures possible, to over one hundred people. Direct voting was now necessary, with a new bylaw that required a two-thirds majority for endorsement. The campus newspaper described the two meetings where four candidates were ultimately endorsed as having an "air of disorganization," but was quick to argue that "long-time members of the Committee accept this as a natural and healthy consequence of the open political process they believe in" (*City on a Hill Press,* January 23, 1975, 2).

Nevertheless, the process was not in fact as successful as it might have been because there was only one neighborhood-based activist on the slate, Carole DePalma, a small-restaurant owner who was one of three key leaders in the Frederick Street Irregulars. The other three candidates, one a quiet Quaker antiwar activist, another a speech therapist who served on the city parks board, and the third a school counselor who had been active on social welfare issues, did not have a strong base in neighborhood work or any ties to the campus. With voter turnout on the campus down dramatically from 74 percent in 1973 to 50 percent, and with bloc voting by students down from 91–97 percent in 1973 to 81–87 percent, DePalma was the only winner, giving the Frederick Street Irregulars two representatives on the council. It was a major setback for the insurgent coalition, even though DePalma immediately claimed that her victory was a triumph for the neighborhoods. In fact, contrary to this optimistic spin, she ran behind the three highest vote getters in twenty-three of the twenty-six off-campus precincts and would have lost to a pro-growth candidate if not for the large margin student voters accorded her (*Sentinel,* March 5, 1975, 1; *Sentinel,* March 5, 1975, 13).

Although the elections were rightly seen by most liberals and environmentalists as a clear defeat, they were not a complete defeat for neighborhood activists. One of the centrist winners, Charlotte Melville, was a member of a new neighborhood association on the far west side of Santa Cruz, Western Limits, just below the university. The group drew most of its members from Western Drive, a street that stretches from Route 1/Mission Street to a roadway 1.5 miles away that parallels the university's western boundary, as seen on the map accompanying this chapter. Western Drive is a narrow, semirural street seen by early planners as ideal for widening to a four-lane entryway to the university, with space on both sides for large apartment and condominium developments that would appeal to new faculty members and upper-division university students. Some environmentalists argued that such large-scale developments in that area made sense because they would save on long automobile trips to the campus for many people, thereby cutting down on the use of gasoline.

The neighborhood had first been galvanized into action to oppose plans for a large apartment complex with 168 rental units near the corner of Mission Street and Western Drive, but that effort had failed. The neighbors then came together more formally and created Western Limits in 1974 in a successful battle against a proposal for 65 condominium units at the other end of the street, close to the university. The group also succeeded in eliminating plans for several side streets off Western Drive that would provide sites for apartments and condominiums.

Ironically, Melville had not been a very active member of the group and had not been endorsed by it in her bid for a city council seat because most of the activists did not agree with her general political stance. Nonetheless, her main agenda became the protection of her neighborhood. She also championed the need for a neighborhood park in the area. Although the plan for apartments and condos in what was still a sparsely populated area seemed sensible to many environmentalists, Melville and the other homeowners in the neighborhood thought otherwise.

In December 1975 Melville joined with DiGirolamo and DePalma of the Frederick Street Irregulars and Muhly to push for a committee to revise the

1964 general plan. Leaders within Western Limits were ready to provide steady input and lobbying, which led to a special master plan for their neighborhood and later to special plans for several other neighborhoods as well. According to the Western Limits plan, adopted in 1978 as part of a new general plan, Western Drive would remain a narrow, two-lane road, leaving it as an unattractive alternative route to the university. There would be sidewalks on only one side of the road, and the area would be zoned for single-family residential homes. As a result, the area did not see much construction for many years. When several dozen houses were eventually approved as part of a major development on several new side streets near the university, the result was bigger and more expensive housing on larger lots.

The Frederick Street Irregulars and Muhly were able to fashion a majority, usually including Melville but sometimes one of the other council members, that opposed high-density projects in other neighborhoods, including one in the Westlake area near the university that was also opposed by the Westlake Homeowners Association. They helped an East Side neighborhood, several blocks from Frederick Street, to stop an apartment high-rise overlooking the river mouth and boardwalk, creating a neighborhood park instead. They supported the plans of the recently formed Downtown Neighbors Association, which would spend the next thirty years defending Chestnut Street from expansionist plans by the growth coalition. In the process, DiGirolamo and De-Palma also achieved their goals for Frederick Street by eliminating the plans for the sixteen-story high-rises and delaying any building at all near the harbor for many years to come, with significant assistance from the Coastal Commission. They brought a neighborhood park to the area near the end of Frederick Street and forced the nearby yacht harbor to be more accessible to non-boaters, including the addition of walking paths and benches along its shores.

More generally, the pro-neighborhood forces also made changes in the general plan that protected single-family dwellings in all parts of the city by making it more difficult for developers to assemble parcels for apartment buildings and by limiting the height of apartment buildings to five stories. Then, too, the new general plan made it much easier to save the many Victorians scattered throughout the city, and it eliminated the call for new highways and the widening of city streets that had been a hallmark of the 1964 general plan. Finally, the neighborhood parks called for by Western Limits and the Frederick Street Irregulars were built in four other neighborhoods in addition to their own, thanks in part to federal revenue-sharing money. Given the votes stacked against them, and the popularity of neighborhood issues, the pro-growth faction on the council seldom chose to make a stand on any of these issues.

In short, even though the slate of liberals and environmentalists lost in the 1975 elections, neighborhoods nonetheless made gains between 1975 and

1977. These successful efforts at neighborhood protection were another clear demonstration that neighborhood politics were becoming important in Santa Cruz and that they were fundamentally protectionist, as growth coalition theory would expect.

NEW CONFLICT AT THE COUNTY LEVEL

Fearful of what might be in store for them, the countywide growth coalition reacted to the victory by Patton in the 1974 supervisorial elections by making plans to have a greater impact in the electoral arena at both the county and the city levels. As a first step, the Santa Cruz County Board of Realtors hired a former Capitola mayor as director of public and governmental relations. His charge was to counter the growing strength of the growth-control movement by launching a "growth is good" ideological counteroffensive. He started attending every city and county government meeting that related to land use, spoke to civic groups, and was quoted frequently in the *Sentinel*. To aid the cause, the owners of the *Sentinel*, who by then also shared ownership with one of their in-laws in a local radio station, provided this former mayor with his own radio show devoted to analyses of land-use issues. A campaign button in his office read: "Get into Politics—or get out of Business" (Glickman 1979, 34).

Despite the efforts by leaders in the growth coalition to use their considerable media resources to paint environmentalists as dangerous to the local economy, environmentalists were able to maintain a 3–2 majority in the 1976 county elections and make Patton chair of the board. A few days after this unexpected turn of events, the county growth coalition stepped up its degree of political organization by forming Advocates for a Balanced Community (ABC) to take back control of the board of supervisors and support pro-growth candidates in city council elections as well. Its seventy-five to a hundred members were mostly large property owners, real estate agents, building contractors, construction union officials, and political leaders. Several were strident right-wingers on social issues, which did not help the growth coalition's cause with the socially moderate voters of Santa Cruz County.

Leaders in the behind-the-scenes ABC group then formed a larger political organization, the Coalition of United Taxpayers (CUT), to lead a campaign to recall the three environmentalist supervisors. The plan could not be announced until the second half of 1977 because new supervisors had to be in office for at least six months before they could be recalled, which meant that the recall vote could not occur until June 1978. However, ABC and CUT immediately involved themselves in the 1977 city council elections by endorsing and raising money for a retired banker active in the chamber of commerce, who was making his first—and, as it turned out, successful—bid for a council seat. They also backed an incumbent moderate who was a local school official. More critically, they ran attack ads and distributed flyers meant to discredit DiGirolamo's reelection efforts, accusing her of seeking to destroy the yacht harbor and turn the local public golf course "into a cow pasture" (*City on a Hill Press,* March 10, 1977, 14).

With the vote on the campus down significantly once again, from 50 percent in 1975 to only 30 percent, and with even less bloc voting by students, candidates backed by ABC and the growth coalition captured two of the three open seats on the city council, with only Muhly winning from the neighborhood and environmentalist side. DiGirolamo's defeat was especially revealing because she had won as a champion of neighborhoods the first time around, finishing in the top three in 55 percent of the off-campus precincts; by 1977 she was among the top three in only 19 percent of the off-campus precincts. Now that the neighborhood-environmentalist-student coalition was reduced to two reliable votes, DePalma and Muhly, it was not likely to have as much impact.

Fresh from its success in the city elections, the Coalition of United Taxpayers focused on everything but growth issues when it launched its county-level recall campaign in the summer of 1977, charging that the three environmentally oriented supervisors "interfered with the operation of county departments, were lax on welfare fraud, and used [the] budgetary process for political retribution" (Santa Cruz *Independent,* August 5–11, 1977; quoted in *City on a Hill Press,* November 10, 1977, 9). After deciding to drop its recall campaign against Patton because he was up for reelection in any case, the county growth coalition far outspent the combined efforts of the two embattled supervisors by $94,000 to $40,000, a better than two-to-one margin (Santa Cruz *Express,* October 29, 1981, 7).

But the real secret to what turned out to be a successful campaign was a decision to link CUT's issues and campaign literature to a statewide initiative on the ballot, Proposition 13, a soon-to-be-famous and widely imitated anti-tax measure that slashed property taxes by two-thirds and thereby severely constrained local government spending from that day forward. CUT's emphasis on taxes and social spending was symbolic politics in the service of "recapturing control of local land use policy," and it worked (Glickman 1979, 1). The symbolic nature of CUT's victory was underscored by the fact that a strong county growth-control initiative won by a 52 percent to 48 percent margin in the same election, along with a new sales tax that made it possible to expand the bus system. The growth-control measure preserved open space and agricultural lands, channeled residential development to urban unincorporated areas, mandated that 15 percent of all new housing in the county be affordable, and made it necessary for the supervisors to set a growth limit each year that represents the county's fair share of the state's growth. CUT had removed two supervisors, but it had not achieved the freedom to build that it really wanted.

THE ACTIVISTS REGROUP AS PROGRESSIVES: THE 1979 CITY ELECTIONS

After losing ground in the city council elections in 1975 and 1977, and suffering the recall of two slow-growth county supervisors in 1978, the pro-neighborhood and pro-environment forces in both the city and the county were clearly on the defensive, and they had lost their ability to energize a large and unified student voting bloc as well. It appeared that the local growth coalition had reasserted its usual ascendancy in the electoral arena even though it had lost on major development projects and on a county growth-control initiative. At this low point the opponents of the growth coalition received new leaders from an unlikely source: the several nonelectoral social movements that had emerged in Santa Cruz—and many other cities—out of the civil rights, antiwar, and feminist movements of the 1960s. These activists for the most part consisted of former university students who had decided to work for what they increasingly called "progressive" social change at the local level, appropriating the word that had been used by the local growth coalition for decades to describe its initiatives. Their previous experience in other grassroots movements and organizations, and their ability to tap into the resources of leftist organizations outside the city, allowed them to create an even broader and deeper base of electoral support for what came to be called the progressive slate (Flacks 1995, 253–255).

The new progressive electoral activists in Santa Cruz had been involved in many different projects, starting with agitation for improved social services at the city and county levels for low-income and elderly people, often led by Community Studies graduates. They had achieved considerable success through the creation of a Community Congress that successfully lobbied the county and city governments for financial support beginning in 1975 (Rotkin 1991, 356–366). Others were feminists who focused their efforts on abortion rights, access to midwives, rape prevention, and the reduction of domestic violence against women. Still others worked for prison reform and rent control, but with little success. As a result of a combination of factors—the passage of the statewide antitax initiative, a decline in federal revenue sharing, and conservative dominance of both the city council and the board of supervisors—the funding for social services they had won through carefully thought-out pressure campaigns now faced the likelihood of drastic cuts. The local activists and their organizations had changed the social and cultural atmosphere of the city and the county, in turn encouraging many student activists to remain in the area after their graduation, but they had not been able to gain control of local government.

The organization at the center of this turn to electoral politics at the city level was an unlikely one: the campus chapter of a nationwide socialist organization, the New American Movement, which had been founded in the early 1970s by one strand of 1960s New Leftists. Known as NAM, as in "wham" or "bam," and numbering from five hundred to a thousand members nationally by the mid-1970s, the organization was originally an attempt to start anew as a nonelectoral socialist movement that would work on specific popular issues as a way to advocate reform programs that could not be accommodated within a capitalist economic system. Building on these "nonreformist reforms," as they were often called, the goal was to develop "ideological hegemony" for organizations like NAM, meaning that working-class people would come to see the limits of capitalism and realize there was a need for a socialist alternative (Gorz 1967; Rotkin 1991). Put in everyday terms, the goal was to identify and address specific local issues that would enhance the quality of people's everyday lives while simultaneously creating a socialist consciousness that would challenge capitalist social relations.

The Santa Cruz chapter of NAM consisted of fifteen to twenty undergraduate and graduate students, primarily in the Community Studies and History of Consciousness departments. It began in 1973 as a reading and discussion group, and then became a formal chapter of NAM in the spring of 1974. According to a retrospective account of the progressive movement in Santa Cruz written by Mike Rotkin, who was to be one of its key leaders for the next thirty years, the new NAM chapter had four projects. First, it contributed to the development of a new socialist-feminist vision through discussion groups and a local magazine. Second, it held educational forums on campus to introduce students to socialism. Third, it worked to create a local progressive coalition of which it would be one part, and fourth, it developed its own off-campus community organization to agitate for a specific reform program (Rotkin 1991, 440). The off-campus organizing project focused on creating support for a community health care center; fewer than half of the members were involved in this effort.

As NAM saw it, these various projects were at distinct levels that did not necessarily complement each other. In fact, they might even conflict with each other in that emphasizing socialism might interfere with grassroots organizing or coalition building (the relationship was "dialectical and inherently contradictory" according to NAM's theorizing). As it is easy to see from the vantage point of the present, the socialist aspect of NAM's work was a failure, but it is still important to emphasize the organization's socialist-feminist orientation because it provided the strong motivation and cohesion for many of those who played a major role in developing the new progressive coalition in Santa Cruz. In addition, even though NAM's grassroots organizing project faltered once the progressive coalition came to power, building it was essential because it taught NAM members the organizing skills that became highly useful in constructing and holding together the progressive coalition.

NAM chose a large neighborhood on the west side of Santa Cruz, about two miles below the university and south of Mission Street, as the place to begin. That neighborhood held out a number of advantages for a socialist organization. To begin with, it was diverse in terms of income levels, with many small bungalows mixed with somewhat larger houses and a handful of venerable Victorians. It was also the area where the few African Americans in the city—a little less than 2 percent of the population—were most likely to live. Many students were scattered throughout the area as well, and the part of it closest to the bay had been at the center of the fight to keep Lighthouse Field from becoming the site for a convention center.

The NAM activists began their efforts by distributing leaflets and making door-to-door visits to residents of the neighborhood, explaining their program and seeking new members. By this time, Rotkin, although still a graduate student in the History of Consciousness program, had become a lecturer in Community Studies as well, and some of his undergraduate students were receiving Community Studies credit for working with NAM. Even with this extra help, the activists had little or no success in their first two years, recruiting only seven new members. When they held a general neighborhood meeting in October 1977, only twenty-six local residents and nine campus activists were on hand.

At this point members of NAM decided to try a new approach by meeting with the leaders of churches and other organizations that already existed in the area. In early 1978 their work received a small boost when they obtained a two-year grant from a progressive foundation in San Francisco, the Vanguard Foundation, which had been created by several wealthy young leftists. NAM used the money to hire a full-time organizer, a former UC Santa Cruz student who had previously received Community Studies credit for his work (Rotkin 1991, 231). He and the other NAM activists organized many specific events within the neighborhood, such as bringing people together to discuss issues of concern to them, which focused in good part on parking problems and traffic congestion, but they made no headway on the health care project.

In part reflecting the growing recognition by NAM's national leadership that they should pay more attention to electoral politics, the Santa Cruz chapter showed its first interest in electoral politics by organizing the widest possible constituency against the 1978 supervisorial recall campaign by ABC and CUT. They were joined in this effort by the Progressive Action Coalition, a forum for activists in a wide range of causes who were willing to include electoral activity as well as marches, demonstrations, and lobbying campaigns in their toolkit of strategies and tactics. Although the effort to defeat the recall was unsuccessful, it did give NAM and Progressive Action Coalition members visibility and credibility with other progressive groups. It also gave them experience in the electoral process and strengthened their ties with activists and elected officials at the county level, especially Patton.

Then two unexpected events outside the NAM activists' control suddenly made them useful in the west side neighborhood, where they had by then become somewhat familiar faces. In June 1978, the Santa Cruz Medical Center, located on Mission Street, a few minutes from the neighborhood NAM had targeted, announced it was moving to the other side of town so it would have more room to expand. Although the new facility was only ten to fifteen minutes away by car, the decision did leave the west side without any medical facility, thereby lending credence to the idea that a community health center would be crucial, especially for low-income and elderly people without cars.

Second, and even more critical in terms of galvanizing the neighborhood into action, the county library board voted a month later to close the small west side branch of the city library, smack in the middle of the area NAM had targeted, for a budgetary saving of a mere $13,000. The cutback was one of several triggered by the passage of Proposition 13 in the June elections. This abrupt shutdown was both a material and a symbolic insult to the neighborhood, and perhaps racially insensitive as well. The library, built in 1915 with money from the famous robber baron and philanthropist, Andrew Carnegie, was only a little larger than a one-story bungalow. But it had a history, and it was used by young children in the neighborhood. Moreover, it was still a place where people from the neighborhood could run into each other, especially senior citizens, and NAM had on occasion used the site as an outreach point.

Sensing the anger and annoyance many members of the neighborhood experienced in reaction to this decision, which occurred without any consultation with people in the neighborhood, the NAM activists called a meeting for mid-July. It was attended by far more people than they expected, approximately sixty local residents, and led to the founding of a new organization, Westside Neighbors, in an attempt to reverse the library decision. When a delegation was treated by the head of the library board in what it saw as an arrogant and dismissive fashion, an increasingly angry and energized group decided it would protest to the city council and demand the restoration of the funds. Soon thereafter three hundred fifty people showed up at a city council meeting and convinced the city council to reopen the library (Rotkin 1991, 239).

Elated by its success, Westside Neighbors now turned its attention to other neighborhood projects as well as resuming agitation on the health center project. The group started a newsletter, began to have social gatherings, and even organized a stamp club. At the same time, the activists were careful not to proselytize for their larger issues in the newsletter or their discussion groups, focusing on the neighborhood issues of concern to the residents. In other words, they had succeeded in organizing the west side, but in the process they were transformed into neighborhood leaders. They stuck to what the residents wanted—the preservation of their neighborhood use values.

Despite continued lobbying efforts and the packing of city council meetings with supporters of the health center, Westside Neighbors was unable to convince the city council to allocate a portion of the city's federal revenue sharing funds for the creation of a community health center. The refusal of funds by the city council was especially frustrating because the council voted to use federal funds from the Housing and Community Development Agency meant for low-income people and neighborhoods to pay for capital improvement projects in the city. In 1978, for example, some of the money from the federal government was set aside to help subsidize a new luxury department store in the downtown, using the rationale that the project could meet federal guidelines because it would provide new janitorial jobs for low-income people. This plan failed, however, when a delegation of Santa Cruz neighbors complained to federal officials, who subsequently rejected the city's application (Rotkin 1991, 243–244).

Although leaders within NAM remained skeptical that there was an electoral road to socialism, they reluctantly decided that formal political representation in local government might be necessary to advance the struggle over health care facilities. Rotkin (1991, 249) overcame what he called his personal "distaste for electoral politics" and threw his hat into the political ring, announcing his candidacy for city council at a Westside Neighbors meeting in the winter of 1979. Lingering doubts among some of the NAM members about the potential divisiveness of entering electoral politics were dispelled, largely because the prevailing view in the group was that Rotkin's bid for office was motivated by his desire to call attention to the continued unmet health care needs on the city's west side. In addition, as Rotkin himself wrote (1991, 250), few of his fellow NAM members seriously believed that a socialist-feminist could actually win elected office, especially in light of the defeats suffered by less radical candidates in 1975 and 1977.

Rotkin was joined in his effort by another socialist-feminist, Bruce Van Allen, one of the leaders of the Downtown Neighbors Association as well as a mainstay in the effort to bring rent control to the city. He, too, was ready to use electoral politics as a springboard after the rent control organization he helped found, the Santa Cruz Housing Action Committee, came within seventy-four votes of passing a city rent control initiative in fall 1978, despite the fact that the real estate interests spent $100,000 to defeat it (*Santa Cruz Express,* February 11, 1982, 8). Van Allen and Rotkin, along with two lesser-known endorsees— one a labor advocate, Vietnam veteran, and graduate of UC Santa Cruz, the other an environmentalist and Sierra Club leader—composed an unofficial "neighborhood and environmental" slate endorsed at an election forum sponsored by Westside Neighbors in the winter of 1979. The slate was then endorsed by most of the nonelectoral activist groups shortly thereafter. Since DePalma had decided not to run again, the challengers would have to win three of the four open seats in order to join with Muhly to comprise a progressive majority.

The decision by NAM and the other previously nonelectoral activist groups in Santa Cruz to challenge in city elections came in a much wider context of progressive analysis, discussion, and political activity at the local level in the 1970s. Its deepest roots were in medium-sized cities such as Madison (Wisconsin), Berkeley, and Santa Monica, although major battles were fought in San Francisco, Boston, and Cleveland as well (Beitel 2004; DeLeon 1992; Dreier, Mollenkopf, and Swanstrom 2004; Swanstrom 1985). The ideas and concerns of the progressive activists in these and other cities were facilitated by the 1974 creation of the Conference on Alternative State and Local Policies, which brought together progressive activists with elected and appointed officials from across the country for annual meetings to exchange ideas (Thompson 2007). Rotkin, who knew several of the conference leaders through his involvement in Students for a Democratic Society at Cornell in the 1960s, was among its founding members. He attended several of its conferences in the late 1970s, thereby providing a direct link between Santa Cruz and the national network.

The Conference on Alternative State and Local Policies published numerous booklets and pamphlets that disseminated what were thought to be the most promising ideas for progressive social change, including various kinds of electoral reforms, such as replacing at-large elections with districts and abolishing the city-manager form of government. Community control of the police was another program of major interest. The group had larger hopes, such as public ownership of "productive enterprise," meaning that cities would own some profit-making ventures, as well as greater citizen participation in all aspects of government. Many of these ideas were brought together in a small book that built in good part on the experience of progressive planners in Berkeley (Bach et al. 1976, 31). Later called "one of the key documents in the visionary history of the city planning profession," the book's blueprint for change started with community-owned public utilities, especially electric utilities, where there was a history of public ownership in a few cities and confidence on the part of progressives that they could be run more efficiently than they are by private companies (Clavel 1999, 139). Ownership of public utilities was understood as a stepping-stone to legitimating public ownership of other enterprises, such as the new industry of cable television, where there were fourteen publicly owned TV systems at the time.

The book held out hope for consumer co-ops and community credit unions as well, and for the idea that cities could sell low-cost home insurance to city residents. In addition, there were plans for the creation of affordable cooperative housing, community-controlled social service agencies that would provide an alternative to city agencies, and a model ordinance that would make it necessary for city councils to widen participation on city boards and commissions through a "fair representation" plan that ensured what is now called diversity and neighborhood involvement (Clavel 1999).

The feasibility of taking these and many other ideas into the electoral arena also gained credibility in the eyes of nonelectoral leftists with the unexpected success of New Leftist and antiwar leader Tom Hayden in the California Democratic primaries for a U.S. Senate seat in spring 1976. Waging a highly visible and forthright campaign that pulled no punches, Hayden received 37 percent of the vote, even though he was challenging a popular incumbent Democratic senator, suggesting there were perhaps ways to use the electoral arena to advance progressive ideas (Flacks 1977). With financial help from his then-wife, the famous and highly controversial actress Jane Fonda, Hayden and his coworkers followed up on this moral victory by founding the Campaign for Economic Democracy to support social movements and electoral campaigns at the local and state level throughout California. Espousing the concept of "economic democracy," which in effect called for a mixed economy that included some public ownership, highly progressive taxation, and improved government social services, the Campaign saw progressive control of local government as a building block for creating a broader national progressive movement (Carnoy and Shearer 1980; Shearer 1982; Zeitlin 1983).

Within this context, rent control also emerged as an important goal on the progressive agenda. The issue had been raised independently in several cities in the early 1970s, including Berkeley, where a strong rent control initiative passed in 1972. The Berkeley initiative led worried apartment owners to try to foreclose further local efforts at rent control with legislation at the state level in 1976. However, a last-minute campaign by activists convinced the liberal

California governor, Jerry Brown, to veto the real estate industry's proposed legislation, thereby encouraging further local rent-control initiatives (Capek and Gilderbloom 1992, 59–71). Capitalizing on this unexpected victory, the Campaign for Economic Democracy helped to create the California Housing Action and Information Network, which quickly became a clearinghouse on tactics, strategies, and substantive proposals for activists throughout the state. Rent control then took off as an issue in several California cities after the 1978 passage of Proposition 13, which had won in part because its supporters claimed it would lead to rent reductions by grateful landlords. Instead, it led to rent increases in most cases, deeply embittering many ordinary citizens, especially elderly ones living on retirement incomes.

Santa Monica became ground zero for rent control in California over the next few years. The failed efforts by senior citizens to pass a rent control initiative there in 1978, combined with arrogant and high-handed rebuffs of renters by real estate interests, who completely dominated the city council, created the motivation for a highly successful coalition effort in 1979. Led by progressive activists, including several who were part of the Campaign for Economic Democracy, a new group called Santa Monicans for Renters Rights passed the strongest rent control measure in the nation in 1979 and carried slates of progressives to city council victories in 1979 and 1981, thereby gaining control of city government in 1981 (Capek and Gilderbloom 1992; Clavel 1986).

THE 1979 SANTA CRUZ CAMPAIGN

Although the progressive campaign in Santa Cruz had some parallels with the efforts in other cities, it was also distinctive. Unlike Santa Monica, for example, a city with many large apartment buildings and 78 percent renters, many of whom were retirees or middle-class people of moderate incomes, Santa Cruz was a city of single-family homes and only 53 percent renters, many of whom were students at the university. In addition, most of the rental properties in Santa Cruz were single-unit dwellings that were often owned by middle-income homeowners living in the same neighborhood. Rotkin reports that "informed local real estate brokers" estimated that there were over three thousand individual landlords in Santa Cruz at the time: "Each of these people, of course, had friends and relatives in the community; in a town where no candidate for city council had ever received over 8,000 votes, an organized and self-interested block of that magnitude was a significant factor" (1991, 402–403).

Nor could there be any thought of focusing on gaining control of the mayor's office, as in Burlington, Vermont, or Madison in order to have a major impact; the council-manager form of government precluded that option. For

Santa Cruz progressives, then, the focus had to be on winning control of the city council through a combination of neighborhood issues and whatever issues might increase the voting turnout by UC Santa Cruz students. In the end, this necessity turned out to be a virtue because the progressives in Santa Cruz gained far more complete and lasting control than did progressives in other cities of any size or consequence.

To reach a wide range of constituencies, the new progressive coalition was careful to embrace and publicize an initiative placed on the ballot by local environmentalists who were convinced that the recent changes in the city's general plan triggered by Muhly and the Frederick Street Irregulars did not go far enough. It was framed as a supplement to the county growth management initiative that passed in 1978 despite the success the Coalition of United Taxpayers had enjoyed in recalling two environmentalist supervisors. This new initiative, commonly referred to as the "greenbelt initiative," prohibited municipal government from providing infrastructure and services to approximately nine hundred acres of privately held land. Much of this land—called the "Pogonip Area" and included on the map that accompanies this chapter—was near the university and owned by the Cowell Foundation, which had recently proposed building several hundred houses on the hillside overlooking the city just below the east side of the campus. Progressives also placed a second measure on the 1979 city ballot, a rent control initiative that insured the fervent participation of the most radical activists and students, who were deeply frustrated, and at the same time hopeful, after their narrow loss on a similar initiative just four months earlier. In fact, rent-control activists may have provided a majority of the campaign workers for the informal slate.

In addition to a UC Santa Cruz student body that had reached 5,754, the progressive campaign also could count on support from the several hundred UC Santa Cruz alumni who stayed in the city after graduation, with perhaps as many as 750 former students living in Santa Cruz County. Although only a handful of these alumni were political activists, most of them were nonetheless part of a new "youth community" that developed in several university cities during the 1970s, such as Berkeley, Santa Barbara, Ann Arbor, Madison, and Burlington, and they supported progressive social change (Flacks 1971; Whalen and Flacks 1989). Many worked in social services or were part of cooperatives. The progressives' day-to-day campaign was augmented by the efforts of the small local chapter of the Campaign for Economic Democracy. Even though the group only had about a dozen members, mostly university students, they were regarded as a crucial addition to the coalition because they could draw on the organization's statewide network of experienced organizers to bring a new level of sophistication to insurgent political campaigns aimed at the city council (Rotkin 1991, 370).

Building on the support of activists from a wide range of city and county groups, both the Rotkin and the Van Allen campaigns cultivated the many neighborhood groups that had developed throughout the city, including the generally conservative Westlake Homeowners Association, which did not feel the incumbent city council was sympathetic enough to its concerns about the proposed shopping center that still threatened their neighborhood. To make clear that he supported these neighborhood groups, Rotkin named his campaign committee "Neighbors for a Change" (Rotkin 1991, 410). Although Rotkin was a socialist-feminist, with a primary focus on class issues, NAM's emphasis on coalition building and his work with the Westside Neighbors made him sensitive to the importance of neighborhood use values.

The growth coalition greatly outspent the progressives, constantly referred to Rotkin and Van Allen's socialist-feminist vision in near hysterical tones, and exaggerated the role of the Campaign for Economic Democracy by claiming that Hayden and Fonda were the masterminds and controllers of the progressive effort. Nevertheless, the coordinated precinct work and ballot initiatives put forth by the progressives resulted in a resounding victory for Rotkin and Van Allen in a field of nineteen candidates. With 51 percent of the registered students voting, the largest turnout since 1973, Rotkin received 84 percent of the possible campus votes and Van Allen 82 percent, which provided them with the margins they needed to finish first and second. Even without the on-campus votes, they would have finished third and fourth, still enough to capture two of the four contested seats, and solid evidence that their work in neighborhoods had a major impact. The importance of neighborhood activism also is revealed in the differential success of Rotkin and Van Allen compared to the other two progressives on the informal slate, who finished third and fourth in the campus vote, but ran well behind Rotkin and Van Allen even in progressive downtown precincts. The fact that one of these defeated progressives was a highly visible environmentalist suggests to us that there are limits to environmentalism in electoral campaigns.

The complex composition of the progressive electorate, and a portent of things to come, can be seen in the fact that voters supported the greenbelt measure 56.3 percent to 43.7 percent, but at the same time rejected rent control by 53.6 percent to 46.4 percent, a much wider margin than the razor-thin loss the previous year. And yet the voters also elected Van Allen, one of rent control's major advocates, to the city council. This unexpected voting pattern suggests that even though progressives won the allegiance of pro-neighborhood voters, electoral support declined on an issue such as rent control because of the significant percentage of neighborhood residents who derived at least some income from rent or had friends who did so (Rotkin 1991, 402–403). Thus, neighborhood residents who owned rental property constituted a potentially influential constituency against rent control even though they were sympathetic to neighborhood use-value politics.

The election of two socialist-feminists to the city council was bothersome to leaders of the growth coalition. However, they could console themselves with the fact that they now had a solid 4–3 majority, since Melville had lost her reelection bid to a more reliably pro-growth candidate, partly because she annoyed students and downtown progressives by unwisely running against Patton for his supervisorial seat in 1978, but also because she had not endeared herself to the growth coalition with some of her pro-neighborhood votes. On the other hand, the vote in favor of the greenbelt initiative deeply upset them because it directly challenged their material interests. When the *Sentinel* reported that the four campus precincts had supported the initiative by a vote of 1,460 to 61 (96 percent to 4 percent), thereby turning a nearly even election in the city into a rout, members of the chamber of commerce were convinced that their setback could be blamed on university voters, especially if the several hundred downtown student, faculty, and staff votes are added to the campus total (*Sentinel,* March 7, 1979, 21). They began to talk about a ballot initiative to de-annex the university campus they had so eagerly welcomed within the city limits just nineteen years earlier (*Sentinel,* March 8, 1979, 1). The de-annexation threat proved to be an idle one, and it probably could have been defeated by campus voters in any case, but it provided a clear indication that the growth coalition had been shaken once again.

Rotkin and Van Allen expressed surprise and pleasure about their new roles as elected officials, but they continued to regard themselves first and foremost as socialist-feminists who had larger goals than simply influencing city government in Santa Cruz. As they made clear in an interview with a New Left journal, *Socialist Review,* they did not see electoral politics as their central focus, and they defined their role as legitimating larger socialist issues as well as bringing about step-by-step changes in Santa Cruz. For Rotkin, electoral politics were one tactic in building a socialist movement in the United States: "I don't think either Bruce or I see the electoral arena as a road to power in and of itself. It's how we use the electoral arena and our positions in the government in a way that will aid building a mass movement, and not as a substitute for it" (Dancis 1979, 110). To aid in building that movement, they planned to use their positions on the city council to legitimate socialist programs. As Van Allen put it, "Mike and I will try to use our prominence as council members to give support and some degree of legitimation to socialist groups and progressive groups in the community by participating, by taking them seriously, by getting them on the [city council] agenda" (Dancis 1979, 111).

They also wanted to use the city council as a forum for speaking on issues that went far beyond the local level and current social movements. Explaining

why he and Van Allen put forth a council resolution calling for the national-
ization of the oil industry, which lost, Rotkin said: "On an issue like national-
ization of the oil companies, there is more than symbolism involved . . .
Having a city council come out for it does make the idea seem more mainstream, more realistic" (Dancis 1979, 114).

As far as the specifics of building on their victory in most Santa Cruz
neighborhoods, Rotkin and Van Allen thought their starting point would be
an expansion of their electoral base by appealing to ideologically nonaligned
voters. This would be accomplished by working with various neighborhood
organizations that they believed to be "populist" in their ideology but lacked
the kind of "class analysis" on key issues that was embraced by Rotkin and Van
Allen. The goal was the development of a "totally politicized populace," which
would allow "people to take control of their lives" (Dancis 1979, 118). At this
point, in other words, Rotkin and Van Allen hoped to move from what they
called populist issues to a socialist consciousness. They did not see themselves
as tethered to neighborhood use values, as growth coalition theory would suggest they were. But they did understand, as Rotkin put it, that the ideological
battle would begin with "sewers and street lights" (Dancis 1979, 113), and that
there was no "inherent force or ideology within capitalist society" that dic-
tated the complex coalition they had helped to create (Rotkin 1991, 442).

TAKING POWER: THE 1981 CAMPAIGN

With their long-term goals always in mind, but with the need to control the
city council in Santa Cruz as their next step, progressive leaders began to plan
for the next election very soon after their 1979 victory. They knew they needed
to sustain their momentum and incorporate even more activists from local
social movements. To that end, Muhly and the two newly seated progressives
started the process of screening and preparing candidates in consultation with
various progressive groups, especially the New American Movement. After
many months of discussion and deliberation, they decided to endorse the candidacy of an activist in the Downtown Neighbors Association, Mardi Wormhoudt, who was also a member of local feminist groups and a participant in
the effort to bring a health care facility to the Westside. She would go on to be
a major figure in Santa Cruz politics for the next twenty-five years, retiring as
chair of the county board of supervisors in 2006. They also agreed to support
a UC Santa Cruz alumnus, John Laird, who was a member of the Westside
Neighbors, the People's Democratic Club, and gay and lesbian organizations.
Employed as a county budget analyst, Laird had helped a wide range of community activist groups prepare their budget requests for presentation to supervisorial meetings in the mid-1970s. He also had taken an active role in the 1978

campaign to defeat a statewide initiative that would have prohibited gays and lesbians from teaching in the public schools.

When Muhly, Rotkin, and Van Allen could find no other woman or a person of color who was also a progressive and interested in running, they endorsed the candidacy of a high school teacher who was a former Lighthouse Field activist, but he did not figure prominently in the subsequent campaign. Nevertheless, the selection of these three candidates to complement the Muhly-Rotkin-Van Allen triumvirate meant that the progressive electoral coalition was linked to virtually every social movement group and social service organization in the city, along with the university community and organized neighborhood groups.

Progressive leaders once again sought to identify issues that would bring out the progressive vote in general and the campus vote in particular. Two such issues were planned as ballot initiatives. The first, which would create a City Commission for the Prevention of Violence Against Women, was created and qualified for the ballot by Wormhoudt and other feminists within the coalition, and was obviously meant to show that the progressives were serious about responding to one of the most serious issues facing all women. However, the conservative majority on the council, realizing that the initiative would draw more women voters to the polls and win overwhelmingly, immediately voted to adopt the initiative as it was written, which the progressives supported as evidence of their effectiveness. The second initiative, created by a NAM task force, which did make it to the ballot, was more symbolic and educational in nature, asking voters if they supported the idea of withholding American aid to the military regime in El Salvador. It was meant to appeal to all progressives, but especially university students (Rotkin 1991, 414–415).

With candidates and ballot initiatives in place, the progressives then focused most of their energy on a grassroots campaign that relied on volunteers from the neighborhood groups and the local social movements in which the candidates had been involved. They also had the help of many university students, some of whom were receiving field study credit for their efforts, usually through Community Studies (Rotkin 1991, 166). Environmentalists once again played a major role because the city attorney seemed reluctant to defend their 1979 greenbelt initiative, which was being challenged in court. In addition, the progressives employed what were then considered to be new campaign technologies, such as targeted direct mailing and computerized voting lists, with the help of experienced political organizers associated with the Campaign for Economic Democracy (Capek and Gilderbloom 1992, 95–102; Rotkin 1991).

The growth coalition, now calling itself "the moderates" who were in favor of "balance," also had a slate, thereby hoping to avoid the dilution of its vote occasioned by the large field of moderate and conservative candidates in 1979. This slate consisted of an incumbent who worked for the county board of education, the owner of a popular grocery store on Mission Street, and an African American woman who worked as a research technician at a local hospital. Ignoring the fact that the progressives were once again running an all-out grassroots campaign focused on neighborhood and student issues, the growth coalition continued to claim that the progressive candidates were dangerous radicals controlled by alien outside agitators financed by Hayden and Fonda. They pointed out that it was outrageous to have a ballot issue on military aid to El Salvador that was totally irrelevant to local politics. Using a strategy formulated by a young paid political consultant, who happened to be one of the rare conservative graduates of UC Santa Cruz, the growth coalition campaign relied on spending many thousands of dollars on direct mail brochures, flyers, and yard signs. The slate and its backers were billed as the "solid locals" for "solid local government," but much of their campaign war chest came from large donations by people from outside the city (*Sentinel,* November 1, 1981, 41; Vermosky 1981b).

The average contribution to the growth coalition candidates was $230, compared to $35 for the progressives, with a high percentage of the largest donations, ranging from $1,000 to $2,400, coming from real estate interests outside the city. Sizable campaign donations of $500 to $1,000 were made by Santa Cruz area real estate and construction firms. The largest single donation, $6,000, came from the Santa Cruz Board of Realtors. By contrast, neither Laird nor Wormhoudt received a contribution for over $500. Wormhoudt had two for $500, one from the Campaign for Economic Democracy, the other from her godmother (Vermosky 1981a; *Sentinel,* October 27, 1981, 16).

Armed with detailed information about the outside funding of growth-coalition candidates by real estate interests, progressive forces were able to turn the growth coalition's claim about running a "solid local" campaign on its head, pointing out that Laird and Wormhoudt, like Rotkin and Van Allen before them, had engaged in years of political work in the city's neighborhood organizations. They were aided mightily in this effort by the local alternative press, including the campus newspaper, which ran exposes on all the pro-growth funders and their ties to conservatives and real estate interests throughout the state. The possibility of outside real estate forces allegedly trying to dictate to Santa Cruz energized the progressive, neighborhood, and student volunteers, who served as canvassers and precinct walkers.

The result was an overwhelming victory for Laird and Wormhoudt, with 7,500 and 7,179 votes respectively. Citywide electoral support was so strong for the progressive frontrunners that they would have finished first and second even if the on-campus precincts were subtracted from their totals. Their victory finally gave the progressives the majority that had seemed within their reach since the 1973 elections. The third slot went to the grocery store owner on the growth coalition slate, with 5,444 votes, who edged out the schoolteacher supported by progressives by 210 votes (*Sentinel*, November 4, 1981, 14).

So, just as the local growth coalition had shown earlier in Santa Cruz history that well organized groups can have a major impact on local government, contrary to Marxist and public choice theorists, the electoral victories for the progressive coalition demonstrate that it is sometimes possible to build on neighborhood and environmental issues to defeat the growth coalition in the electoral arena, in this case with the aid of university student voters who cared about environmental and social welfare issues. Now the progressives had to see if they could turn their electoral coalition into a governing coalition without developing alliances with other groups, thereby challenging the claim by regime theorists that "an electoral coalition, even when it wins, is not the same as a governing coalition" (Stone 1989, xi).

4

~~~~~~

THE PROGRESSIVE
COALITION IN POWER:
1981–1989

Once they assumed office, the progressive majority immediately began instituting new programs. First, and most important from their point of view, they increased spending on social services, doubling it during their first year in office (Moberg 1983, 13). The increase in funding for social programs was made possible by a decision to postpone infrastructural maintenance projects by one year, creating a rolling fund of several hundred thousand dollars. It was a clear demonstration of the difference in priorities between a growth coalition focused on bricks and mortar and a progressive coalition focused on social services and use values. By the close of the decade, the progressives had increased social service spending tenfold: from $150,000 in 1980 to over $1.5 million (Rotkin 1991, 420–421). Among the programs funded was the Westside Community Health Center that had been NAM's original organizing objective.

The funds for social services represented only a small part of the city budget, but a million dollars can mean a very large increase in health and well-being for low-income and elderly residents. The new city council's focus on social welfare was aided by the fact that progressives also won a majority on the county board of supervisors in the 1981 elections, making it possible for the city and county to coordinate their funding of social programs. As a

result of the large sums of money spent by Santa Cruz County on social services of all kinds, progressive control of county government played an important role in improving the quality of life for many low-income and otherwise
marginalized people in the Santa Cruz area.

The victory at the county level once again elevated Gary Patton to the leadership role on the board of supervisors, even in the years he was not serving as
its chair, and in effect made him the de facto leader of all progressive forces in
the county for the next thirteen years, until he made an unsuccessful run for
the state assembly. He then retired from the county board and accepted a position in Monterey as the director of a land-watch organization that tried to
protect open lands in a county dominated by its growth coalition. In keeping
with the powerful role Patton played between 1974 and 1993, and especially
between 1981 and 1993, the *Sentinel* later judged him to be one of the two
most important people in Santa Cruz in the twentieth century, rivaled only by
the colorful boardwalk booster and mayor, Fred Swanton.

The relationship between the city and county on social and environmental
programs was in good part coordinated by a former neighborhood activist in
the Lighthouse Field controversy, Andy Schiffrin, who also had played a significant role in bringing some semblance of order to the deliberations of the
Bicentennial Committee in 1973. He became Patton's key aide after Patton
was first elected to the board of supervisors, working with him to preserve
open space and provide affordable housing. Raised in a leftist family and a
veteran of the 1964 Mississippi Freedom Summer, Schiffrin studied sociology
at UCLA and planning at MIT, where he became part of the trend toward advocacy planning, and then worked for the Boston Model Cities program as a
planner and director of housing development (McAdam 1988, 217). He came
to Santa Cruz in 1972, and from the late 1970s until his formal retirement
from county government in 2006, he met regularly with progressive members
of the city council to help coordinate the city's and county's agendas on a wide
range of issues. It was only in 1981 that those meetings took on major signifi-
cance because of progressive control of both the city and the county governments. He also served in appointed positions in city government concerning
planning, housing, and water supply. He had his hands on so many levers that
he was described to us as "Patton's octopus" by one longtime observer of city
and county government in Santa Cruz.

The increases in social services spending by the city council were achieved
even though Proposition 13 left municipalities with less tax revenue and the
"New Federalism" of the Reagan era meant less federal support for cities. To
fund their new programs, the progressives not only delayed spending on the
infrastructure projects advocated by members of the growth coalition but also

created or increased several taxes. In 1985 they created a tax on tickets for movies and live performances and on concessions in the beach and boardwalk area (the "amusement tax"). To forestall any possible organized opposition to the tax, they struck a deal with the highly conservative president of the Seaside Company, Charles Canfield, to spend half of the proceeds in the beach and boardwalk area. They also increased taxes on lodging at hotels and motels (the "bed tax"). Both of these taxes were ideal from the point of view of the local citizenry because they were in good part paid by out-of-town tourists, who were not likely to stop coming to Santa Cruz because of somewhat higher costs (Rotkin 1991, 420–421). Finally, the progressives increased the tax on utility, cable, and phone bills, making these services a little more expensive for local citizens.

Because of their concern with better working conditions for everyone, the progressive majority started an affirmative action program for city employees and allowed them to unionize without resistance. A few years later they passed a resolution asking the virulently anti-union Canfield to enter into "good faith" negotiations with his employees at the Seaside Company, which he viewed as an unwarranted government intervention into the prerogatives of private enterprise. The bite in the resolution called for the city to discontinue renting the company's banquet and reception facilities for meetings and other events until negotiations began, but the Seaside Company was never unionized, showing once again government's limits in shaping capital-labor relationships.

To ensure that their policies would be carried out, the progressives promoted an assistant city manager they were confident would be willing to follow their directives. He proceeded to gradually replace the managers of city agencies with people he knew to be professional enough to accept the new directions. When a police trainee revealed to a progressive council member that some local police had been systematically brutalizing homeless transients, the ensuing investigation led to the prosecution of six officers and resignations or early retirements by nearly one-third of the police force (Rotkin 1991, 427). In the course of dealing with these and other issues, the progressive majority demonstrated competence in governing at the local level, which the socialist-feminists in the national NAM organization believed to be an essential first step in developing a greater socialist presence at the state and national levels. This competence was especially evident in the way the progressives were able to coordinate city, county, and state governments in response to a major flood in 1982 that destroyed one of the bridges over the San Lorenzo River and nearly overflowed the supposedly impregnable river flood banks.

As part of their efforts to create a popular consciousness that would be supportive of socialism in the future, the progressives held public hearings on a wide range of issues, with the goal of involving more people in government. They passed symbolic resolutions criticizing federal spending priorities, supported disinvestment in South Africa as part of the battle against apartheid, and declared the tiny Santa Cruz Harbor a free trade zone with Nicaragua as a protest against the Reagan administration's effort to overthrow the Sandinista government. They vetoed plans for an unnecessary dam in the mountains that would have created an oversupply of water that the growth coalition wanted in order to provide a basis for future growth, and they instituted a recycling program.

But for all their successes and their mutually beneficial coordination with the progressive county government, the progressives on the city council were unable to realize their most ambitious plans. First, and ironically, control of the city council did not lead to an expansion of Westside Neighbors and the creation of new neighborhood groups. If anything, the electoral victory had the opposite effect: the group quickly lost members and declined in importance. Not only did several activists join the city government in one way or another, but most neighborhood residents seemed satisfied to go back to their everyday lives once they had representatives they felt they could trust to look out for their interests. To the degree that new members could be attracted into Westside Neighbors, they tended to be young leftist university students who wanted the group to take stands on controversial social issues and support third-party candidates at the state and national levels, which tended to alienate the remaining "old timers" who had diverse political views beyond the neighborhood level (Rotkin 1991, 264).

For a variety of reasons, then, the hopes that NAM, Mike Rotkin, and Bruce Van Allen had for neighborhood groups as a way to create a politicized populace could not be realized, as also proved to be the case in other cities where progressives triumphed (Capek and Gilderbloom 1992; Clavel 1999). Socialist-feminists were dismayed, but we believe neighborhood use values trumped the activists' belief that victory at the local level might lead people to become interested in working toward a socialist alternative concerned with class-based issues that involve wages, hours, working conditions, social benefits, the right to unionize, and control of the production process. Instead, people showed a stronger commitment to the pleasures and values that are part of their everyday lives, such as partners, children, friends, hobbies, and athletic interests, which tend to take priority as long as it is possible to enjoy these routine and often taken-for-granted involvements without fear of disruption or turmoil (Flacks 1988; Logan and Molotch 1987).

In addition, several of the progressives' major economic plans were blocked, starting with a successful pushback by local merchants when the progressives wanted to earn extra revenues for the city by renting beach umbrellas, surf boards, and wet suits (Rotkin 1991, 428). Other plans to raise revenues were stopped by legislation at the state and national levels sponsored by business lobbyists. The banking and insurance industries, rightly sensing they might be subjected to new local taxes by progressives in many cities, successfully lobbied for state legislation that prohibited cities from levying taxes on them; moreover, the insurance industry convinced the state legislature to make it illegal for any city to sell housing insurance to its citizens, thereby creating a private-enterprise monopoly (Rotkin 1991, 46). Then a 1984 congressional telecommunications act made it all but impossible to challenge license renewal for private cable companies, dashing the progressives' hopes of having the city or a friendly local progressive group take over this operation (Rotkin 1991, 428). These defeats underscore the fact that cities have limited power in the United States, with the exception of "home rule" on many important land-related issues where few state legislatures would dare to tread. One legal expert goes so far as to say that state governments "have absolute power over cities," and that the federal government "has taken an increasing part in determining city policy, sometimes by mandating city action but more often by attaching strings to federal grants-in-aid" (Frug 1999, 1).

Two issues closer to home caused divisions among the progressives and at the same time inspired the growth coalition to return to the attack. The first was the growing number of homeless people who were congregating in the downtown business district, where some of them began to panhandle in a more assertive fashion. The other was rent control, the issue that had gone down to defeat on ballot initiatives in 1978 and 1979. Based on these two issues, along with the larger socialist goals openly championed by Rotkin and Van Allen, the growth coalition mounted spirited campaigns in the 1983 and 1985 elections that were all-out efforts to regain control of the city council. The progressives could not afford to rest on their laurels or allow the differences among them, which had been papered over during the 1979 and 1981 campaigns, to lead to electoral defeat.

HOMELESS BY CHOICE?

Progressives faced a major unexpected problem that plagued them throughout the 1980s and gave ammunition to their critics—the rising number of homeless people hanging out in the downtown. The landlords and merchants claimed that the problem began with the hippies of the 1960s, who were relatively few in number but highly visible and notable for their dress and idiosyncratic behavior. Worse, they were often said to be "homeless by choice," which was puzzling and annoying to many members of the growth coalition, not to mention most other adults of that era. Contrary to the growth coalition's version of the issue, however, the homeless population changed in the 1970s when the state's mental health system adopted a policy of deinstitutionalization for its very large hospitalized population of mentally ill people. While partly motivated by the benign intent of liberal reformers to move patients from large impersonal institutions to smaller community-based facilities, deinstitutionalization was driven primarily by conservative concerns with rising taxes in the face of state fiscal constraints. The result of this liberal-conservative alliance was more and more mentally ill persons on the streets without adequate state funding to coordinate their care (Rosenthal 1994; Wagner 1993).

The increasing number of homeless was also caused by changes in the economy that began in the 1970s, which were then exacerbated by Reagan administration policies that cut back on federal funding for subsidized housing by 80 percent, thereby drying up the construction of affordable housing until community development corporations began to pick up a meager amount of the slack in the 1990s (Domhoff 2005a; Guthrie and McQuarrie 2005; Liebow 1993, Chapter 7). The problems generated by the lack of low-income housing were then dumped in the laps of city and county governments. This sequence of events created a special dilemma for progressive elected officials in Santa Cruz and elsewhere because their overarching value orientation toward providing social welfare ran the risk of drawing fire from landowners and merchants if they did anything that might "attract" people who were allegedly choosing to adopt a homeless lifestyle.

Progressive city administrations across the country slowly began to fund homeless shelters and soup kitchens in the 1980s, but they did so cautiously, mindful of potential political backlash. Van Allen, who served as mayor in 1982–1983, stated the problem concisely when it came to dealing with the issue in Santa Cruz:

Well, in the '80s the street scene changed because of the rise of homelessness. And the year I was mayor, which was '82–'83, was really the year in which there was dramatically more people on the street in Santa Cruz. It was assumed that you were a drop-out, of the counterculture, a street person, a hippie, and that there was an aspect of voluntarism to it, or of just being a social breakdown, a klutz, you know, who couldn't handle it and therefore didn't have a place to go. And that image really died hard here. In fact, it's not dead, really. Homeless people are still regarded mostly as doing it for a lifestyle choice, or people who are ne'er-do-wells, and who have substance problems or whatever. And a real denial of the economic origins of homelessness. But it began happening in '82 very dramatically. In fact, the way I got involved was that the head of the Salvation Army had come in to see me as the new mayor, and she said, "You know, we can't handle it any-more." But it was not politically viable to attempt to, the year I was mayor, to put any city money into doing anything for the homeless. So what I did, I organized a homeless shelter network of churches and social service providers and others, and we didn't go to the city for money because it was too politically volatile. And, I mean, I have to say that again I feel the people we had in at that point—which was me, and Mike [Rotkin] and John [Laird], and Mardi [Wormhoudt], the council majority—collectively we failed; we chickened out because of politics in that very initial period of dealing with homelessness. I was literally told by my progressive comrades, "Don't touch it with a ten-foot pole." And yet, for me, I couldn't do that. So, the best strategy I could come up with was getting people going without any city money. By 1985 or so, the city was involved, and the need for services and shelter was increasingly recognized. And yet there was still the battle over whether Santa Cruz was somehow a magnet for drop-outs or whatever. And so if we were going to somehow provide shelter or more food pro-grams, that meant that hordes would be coming here from all over the country. That was the political battle over doing anything for the homeless. (Interview with Bruce Van Allen, August 19, 1993)

TENSIONS OVER RENT CONTROL

The other difficult issue, and the one that gave renewed hope to the growth coalition, was rent control. Despite the defeats suffered on their ballot initia-tives in 1978 and 1979, members of the Santa Cruz Housing Action Committee lobbied the progressive majority to institute a strong rent control administra-tion through legislation. The presence of one of their leaders on the council, Van Allen, made them especially hopeful, and Rotkin had expressed support for rent control as well. Advocates also noted that rents had been rising rapidly in Santa Cruz, from a median monthly rate of $112 in 1970 to $290 in 1980, an increase of 159 percent that outstripped the California average of 125 percent and the nationwide average of 120 percent (U.S. Bureau of the Census 1972, 1983). Between the time the first rent control initiative went down to defeat and the progressives won control of the city council in 1981, Santa Cruz rents increased by 58 percent, almost three times greater than the increase in in-comes (Fisher 1982, 8).

As for the real estate interests, they were equally aware that the council could enact rent control through a majority vote. They therefore worked to organize landlords as a constituency to turn the often dull, routine proceedings of city council meetings into an ideological battleground that one observer described as "a months-long public spectacle that all four of the Council majority would rather not repeat" (Johnson 1982b, 8). In classic social movement fashion, the landlords adopted many of the successful tactics of the tenants' movement, including staging public protests at city hall, just as they had done earlier in Santa Monica (Capek and Gilderbloom 1992; Gale 1986; Zald and Useem 1987). The flavor of their efforts is captured in this account by a local alternative journalist who followed Santa Cruz politics closely in the 1980s:

> Landlords came to every meeting where the issue might be discussed. And they came in large numbers, with a hostile attitude and a willingness to be vocal about it. The new Council was indecisive, and at times looked inept in finding a solution to the rent control question. Eventually the majority was backed into a political corner where it was charged with being heavy-handed while taking the cautious route of placing rent control on the ballot for the voters to decide. (Johnson 1982a, 8)

But it was not just organized real estate interests who opposed rent control. So did some committed members of the progressive coalition. David Moberg, a left-wing journalist for *In These Times*, trained originally as an anthropologist, spent several weeks in Santa Cruz about this time and found that rent control was not supported by otherwise stalwart supporters of the progressive agenda. For example, after one city council meeting on rent control, two gay couples told city council member Laird that they "still supported him but were landlords and would vote against rent control" (Moberg 1983, 13).

Even before all these tensions, Laird and Wormhoudt had been wary of advocating rent control during the 1981 campaign (Cone 1983, 14). Behind the scenes, the elected progressives tried to find a compromise position, but the rent control activists did not like that idea. In addition, it seemed likely that real estate interests would be able to put an initiative on the ballot in an attempt to overturn any rent control legislation passed by the council. This possibility had already been demonstrated by the fact that in just two weeks they had collected enough signatures to create a ballot initiative opposing "just cause" eviction legislation passed by the city council (Rotkin 1991, 425–426). The progressives therefore opted to have the issue of rent control contested at the ballot box once again in June 1982, but not before they repealed their "just cause" eviction law in order to keep the issues as clear and simple as possible. The third time for rent control was not the charm—the initiative was rejected by over two thousand votes, and this decisive defeat effectively ended any subsequent efforts to enact rent control in the city of Santa Cruz (Rotkin 1991, 426).

The defeat was especially difficult for Van Allen to accept:

> That was a tough one. I was very closely involved with rent control campaigns and the tenant organizing. That was really a lot of what got me to run for office. And we had rent control on the ballot twice, and then we got the [council] majority, and then the two new people—John and Mardi— for whatever reasons or strategy, refused to go along with me and Mike and pass it directly. So it went to the ballot for a third time, and lost by a decisive margin. So, that pretty much killed rent control as an issue in Santa Cruz. (Interview with Bruce Van Allen, August 19, 1993)

While the growth coalition exulted in this victory, it is not likely that it was theirs to claim because the homeowners who were also landlords did not have to choose between their use values and exchange values on this issue. That is, they did not see the absence of rent control as a threat to their neighborhoods. From their point of view, most renters were university students who would only be living in the city for two or three more years and whose parents could well afford to pay a little extra rent. Rent control, for all its contentiousness, was not a neighborhood issue in Santa Cruz that involved preservation of neighborhood integrity and quality of life.

BUILDING AN ELECTORAL MACHINE

After failing to sustain neighborhood organizations that would lead to greater politicization, with the important exception of the Downtown Neighbors Association, the progressive coalition decided to create an umbrella organization that could bring representatives of many different progressive organizations into one group for the purpose of maintaining the electoral coalition. Many of its members came from the social welfare organizations that the city and county governments were now supporting. The result was the Santa Cruz Action Network (SCAN), founded in late 1981 as a way to sustain political involvement between elections and as a bridge between the movement base and its elected representatives in local government. In effect, SCAN operated as a highly effective campaign organization for progressive politicians. It conducted voter registration drives, hosted a forum at which candidates were endorsed, and organized precinct walking and other election-related work on behalf of its endorsees. SCAN enjoyed remarkable success at electing progressive candidates to local political office. Considering just the three city council elections after the 1981 takeover, eight of nine SCAN-endorsed candidates won or retained their seats, ensuring progressive-neighborhood dominance of the city council throughout the decade.

This success earned SCAN the enmity—as well as the grudging respect—of its political opponents, who wrongly labeled it a "political machine," as if it had the financial and governmental wherewithal to reward its friends and punish its enemies. This label, widely used throughout the city, was repeated in many of our interviews, usually by conservative politicians and businesspersons, but sometimes by self-described progressives. The most common characterization of SCAN—by both its strong opponents and somewhat sympathetic critics on the left—was that it functioned much like the rough-edged Daley Democratic machine in Chicago, even though it had no public power and could not reward its friends or punish its opponents in any material way. Other, more bitter adversaries portrayed SCAN as the frontline troops of left totalitarianism.

With Rotkin and Van Allen running as incumbents, the progressives started the 1983 campaign season in a strong position. Their position was further bolstered by the candidacy of a third SCAN-endorsed candidate, Jane Weed, a recent graduate of UC Santa Cruz with a major in Community Studies. She was also a neighborhood activist through her involvement in Westside Neighbors and served on the board of the Westside Health Clinic. In addition, the progressives made the same kind of symbolic appeal they had used in the past by putting an initiative on the ballot. This one allowed students and downtown voters to express their antipathy toward university administrators, who had placed the campus on a growth path that would lead it well past the seventy-five hundred students that had been set as the target for 1990 (in fact, the campus enrolled just over ten thousand students at the start of the 1990–1991 academic year). The initiative basically asked voters if they approved of a new research and industrial park on the outskirts of the campus that had been proposed by the university leadership. Although the university argued it could do what it wanted to on its own land, it was not clear that a court would rule that a park that included industry was part of the university's educational mission and exempt from the local planning process. Either way, the initiative was likely to send local university administrators a message and increase voter turnout.

At the outset, the new progressive-neighborhood electoral organization did not look as unbeatable as it turned out to be. To the contrary, the pro-growth forces felt confident in 1982 that they could win back the city council, thanks to their decisive defeat of rent control for a third time in the spring of that year. Just as the rent control activists had been essential in the progressive campaigns of 1979 and 1981, now leaders within the growth coalition hoped that opponents of rent control would be their foot soldiers in a return to power. This time they called themselves Alert Santa Cruz. They first mulled over (and ultimately rejected) the possibility of launching a recall against council members Rotkin and Van Allen, then decided to focus their energies on defeating the two socialist-feminists in the 1983 municipal election (Johnson 1983c, 8).

Alert Santa Cruz began with a seven-person board of directors that, with one exception, was not composed of the usual faces from the growth coalition. There also seemed to be a new public face for the group, a former professor of geography at UC Santa Cruz, who had left the university to work on the renewal of downtown housing and to serve as a consultant to local real estate and construction interests. As this genial moderate Republican put it, "We can't go with conservative candidates" (Johnson 1982b, 8). His group argued that it represented the whole city, that is, the "public interest," whereas progressives made "brazen political payoffs to its neighborhood activist support factions" (Johnson 1983b, 8).

This approach also included an attempt to connect with neighborhoods. In particular, the group developed a relationship with a newly formed group of dissident neighbors near the downtown area, who did not like a program to erect street barriers and diverters proposed by the Downtown Neighbors Association. This nascent neighbors' group, which turned out not to have much staying power, provides an instance of one of the general problems facing neighborhood politics: the interests of residents may not always be the same. If this backlash effort had been successful, the progressive coalition would have faced political risks on two fronts—criticisms by the growth coalition for attending to the "special interests" of neighborhoods and protests from residents who claimed that their real interests were not being served.

Moreover, Alert Santa Cruz came up with a moderate four-person slate. It consisted of a retired public school administrator, a retired city official who had been head of the public works department, a real estate agent, and a local computer industry businessman who owned land near the greenbelt that he wanted rezoned for high-density development (Johnson 1983a, 10). While the attacks on progressives in the Alert Santa Cruz newsletter were pointed and caustic, the usual fear of "creeping socialism" was not raised in the early stages of the campaign.

By the height of the campaign season, however, indications that this race might be run with less emphasis on incendiary symbolic issues had vanished. The moderate former geography professor was pushed aside, and the other board members reconstituted themselves as the All Santa Cruz Coalition. The campaign was by this time in the hands of Marathon Communications of Los Angeles, which earlier in the year had directed a successful campaign against the progressive mayor of Santa Monica, using the name All Santa Monica Coalition. The Santa Cruz growth coalition soon adopted Marathon Communications' well-practiced "creeping socialism" strategy (Johnson 1983a, 10; Capek and Gilderbloom 1992, 158).

The new campaign strategy started somewhat modestly, although absurdly, with a conservative council member writing a letter in which he attacked the progressive majority for seeking "the suspension of representative government in Santa Cruz" (*Sentinel*, November 3, 1983, 1). The letter was reprinted and distributed in a direct mail piece that went out to Santa Cruz residents under the auspices of the All Santa Cruz Coalition. While it was not an all-out attack on the evils of socialism, it did label each member of the progressive majority as a "socialist," even though Wormhoudt and Laird took pains to distance themselves from that political identity. In other campaign pieces, the All Santa Cruz Coalition continually pointed out the connections between the Campaign for Economic Democracy and Santa Cruz progressives, decrying the pernicious influence of "outside agitators." The All Santa Cruz Coalition also put out a series of campaign fliers and mailers that had as their central theme the desire of "socialist ideologues" to take "absolute control" of city government to implement their "hidden agenda" (Johnson 1983b, 16).

The renewed attempt to create moral panic over the long-term socialist goals espoused by key members of the progressive coalition, which by then had suffered serious setbacks in Santa Cruz and most other cities, reached its peak in a letter sent to Santa Cruz businesspersons by the realtor who led the charge against rent control and was a founder of Alert Santa Cruz: "We have been operating at the mercy of a socialist progressive City Council that works with constant unrelenting determination to limit free enterprise." To underscore the message that the worst was yet to come, he included a reprint of an article that he had used during the earlier rent control battles, "Socialism: On the Street Where You Live," produced by the anti–rent control forces in Santa Monica. It warned of the "10 steps to socialism," beginning with seemingly innocuous projects such as bicycle lanes, recycling programs, and the creation of food co-ops, and culminating in full-blown socialist control of local government (Johnson 1983b, 15).

The alleged organizational nexus of socialism in Santa Cruz continued to be the Campaign for Economic Democracy, even though it was located in Santa Monica and did not advocate socialism. The All Santa Cruz coalition seized on the fact that one of Rotkin's most active campaign workers, a Community Studies major in the 1970s and also a member of the early group of students and NAM activists who created Westside Neighbors, was by then a member of the Campaign for Economic Democracy (Rotkin 1991, 274). Furthermore, the All Santa Cruz coalition had learned that this activist sent a postcard to the group's members requesting that they come to Santa Cruz to "save the progressive majority [on] the Santa Cruz City Council" (*Sentinel*, October 26, 1983, A-1). With the three growth coalition supporters on the city council acting as spokespersons, All Santa Cruz called a press conference to decry the postcard. They raised the fear of an "invasion" of "our little city by the sea" by hundreds of leftist activists (Johnson 1983b, 15).

Beyond the ideological rejection of socialism, the growth coalition and its candidates offered a few general substantive critiques of the progressive/socialist regime: "heavy-handed" control by "big government" ignored more efficient market solutions to problems of housing, the incumbent administration had drained the city's budget reserves "without the benefit of a major capital improvement project to show for it," and "socialistic candidates" put forth the idea of "government intervention in hiring practices" by private business. Most ominous of all, a 5–2 progressive/socialist majority would be able, under the existing city charter, to revamp the actual form of the local government by ending the council-manager form of government with its "built-in checks and balances." Santa Cruz was now portrayed as the socialistic commune of the West Coast, as the "People's Republic of Santa Cruz" (*Sentinel*, November 6, 1983, A-17).

Uncharacteristically, the pro-growth forces also engaged in precinct-level political organizing, even though they once again were able to build a roughly two-to-one advantage in campaign contributions, approximately $100,000 to $50,000 (*Sentinel*, November 9, 1983, 1). Unlike the previous election campaign, when the bulk of the contributions to moderate and conservative candidates rolled in through large donations from outside real estate interests, less than 10 percent of campaign contributions came from real estate interests outside of Santa Cruz County. About two-thirds of the total was raised from local residents (Johnson 1983b, 16). While some of the "old hands in local politics" provided some of that money, as did "people in the real estate and development business throughout the county," the All Santa Cruz Coalition succeeded in broadening its base of local support: "More relatively small landlords, businesspeople, and professionals have given to All Santa Cruz than to any other campaign in the city's history" (Johnson 1983b, 16).

The real drama of the campaign proved to be an unexpected and unprecedented challenge to the student vote shortly before the election on the grounds that many students did not provide their correct home addresses when they registered. Led by a real estate agent and anti–rent control activist, a new group called Citizens Against Voter Fraud filed a court challenge against seventeen hundred of the twenty-seven hundred campus voters, who were singled out by name. The challenge asked the grand jury to petition the county clerk to have the voters disqualified, but the Santa Cruz County District Attorney's office denied their request, arguing that such a "late challenge" could "have a chilling effect on voting" (*Sentinel,* November 7, 1983, A-1). Undaunted, Citizens Against Voter Fraud, which was later revealed to have a considerable overlap in personnel and funding with the All Santa Cruz Coalition, made it clear that it would take its case to court after the elections in an effort to overturn the results.

The argument by Citizens Against Voter Fraud had two aspects. First, there was a danger that former students who continued to be registered at a campus address could vote even though they might not live in the city any longer. Second, students who lived outside the city limits could vote in the city using their campus address and vote at their home address as well.

Despite the challenge to student voters and the all-out campaign by supporters of the growth coalition, progressives held on to their 4–3 majority, thanks once again to their overwhelming support on the campus. Although only 52 percent of students registered in the campus precincts voted, which was lower than the 57 percent citywide turnout, the solid voting bloc among students was decisive, with 81 percent of them supporting the progressive candidates. In both 1979 and 1981, the progressives who won would have been elected even if the student vote in the campus precincts were subtracted from the final vote count. This time, however, the All Santa Cruz Coalition would have enjoyed a clean sweep if the student vote had been eliminated, giving the growth coalition a 5–2 edge on the city council. Even with the student vote included, Van Allen lost his seat by the narrow margin of thirty-four votes to Weed, the third member of the progressive slate. According to the alternative press, the rent control issue may have come back to haunt Van Allen, who made firm public stands at council meetings and made a strong critique of the failings of the private housing market using a leftist political economy framework (*Santa Cruz Express,* October 13, 1983, 11). On the other hand, voters on and off the campus expressed their displeasure with university growth plans by voting against the proposed university research and industrial park by a 72 percent to 28 percent margin.

The effort by Citizens Against Voter Fraud to disqualify student voters took on added weight after the election because Weed would be replaced by an All Santa Cruz Coalition candidate if the judge found in the postelection hearings that the charges had merit, returning majority control of the council to the growth coalition. However, the Superior Court judge who heard the case decided in April 1984 that voter fraud had not taken place. After hundreds of students were forced to testify, he concluded that votes had been miscast, but he did not overturn the election results. At the same time, he wrote that the plaintiffs were right to say that the campus represented an "ideologically discrete enclave in the body politic." Other comments by the judge were critical of the effect of the student vote on Santa Cruz political contests, raising the possibility that the complaints by the Citizens Against Voter Fraud/All Santa Cruz Coalition might have an impact on the next election. Whether this was one of the intentions of the plaintiffs or not, there is some evidence that the lawsuit dampened student participation in the next election: voter turnout on campus declined from 52 percent in 1983 to only 42 percent in 1985 (*Sentinel,* November 9, 1983, A-11; *Sentinel,* November 7, 1985, A-9).

1985: Students Make the Difference Again

The 1985 elections were basically a rerun of 1983, with SCAN endorsing the two progressive incumbents, Laird and Wormhoudt, along with a Latino high school teacher who added to the ticket through his association with Jesse Jackson's Rainbow Coalition, which had energized progressives nationwide in the 1984 Democratic primaries. The All Santa Cruz Coalition once again spearheaded the growth coalition's campaign, endorsing a former council member, Joe Ghio, who had to sit out for two years after serving from 1975 to 1983. Ghio was joined on the slate by a captain in the campus fire department and the owner of a real estate firm who was married to a former chamber of commerce executive.

As before, the All Santa Cruz Coalition claimed that progressives polarized the city and that the Campaign for Economic Democracy, by then all but dead, was the red menace behind the progressive agenda. Although the coalition said nothing positive about either of the progressive incumbents, it adopted the strategy of portraying Laird as a reasonable person who fostered a spirit of cooperation. Then it concentrated on trying to defeat Wormhoudt as an extremist (*Sentinel,* November 6, 1983, A-13). The *Sentinel* endorsed Laird on the basis of his ability to "get around the rhetoric and focus on the jobs that need to be done" (*Sentinel,* October 31, 1985, A-11).

The progressive candidates ignored the taunts, stressing that the local economy was strong and the city enjoyed a sound financial footing. They noted there had been a 40 percent increase in sales tax revenues since they took control in 1981, so they must be doing something right. While this was no quantum leap compared to the 38 percent increase for the preceding five-year period, when the growth coalition controlled the city council, it did blunt the opposition slate's charge that progressives were responsible for leading the city to the brink of economic ruination.

The progressives also countered with their usual charge that the All Santa Cruz Coalition candidates would favor the rapid development of the city, implying that Santa Cruz would become another San Jose. Addressing the standard claim by the local growth coalition that growth brings more jobs, Wormhoudt offered a rejoinder that illustrates that local progressives had developed a more sophisticated analysis based on research showing that local growth does not reduce the unemployment rate and often leads to increases in housing costs (Applebaum 1978; Applebaum and Gilderbloom 1983). "Jobs" she said, "are the biggest cause of immigration [to Santa Cruz county]. New jobs in electronics have never lowered the unemployment rate—new people simply come here to take them. Our stable population is not served by those jobs—if those jobs bring more affluent people who squeeze residents out of housing" (*Sentinel*, October 31, 1985, A-16).

Although progressives presented a sophisticated analysis of the political economy of job creation, housing, and unemployment in their literature, they nonetheless stressed symbolic politics to turn out the vote and to win the election. Just as the growth coalition presented its opposition to progressives as taking a stand against socialism, progressives attempted to portray their continued political success as critical to establishing a bulwark against the rising tide of right-wing Republicanism. In so doing, they constantly called attention to the Reagan administration's desire to lift the moratorium on oil drilling in protected coastal waters, which included the Monterey Bay (*Santa Cruz Express*, October 17, 1985, 10). Despite the fact that the moratorium was a matter for Congress to decide, progressives placed a measure on the ballot to ban oil drilling off the Santa Cruz coast. It was clearly understood by both sides as a way to draw progressive supporters to the polls, the equivalent of the 1981 measure opposing the government's support for the right-wing regime in El Salvador and the 1983 measure opposing the university's research and development park (which never was built).

In spite of the new strategy employed by the growth coalition, Laird finished first in the voting and Wormhoudt finished third, and the progressives retained their 4–3 majority. At the first meeting of the newly elected council, Laird credited his and Wormhoudt's victories to the fact that they both enjoyed support throughout the city. Addressing the claims by the "conservative faction" that the student vote was the key to the progressives' ability to win local office, Laird said, "People have not been complaining this time. I think people realize this is not what decides our elections. Santa Cruz as a whole is a generally progressive city" (*Sentinel*, November 13, 1985, 1).

Nevertheless, it was in fact another close call for the progressives, who needed the student vote to return Wormhoudt to office. Although voter turn-out in campus precincts was about 10 percentage points lower than in 1983, the overwhelming student support for the incumbent progressives (78 per-cent for Wormhoudt, 71 percent for Laird) once again made the difference. Without the campus precincts, Joe Ghio, the moderate who finished second, would have been first, Laird would have dropped to second, and Wormhoudt would have been out of office, with the third spot going to the campus fire captain. The fact that the student vote was especially critical in Wormhoudt's victory suggests that the strong focus on her alleged "extremism" by the pro-growth forces may have had an impact in some parts of the city.

For all the progressives' talk about their strong support throughout the city, they were extremely worried after the 1985 elections about the fact of declin-ing voter turnout among university students. They therefore took a page out of the growth coalition's playbook back in 1972, when it tried to move the date of the local elections from April to October. The progressives fashioned a ballot measure for the 1986 elections that would move local elections from odd to even years, hoping to increase participation in local voting because of the pull of state and national issues. In so doing they were following the lead of the progressives in Santa Monica and Berkeley, who made the same change in 1984. They were also undoing one of the key "reforms" by the growth coali-tions in the Progressive Era that had worked to lower voter turnout. The mea-sure passed by a two to one margin.

1988: Solidifying the Progressive Electoral Machine

The successful ballot measure in 1986 meant that the next city election was in 1988, not 1987, by which time the economic scene appeared to have changed for the worse in Santa Cruz, generating new pressures on the progressive coalition. Critics of the progressives claimed that the downtown mall was in economic decline, as evidenced by the fact that city tax revenues from the downtown area had decreased by 8.8 percent between 1986 and 1988. As a re-sult, the city budget ran a $1 million deficit in 1988–1989, which was covered by tax increases and budget reallocations from other revenue sources, such as highway maintenance funds (*Sentinel*, October 18, 1988, A-4).

The claims about the decline in retail sales proved to be off the mark: they were due to the relocation of downtown auto dealers, located several blocks from the mall. Although the progressives had offered the car dealers a large plot of land near the river to keep them within the city, the dealers thought the space was too cramped, so they moved to open space near the Capitola

Mall, where there was more room for expansion and easy freeway access for shoppers. Nevertheless, their departure allowed the growth coalition to blame the progressives for the city's shrinking tax base. The alleged decline in downtown sales also provided the occasion for a renewed attack on the progressives for supposedly ignoring the homeless population on the mall, which had increased in its size and restiveness despite the palliative efforts by the city and various nonprofit agencies. Even though the problem had been created by national-level policies supported by most members of the growth coalition, its local leaders wanted to push homeless people out of the downtown and make them someone else's concern. At the same time, the elected progressives at both the city and the county level were excoriated by some liberal and left advocates for the homeless, often based in churches, as being overly bureaucratic and having the wrong budgetary priorities (Lee 1992).

Although the economic problems appeared to create an ideal situation for the growth coalition to reverse its declining fortunes, in fact its leaders had all but given up politically. Gone were the outside consultants and the behind-the-scenes discussions that would have led to a slate of three or four candidates. Gone was any evidence that the leaders of the chamber of commerce or the Board of Realtors were actively supporting a few favored candidates. The result was a field of nine moderates and conservatives, along with a clearly defined three-person progressive slate and several candidates in the middle. This meant that the many pro-growth candidates were likely to divide the vote so widely that a focused progressive slate would have a strong edge. Four straight electoral defeats dating back to 1979, along with the change in the year of the elections, had taken the heart out of the growth coalition as a political force.

Still, the progressives by no means felt confident of their position after the close elections in 1983 and 1985. Nor could they know in advance that the growth coalition would not run a strong campaign. Laird and Wormhoudt would not have to vacate their seats because of term limits until 1990, but Rotkin had to rotate off the council after two terms, and Weed had decided not to run again. So the progressives had to field three new candidates, all of whom felt they needed to stress their pro-business orientation to counter the growth coalition's attempt to blame progressives for local economic problems. This decision disappointed some of the old-line progressives and neighborhood activists, who did not see seven years in the majority as any assurance of long-term dominance.

One of the new candidates, Don Lane, was a UC Santa Cruz graduate long involved in progressives politics, especially as an organizer of successful campaigns for the state assembly and U.S. House of Representatives. He was also the founder and owner of a small restaurant, the Saturn Café, which catered in good part to university students, making him appealing to both students and downtown progressives. Another was an independent accountant and gay activist, Mo Reich, who worked for small businesses, giving his pro-business comments a considerable degree of legitimacy. The third, Jane Yokoyama, a one-time UC Santa Cruz Spanish language instructor, was employed as a staff member of the Santa Cruz Housing Development Corporation, where she worked on a project to improve low-income housing in the Latino neighborhood—Beach Flats—adjacent to the beach and boardwalk. She was a supporter of the Rainbow Coalition who had ideal credentials as a woman of color and an advocate for the poor.

At times it was difficult to distinguish the positions the three new progressive candidates took on specific development proposals from those of the growth coalition candidates. For example, two of the three supported the development of a beachfront hotel, a key component of the growth coalition's economic development plan but anathema to most progressives. They also discussed the possibility of annexing unincorporated areas to broaden the city's economic base, but many grassroots progressives took a dim view of this plan, viewing it as growth-inducing (*Sentinel,* October 17, 1988, A-4, A-10). Unlike the pro-growth candidates, however, they made clear they were progressive on social issues, and Lane stressed that he would try to do more for the homeless.

Although progressives felt they would have an advantage in turnout because of the change to even-year elections, they did not leave anything to chance. Once again they offered a ballot initiative that would appeal to both students and downtown progressives. It asked voters to oppose a recent decision by the top officials of the University of California to accelerate the growth of the Santa Cruz campus, which would take it to fifteen thousand by 2005. The initiative was called Slow University Growth, known by the acronym SLUG, which in Santa Cruz is shorthand for Banana Slug, the unusual mascot picked for campus sports teams by the students in the 1970s. In keeping with the liberal and activist campus culture, this slimy yellow indigenous invertebrate is meant to symbolize the students' disinterest in highly competitive college sports teams. (Even in the late 1980s, most of the Santa Cruz teams were mere "clubs," with only a few of them playing in Division III of the NCAA.)

Although the SLUG initiative was at best advisory, it did allow the neighborhoods—along with most students, faculty, and staff—to express their desire to keep the campus small and personal. Even more than the failed plan for a research and industrial park, the university's growth plans rekindled the running battle between the campus and the city that has continued ever since. The conflict was made all the more ironic because the university activists and voters were so obviously important to the progressive coalition, which was now beginning to turn its attention to limiting the growth and expansion plans of the university itself. And by this point we estimate that the "campus vote" was being supplemented by as many as one thousand alumni who had settled in the city. Several of the prime movers behind the initiative originally came to the city to attend UC Santa Cruz in the late 1960s and early 1970s.

Whether it was the presidential election occurring at the same time, the pull of the SLUG initiative, or the local issues that faced the community, voter turnout rose to 75 percent, with 75 percent of those voters endorsing the anti-university position on the SLUG initiative. And despite all the problems related to the economy and homelessness that the growth coalition candidates tried to blame on the progressives, the three progressive candidates swept the first three open seats. A widely known and amiable physician and real estate owner, John Mahaney, who had been a pro-growth council member in the 1970s, picked up the fourth council seat. The unexpected success for all three of their candidates gave progressives a 5–2 majority on the city council for the first time since they gained control of city government in 1981. Moreover, there was a further surprise. For the first time since 1981, the progressives would have won a majority without the campus vote, a fact they used to reinforce their claim that they had support throughout the city. Student support for SCAN candidates, which had declined from 81 percent in 1983 to 73 percent in 1985, dropped to 61 percent for Yokoyama, 46 percent for Lane, and 43 percent for Reich in 1988, suggesting that their pro-development appeals did not sit well with students.

PROGRESSIVE SUCCESS BUT SOCIALIST DECLINE

By 1988, it was the progressives who had a strong electoral machine, based not only in neighborhoods and the student vote but in the employees and volunteers of the many new and well-funded social service organizations in the city and county. A community credit union, a community printing company, a cultural council, and many unionized government and service workers were also supporters of the progressive electoral coalition. Just as local land and business owners had earlier shown that initiative and organization can matter at the local level, now their opponents had shown that local progressive electoral coalitions can be developed that deliver tangible benefits to their supporters in the form of better support for neighborhoods, increased spending for social services, environmental protection, respect for the rights of gays and lesbians, and support for city employees. This electoral coalition had shown that it also could be a governing coalition, able to work with business but not bending to the will of the growth coalition. According to regime theory, such an outcome is not a likely one. Nor does the progressives' ability to support a variety of "redistributive" programs fit with public choice theory's claim that such programs are not possible at the local level.

By this time, however, the socialist-feminists' hopes of building a larger socialist movement had been completely dashed, not just by the election of Ronald Reagan for two terms and then George H. W. Bush in 1988, but by defeats on the kinds of local economic proposals progressives had hoped to use to advance their cause—modest ones, such as renting beach umbrellas and surf boards, and more ambitious ones, such as selling home insurance and owning the local cable TV outlet. Aside from symbolic issues, the progressive coalition in Santa Cruz had succeeded on neighborhood issues, the preservation of open space, improved social services, and better treatment for city employees, which liberals and even some moderates could endorse. In effect, the socialist-feminists in the New American Movement and other leftist organizations had hoped to leverage neighborhood use-value conflicts into class struggles over economic redistribution and ownership of productive enterprises. But they had ended up primarily as neighborhood leaders, protectors of the environment, social welfare providers, and good employers.

Even the Santa Cruz chapter of NAM, which had played such an important role in organizing the takeover of the city council through victories in the 1979 and 1981 elections, was disbanded in 1982. This was partly due to the enormous amount of effort that its small membership put into exercising municipal power in the early 1980s. But it also crucially involved the fact that the national NAM had merged with a slightly larger and less militant nationwide socialist organization, the Democratic Socialist Organizing Committee, whose three thousand members tended to focus on influencing labor leaders and liberals within the Democratic Party rather than trying to work at the grassroots and create participatory organizations. Feeling that their efforts at the local level would not be supported within the new organization that emerged, the Democratic Socialists of America, the Santa Cruz chapter of NAM disbanded (Rotkin 1991, 323–325).

More generally, progressive hopes had been dampened nationwide by the fact that progressive governments in other cities had suffered losses or had been forced to moderate their programs. In Burlington, the socialist mayor, Bernie Sanders, who was elected and reelected between 1981 and 1989 and who went on to win a seat in the House of Representatives in 1990 and in the Senate in 2006, could never convince the electorate to provide him with a majority on the city council. His coalition only gradually made any inroads on housing and neighborhood issues (Conroy 1990). In Santa Monica, the renters' rights coalition temporarily lost control of the city council at one point in the 1980s, then won control again with a more modest agenda (Capek and Gilderbloom 1992). In Madison, the progressive coalition of the 1970s continued to pursue a limited progressive agenda in the 1980s and 1990s, but it never gained full control of the city council (Thompson 2007).

Perhaps most dramatically of all, the progressive coalition in Berkeley, which had a working majority on the city council from 1979 to 1981 and then won an 8–1 majority in 1984, nearly lost control of the city council in 1986. At that time angry neighborhood leaders broke with the leftists from the university community over a plan to disperse federally financed low-income housing into eleven neighborhoods. The result was a successful ballot initiative strongly supported in upper-income neighborhoods in a special June election when most UC Berkeley students had already departed for the summer. It created district elections in the city, thereby reducing the importance of the university student vote and forcing the reconstituted progressive coalition to focus more fully on neighborhood issues. This unexpected turn of events is support for the emphasis that growth coalition theory puts on neighborhood use values. More recently, the relatively few examples of municipal ownership of retail outlets and public utilities are as likely to be in conservative or centrist cities—e.g., Cincinnati, Louisville, San Antonio, and San Diego—as in progressive ones (see Alperovitz 2005, Chapter 8, for a detailed catalogue of "enterprising cities" and the income-producing projects they own).

Still, for all the setbacks their cause had suffered locally and nationally, progressives in Santa Cruz had some reason to feel hopeful about their successes. They had defeated the local growth coalition on every major development project since the late 1960s and had kept it from winning back control of the city council despite its well-organized efforts in the 1983 and 1985 elections. Furthermore, the growth coalition's failure to mount a serious challenge to progressives in 1988 seemed like a signal of acquiescence to progressive dominance of city government.

Even so, the politically defeated landowners and merchants could take solace in the fact that commercial rents and tourist revenues had increased throughout the 1980s, a fact that the progressive coalition often pointed out. Moreover, even though progressive candidates took three of the four seats in the 1988 elections, many members of the growth coalition were heartened by the support the new progressive council members expressed during the campaign for economic development. As it turned out, however, there was little movement on any of these issues in the first ten months of the new council. Instead, downtown leaders and progressives continued to argue about issues such as homeless people on the mall, which led to a Social Problems Task Force that was asked to analyze the problem yet again and offer recommendations for improvements.

For all the seeming moderation during the electoral campaign and its aftermath, tensions increased when the newly elected Mo Reich resigned in late February 1989 because he publicly lied about sending an inappropriate unsigned Valentine to a conservative political leader in a nearby town. This brouhaha provided the occasion for the city's most extreme right-wingers, who were already angry with the city council for refusing to welcome a naval vessel into the harbor on the previous Fourth of July, to mount a recall campaign. Although the recall campaign never made it to the ballot, the rightists had stirred up enough trouble to cause progressives to wonder if their majority on the council would be in danger in 1990. Meanwhile, Reich was replaced through appointment with one of the key neighborhood activists in the Lighthouse Field struggle, Katherine Beiers, who was also an administrator in the university library.

And then the earthquake struck, heavily damaging the downtown, shaking up the power structure of the city, and creating the possibility of new fault lines of power. The massive destruction in the context of moral and patriotic anger toward the council majority suddenly provided new hopes for the growth coalition—and new threats for the progressives.

5

~~~~~~

SHAKING UP
THE POWER STRUCTURE

The major earthquake that began at 5:04 PM on Tuesday, October 17, 1989, lasted only fifteen seconds, but it took sixty-three lives, injured hundreds, and left thousands homeless in the overall San Francisco Bay Area.[1] (The earthquake was originally thought to be 7.1 in magnitude, but in 1999 seismologists adjusted the strength to 6.9.) Santa Cruz County as a whole experienced the most deaths and damage in relative terms. With a much smaller population base, the county suffered six of the sixty-three deaths, had the most homes destroyed (774) or damaged (13,329), and had greater damage to businesses, with 310 businesses destroyed and 1,615 damaged. Of the $36 million in funds disbursed statewide by the Federal Emergency Management Agency, $12 million were earmarked for Santa Cruz County (*Sentinel*, October 13, 1991, A-8).

Although Watsonville also incurred considerable damage, the greatest concentration of deaths and destruction was on the Pacific Garden Mall in downtown Santa Cruz. From nearly one end to the other, brick buildings were reduced to piles of rubble; storefront windows were blown out, littering the

---

1. Some of the arguments and analyses in this chapter, as well as some parts of the text, first appeared in Richard Gendron, "Forging Collective Capacity for Urban Redevelopment: 'Power To,' 'Power Over,' or Both?" *City and Community* 5 (2006): 5–22, copyright 2006 Blackwell Publishing. Reprinted by permission of Blackwell Publishing.

street and sidewalk with thousands of shards of glass; and cars were crushed by fallen trees. It was originally estimated that one-third of the buildings on the mall either were destroyed or needed to be demolished. Later assessments pegged the extent of the downtown damage even higher, with the local redevelopment agency calculating that over 50 percent of the commercial buildings in the downtown core were destroyed or so badly damaged that they needed to be demolished (Santa Cruz City Redevelopment Agency n.d.). President Bush and other federal officials toured the wreckage. Cities as far away as Charlestown, South Carolina, sent police officers to help out.

When the well-known and well-liked owner of the main downtown bookstore, Neal Coonerty, soon to be a major player in the rebuilding effort, pleaded with his progressive friends in city government for a day or two to save books and avert bankruptcy before the remains of the building were torn down, four hundred volunteers lined up to help the next morning. They signed waivers agreeing that the city would not be responsible for any injuries they suffered if the building collapsed, and then they carried thousands of books into the tent-like pavilions, which were erected on city parking lots without charge by members of local construction unions and would house many displaced stores and restaurants for the next three years at very low rents. Other business owners went through similar harrowing experiences as they struggled to salvage inventory in a chaotic and uncertain situation—no one was certain if it was safe to go into the buildings.

On the other hand, few city buildings and houses outside the downtown area lost much more than a chimney or a plate-glass window. For example, windows were broken on the UC Santa Cruz campus, books were knocked off shelves in the university library and faculty offices, and one building suffered cracks in its foundation that required major repairs, but no one who was on the rock-solid hillside underlying the campus had any idea of the extent of the damage in the downtown. The fact that the central business district was built on a floodplain had once again come back to haunt the city. Not only did the ground turn to liquid and destroy foundations, but the unreinforced, limestone-based masonry used in the old commercial buildings left them even more vulnerable to collapse.

But floodplain or no floodplain, rebuilding would have to occur on the same downtown sites, mainly because of property ownership and the lack of available open land in the city. Besides, the downtown was essential to city finances, providing about 25 percent of citywide retail sales as well as jobs for an estimated 15 percent of the city labor force (U.S. Bureau of the Census 1993). Immediately after the quake, the city's public information officer estimated that Santa Cruz would lose about $1 million in sales tax revenue as a direct result of the closure of the mall (*City on a Hill Press,* October 21, 1989, 9).

The earthquake did not simply damage the physical infrastructure of the city. It opened up the possibility for significant changes in the power structure. Some leaders within the growth coalition believed they had an opportunity to regain power if they could take the lead in the rebuilding process. On the other hand, the progressives were quick to realize their vulnerability because they could lose revenues for their social programs and the confidence of voters if they did not assume leadership in a situation in which property rights and the ability of the major landholders to outwait them might put them at a distinct disadvantage.

Rebuilding turned out to be a slow process for a variety of reasons. Not only were there tensions between property owners and progressive elected officials, but the nation, and especially California, was headed into a recession as well, which was deepened as a result of the credit crunch caused by the collapse of the savings and loan industry in the 1980s. The recession also led to a precipitous decline in funds transferred by the state of California to its cities (Barnhill 1990). Nor could there be any thought of fully reopening the mall until the electric, gas, and sewer lines under the main street were replaced, which took three years. The one saving grace was a half-cent increase in sales taxes approved by Santa Cruz County voters in the fall of 1990, which provided $43 million for downtown repairs over a six-year period, beginning in the spring of 1991. The city also received millions of dollars in grants from state and federal agencies, along with $1 million from the American Red Cross.

Many business leaders ignored the larger economic problems when they blamed progressives for delays in a new planning process that they all but demanded. They claimed the new planning group was more concerned with "process" than they had anticipated and too focused on technical details best left to planning experts on the city staff. Still, most of them did realize that broader economic forces were far more to blame for the slow pace of earthquake recovery than any failings of the planning process adopted for rebuilding. As Harvey Nickelson, the president of the local Coast Commercial Bank and a key player in the rebuilding process, later put it, "You never want to have a disaster followed immediately by an economic recession" (Interview with Harvey Nickelson, January 20, 1993).

Because of this combination of problems, only one building had been rebuilt by the elections in November 1990, and only four had been rebuilt, with eight more under construction, as the 1992 elections approached. A new museum of art and history opened in 1993, and by 1995 there was a new multiscreen movie theater, which became the stimulus and magnet for a downtown revival. Still, gaping holes in the ground were readily apparent until the late 1990s. Even as late as 2006, there were two remaining empty lots where construction had just started. One was owned by the family of a very conservative multimillionaire, Louis Rittenhouse, who will figure prominently in this and the next chapter. The other belonged to a sentimental environmentalist, who was so particular about what his new building would look like that his friends on the city council finally sued for control of the property—to the shock of extreme conservatives and strong environmentalists—and forced him to turn rebuilding over to his adult children (Egan 2005).

As we show in this chapter, the arguments over rebuilding were first fought out over the creation and functioning of a public-private partnership, ostensibly designed to establish a harmonious setting in which all the "stakeholders" would have an equal say. While some cooperation and social learning were achieved, as regime theory would expect, neither side made any serious changes in its preferences. Moreover, this cooperation could only begin after the growth coalition and the progressives first battled to a near standstill on key substantive issues, with the most assertive landowners first attempting to expand the downtown, to the dismay of all progressives. Then the most radical environmentalists and neighborhood activists tried to expand their use-value orientation into the downtown through more open plazas and public meeting areas, to the horror of all members of the growth coalition.

Once those two overarching initiatives failed, conflicts within the rival coalitions—not between them—created most of the delays and many of the compromises. In the face of the new crisis conditions, differences between landowners interested in rents and storeowners interested in profits often came to the fore, as symbolized most dramatically in one retailer's comment that landowners are the "natural enemies" of storeowners. On the progressive side, long simmering but previously less salient differences soon surfaced between the socialist-feminists and social-welfare liberals, on the one hand, whose desire for greater revenue for expanding social services led them to support some new developments, and the most radical of environmentalists and neighborhood activists on the other, who did not want any developments that might threaten use values. This disagreement within the progressive coalition made the social-welfare progressives look like moderates who were selling out to the growth coalition, or so some of their critics contended. However, we think the disagreement was rooted in the conflict between the class-oriented concerns of the socialist-feminists and social-welfare liberals and the exclusive focus on the use values of land on the part of environmentalists and neighborhood activists.

THE ORIGINS OF VISION SANTA CRUZ

While progressive elected officials were busy with the details of restoring basic services, such as gas and electricity, and conferring with state and federal officials about providing help for dislodged citizens in and around the downtown area, the growth coalition swung into political action a day or so after the earthquake. In doing so, it drew on the resources of the International Downtown Association, one of several organizations in the nationwide urban policy-planning network that provides local growth coalitions with technical expertise as well as ideological support. By coincidence, one of the major property owners in the downtown area, Rittenhouse, was serving as the president of the Santa Cruz Downtown Association and had attended a meeting of the International Downtown Association just a month before the earthquake. As he explained in an interview in August 1993, he had been introduced to new ideas on how to revitalize a downtown and met the president of the international group, Richard Bradley, so he was in an ideal position to reach out to Bradley for ideas: "So we got in touch with Rich [Bradley] in Washington, and made arrangements to get him out here. So he was here within a week of the earthquake. . . . When Rich was here, we really got more into this issue of now what are we going to do with this mess. Because within a month to two months, the crap's going to be gone, and now we have to rebuild it, and how are we going to make this happen?" (Interview with Louis Rittenhouse, August 23, 1993).

According to John Lisher, executive director of the Santa Cruz Chamber of Commerce at the time, the chamber also was involved in bringing in Bradley: "After the earthquake we called out Rich Bradley, who is the president of the International Downtown Association. He was out the next day after the earthquake, flew in from DC. The next day we were thinking about rebuilding; it was that fast" (Interview with John Lisher, August 23, 1993). Although their recollections of the exact day that Bradley came onto the scene vary somewhat, Rittenhouse's and Lisher's accounts indicate how connections between local growth coalition organizations and national urban advisory groups allowed for a quick mobilization of resources to aid Santa Cruz landowners in planning for the rebuilding. Bradley visited Santa Cruz three times between the early days after the earthquake and December 12, 1989, when the city council announced how it would plan for rebuilding. On two of those trips, he was a keynote speaker at events hosted by the Santa Cruz Downtown Association, where he met with local economic and political leaders and presented his pitch about the need for the city to create a public-private partnership to guide the rebuilding of the downtown.

While the idea of a partnership between government and business is not a new one, the use of the term "public-private partnership"—and the explanation of its principles and operating assumptions—began to appear in urban policy journals in the late 1970s, when national-level corporate leaders called for cutbacks in government spending as part of their attempt to deal with inflation and the growth in spending for social services (De Neufville and Barton 1987; Piven and Cloward 1982). By the mid-1980s, public-private partnerships were established as the principle new public policy mechanism to guide urban redevelopment, a key part of a "new federalism" that shifted the provision of urban service delivery—and ways to generate revenue to pay for it—from the national level to the states and municipalities (Woodside 1986). Cities were thereby constrained more than ever to compete with one another to attract capital investment to augment the local tax revenue base. This was especially the case in California, where the passage of Proposition 13 in 1978 severely cut into tax revenues raised from residential properties (Schwadron and Richter 1984).

The specification of the operational mechanisms that serve as a blueprint for implementing public-private partnerships came from the Committee for Economic Development, the same national-level policy discussion group that led the effort to rejuvenate cities after World War II. This is best seen in the CED's 1978 policy statement, *An Approach to Federal Urban Policy*. Drafted by its Subcommittee on Revitalizing America's Cities, which consisted primarily of insurance and banking executives, with assistance from six economists and urban policy experts, the statement advocated an increased role for private capital in solving urban problems (Fosler and Berger 1982). A critique of top-down, bureaucratic, and externally imposed federal programs was a central feature of the proposal. It enjoyed initial support from both sides of the political spectrum because at first glance it dovetailed with conservatives' long-standing espousal of "local control" as well as with progressives' emphasis on decentralization and community-based decision-making (De Neufville and Barton 1987). At the same time, the report criticized local governments for "inefficiency" and encouraged them to model themselves after business firms by becoming more rational and efficient through public-private partnerships.

Then, in a follow-up report in 1982, *Public-Private Partnership: An Opportunity for Urban Communities,* the CED urged local governments to become more "entrepreneurial" and to "encourage coalitions of public and private efforts" (Committee for Economic Development 1982, 2). In apparent agreement with growth coalition theory, the CED's 1982 report noted that cities are forced to compete to attract footloose capital. It pointedly stated that if private investment did not occur in one locale, because its political leaders did not create the requisite partnership with business interests, it would "lose position to those that respond more energetically" (Committee for Economic Development 1982, 2). The corporate leaders obviously recognized that this competition worked in their favor, a belief supported by several case studies of "who benefits" from public-private partnerships (Feagin and Parker 1990, 256; Squires 1989). Not surprisingly given the circumstances, city leaders often feel pressured to enter into such partnerships, where they are usually "excessively concession-prone, tipping the balance toward exclusively private benefits" (Cummings, Koebel, and Whitt 1989, 218).

As duly reported in the *Sentinel,* Bradley's speeches emphasized all the basic features of public-private partnerships that are discussed in documents developed by the Committee for Economic Development and later the International Downtown Association. For example, he spoke of the need for the city to develop a common "vision" for the downtown, to work toward fostering broad participation in the partnership by including all "stakeholders" in plans to rebuild, and to cultivate political leadership that was willing to "share power" with the business community. Bradley stressed the final point over and above the others: "The political structures have a chance to behave differently, to be for things . . . previously in the city, forces have learned so well how to block things" (*Sentinel,* December 4, 1989, A-2).

Invoking the time-honored values of cooperation and negotiation, and calling for a new role for "political structures," the overall message in Bradley's speeches was predicated on three key assumptions that underlie public-private partnerships: (1) equal representation of all stakeholders' interests; (2) pluralist decision making through negotiation; and (3) the partnership forum as a neutral arena for rational planning (Jezierski 1990, 217). In this formulation, the goal is an outcome that is supported by all parties because it is arrived at through a process of "consensus." Public-private partnership proponents argue that "politics" has no place at the negotiation table, but as Humphrey, Erickson, and Ottensmeyer (1989, 628) conclude, "The partnership provides both the advice and the *pretense* of decision making outside of politics" (emphasis added).

In his speeches, Bradley directly addressed—and criticized—the past political positions and practices of Santa Cruz progressive leaders. He claimed their concerns for preservation of neighborhood quality of life and protection of the environment led them to defeat many different development proposals, to enact growth control measures, and, in general, to use their political control over land-use and zoning ordinances to stymie the plans of the growth coalition. In effect, what Bradley and other proponents of the public-private partnership were calling for was a depoliticization of planning, in diametric opposition to the advocacy planning that the political leadership of progressive cities was trying to institutionalize (Clavel 1986). Along with most urban policy think tanks and advisory groups, Bradley urged the adoption of a rational, technocratic model of city administration and urban governance that is claimed to be value-free.

Bradley's rapid and frequent arrival on the scene also served as a galvanizing force for generating greater cohesion within a fragmented growth coalition that had not had its way on any issue of any importance since the late 1960s.

Rittenhouse's home became a kind of headquarters where members of the local growth coalition—which he, of course, calls the "business community"—mapped out plans for implementing salvage operations, securing unsafe buildings, and realizing their long-standing desire to redevelop the downtown and reroute traffic in such a way as to link the central business district to the beach and boardwalk. The main feature of this grand plan entailed expansion of the central business district and construction of a more direct highway to the tourist-serving destinations along the main beach. Rittenhouse knew that the growth coalition would be "pushing buttons" with progressive politicians by pressing for both of these elements as cornerstones of post-earthquake redevelopment. Progressives had always opposed such plans, particularly the Beach Loop, which had been defeated in the epic battles of the early 1970s. But Rittenhouse and other business leaders were feeling a new sense of possibility:

> I started pushing the whole subject of the Center City Project, and, of course, Mardi [Wormhoudt, serving as mayor when the earthquake struck] just went ballistic. I mean, she was bouncing off walls. Here comes the arch-enemy, who not only now may have a say at the table—she and a [progressive city council] majority aren't going to just do this their way—they're going to have to communicate. And now this son-of-a-bitch [referring to himself] is going to blow the walls out and go from Church Street to Ocean Street and from the freeway to the sand. And the press was catching on with it . . . The press started to hammer on it. (Interview with Louis Rittenhouse, August 23, 1993)

Moreover, the downtown business leaders hoped that the earthquake had provided them with an opportunity to recapture control of the city council in the 1990 elections, which were just a little over a year away, with three seats up for grabs. It soon became apparent that Rittenhouse himself was going to use the rebuilding process as a platform for his own candidacy. In addition, the Downtown Association used its meetings to discuss county politics. According to one disgruntled member, a family therapist with a downtown office, one meeting called to discuss the promotion of downtown businesses was devoted entirely to the question of how to defeat Gary Patton in the county elections and progressive council members in city elections in 1990 (*Sentinel*, June 13, 1990, A-1).

Bradley's visits to Santa Cruz, along with the extensive press coverage of his public proclamations, made it difficult for progressives to balk at "sharing power" with business interests because he seemed to be playing the role of an impartial outside expert, providing evidence of how public-private partnerships had worked in other cities and using the compelling language of the partnership concept. Moreover, if the progressives balked at embracing the idea of a partnership with business, not only would they risk being seen as the anti-business contrarians the local growth coalition had long portrayed them to be, they would also be open to the charge of opposing such widely shared values as "cooperation" and "consensus." In addition, the appeals to progressive leaders to work for things rather than block them was designed to cast their previous policies in a negative light and as failing to serve the community-wide interest, a common accusation in times of crisis.

Progressive leaders and activists realized that the obviously large-scale rebuilding project facing the city presented an opportunity for the growth coalition to resurrect its thwarted growth plans. They also knew that the landowners and store owners were busily making big plans, so progressives, too, quickly began having private meetings to work out their strategy, bringing in former city council members such as Mike Rotkin and Bruce Van Allen. One key informant from the progressive inner circle described the reaction among progressive leaders when they discovered that leaders within the growth coalition had been meeting at Rittenhouse's headquarters and elsewhere:

> Once the extent of the damage was clear, which was within a couple of days, people realized through Neal [Coonerty, the owner of the bookstore saved by the four hundred volunteers, and a supporter of the progressive coalition] that there was a meeting of a group of major downtown property owners, most of them old guard who had owned their property for a long time, and some of the bigger business people who were essentially saying, "Let's just level the whole thing." And that had veracity to a lot of us because some of us knew about earlier plans for totally redeveloping downtown. And so we felt that this was a threat that we had to take seriously. So that really led to, in spite of a lot of nice talk about how we're all going to pull together, that kind of stuff, there was a very dramatic and very quick hardening of sides over exactly how we were going to do it.

For at least some progressive leaders, this was not just a crisis about how to rebuild the downtown; it was also a potential political crisis. If the Downtown Association led the rebuilding process through rallying property owners, this might provide political capital that could be used by the growth coalition to champion pro-growth candidates in the next city council election. These progressives therefore worried that they could jeopardize their control over local government if they did not enter into a partnership with the business community.

It was in this context of mutual suspicion and strategizing that leaders in the Downtown Association formally proposed the idea of the public-private partnership, which would later be named Vision Santa Cruz. They were quite proud of their accomplishment. As John Lisher of the chamber of commerce explained, he and other business representatives met with the mayor: "And so we championed this cause with the city government. And we were met with a lot of resistance: 'We don't need to do this, we can handle it, we're in charge.' Alexander Haig was alive and well, I guess. But we arm-wrestled them down, and we said we had to do it—we want it to be broad representation. We're not trying to save only the business community" (Interview with John Lisher, August 23, 1993).

Publicly, the progressives took credit for creating Vision Santa Cruz, but, behind the scenes and after the fact, several progressives said that business leaders had forced the issue. According to a member of Vision Santa Cruz, who self-identified as a strong progressive and had supported progressive political leaders in their electoral campaigns:

> [Vision Santa Cruz] was a situation that had been forced, and it always intrigued me, you know, nine months into the actual Vision Santa Cruz process, hearing board members of mine who I would have anticipated being much more aware of how it had come to be and how it had happened, say, "I don't understand why we are hearing this level of obstructionism from Mardi [Mayor Wormhoudt], when this whole thing was her idea." And the simple truth was, it wasn't her idea, she was forced to swallow it, and then being the wise politician she is, she made the best of the situation and said, obviously this is what Santa Cruz needs and what we'll work for.

Coonerty, who was appointed to Vision Santa Cruz, explained why the idea of a partnership was eyed with suspicion by progressive leaders:

> There was a lot of worry about that. Out of Vision Santa Cruz was going to come a coherent vision from the other side that they wanted to implement, and that they were going to come together to implement it, and that the other side—the city government side—had to recognize that, and deal with it, and analyze what was going on in terms of that, and respond to it. And that there wasn't going to be some kind of shadow government created in Vision Santa Cruz or a power base that could transform itself into electoral politics. . . . I mean there was a small group of people that met informally centered around Mardi and her concerns, which were political concerns. They would do this analysis—I was part of it, Denise Holbert [longtime

neighborhood activist, progressive insider, and also an administrative aide to County Supervisor Gary Patton] was part of it. And they took what was going on with Vision Santa Cruz and gave it a very political viewpoint. Sort of in the sense that the players represented certain power factions in Santa Cruz. And they wanted to make sure it didn't go awry politically. (Interview with Neal Coonerty, February 19, 1993)

Very early on in their discussions of the public-private partnership, the progressive leadership and their advisors also decided that the prerogatives of private property—in regime theory terms, the potential of "systemic power"—imposed serious constraints on them in the rebuilding process. They therefore concluded they had to negotiate with the business leaders and agree to the public-private partnership even though they were reluctant to do so. As Van Allen put it, "It was really clear also that the progressive side couldn't just figure out what to do and impose it on the city, because we didn't own the property. And this was predominantly a private property problem, as far as rebuilding. So it was really clear that we needed to have everybody work together, but at the same time, there was great suspicion and paranoia about what the agendas of the various sides were" (Interview with Bruce Van Allen, August 19, 1993).

Rather obviously then, progressive political leaders believed that their official responsibilities and political future required greater cooperation with business interests and even necessitated granting significant concessions to those interests. Nor did they think the public sector was in a strong position relative to the private sector in terms of either local economic conditions or intergovernmental support. It was weak in terms of the "distribution of bargaining advantages" that in general dictate the terms of cooperation between business and local government (Kantor, Savitch, and Haddock 1997, 350).

From our point of view, however, the progressive leaders' beliefs about the systemic power of their opponents did not take hold independent of the concerted actions by leaders in the growth coalition. It mattered that Rittenhouse and the chamber of commerce brought Bradley of the International Downtown Association to Santa Cruz shortly after the earthquake, and that they pressured for the creation of Vision Santa Cruz. As regime theorist Stephen Elkin (1987, 98) argues in his analysis of structural constraints on urban policy, the responses of political leaders to "structural imperatives" are mediated by their interpretations of those seeming imperatives, which also involve gauging the meanings and intentions that seem to lie behind the actions of other social actors. In this case, the vigorous and visible efforts by growth coalition leaders, along with their informal meetings and grandiose plans, signaled very directly to progressive political leaders that business interests were determined to take an active role in formulating redevelopment planning and policy.

So, for what they understood as structural or systemic reasons and for the purpose of maintaining their legitimacy, the progressive leaders entered into the formal partnership that had been demanded by the growth coalition. In addition, because only the city council could formally establish the public-private partnership, progressives figured they would be perceived by the populace as having taken the lead in creating the partnership. But even as progressive leaders recognized that moving expeditiously was critical to the city's economic well-being and to their own political fortunes, they remained deeply skeptical about the much-vaunted partnership proposal. Even though Wormhoudt called for an end to the divisiveness between the business community and progressive political leaders in a "state of the city" speech shortly after she announced the creation of Vision Santa Cruz, she was wary. As she told us in the summer of 1993, "I think there's a real reason for people to be suspicious of each other, frankly. I think there are different agendas. I think we care about different things. . . . I think it's sometimes important to realize that problems are not just [lack of] communication, and are not just that we don't sit down and talk. Sometimes the problems are real. There are real, structural, basic differences in what we want" (Interview with Mardi Wormhoudt, August 9, 1993).

Moreover, the progressives knew that they had an ace up their sleeves because members of the city council had served as the directors of the city's Redevelopment Agency ever since the early 1970s, after the appointed directors of the Redevelopment Agency notified several hundred downtown homeowners that their homes had been designated for redevelopment as part of the plan to enlarge the downtown. Thus, any and all rebuilding plans formulated by Vision Santa Cruz were subject to final approval by the city council, acting as the Redevelopment Agency. The elected progressives' intention to make use of this power was made clear at the same city council meeting where they approved the creation of Vision Santa Cruz. At that meeting they also agreed to a proposal by the city manager, a person selected for the job by progressives because they knew he would not try to countermand their decisions, to hire a full-time executive director for the Redevelopment Agency (*Sentinel*, December 13, 1989, A-3). Ceil Cirillo, the person they hired two months later, who had worked for a private developer in Los Angeles, was given two tasks: to identify and deal with any problems property owners were experiencing with their rebuilding plans and to recruit investment capital into the city.

Furthermore, the progressive leadership facilitated new communication links between the city staff and private developers by introducing modifications of bureaucratic functions and responsibilities. In addition, and again following the recommendation of the city manager, the city council instructed the planning department to work more closely with developers so that their redevelopment and rebuilding plans could be fast-tracked through the planning process.

Beyond all this direct control through the city council and the Redevelopment Agency, the elected progressive officials had one more ace up their sleeves: they had agreed among themselves that they would terminate Vision Santa Cruz as soon as possible, making sure it did not last long enough to become a political platform for the growth coalition. Closing down Vision Santa Cruz as soon as it was feasible to do so, they believed, would lead to a fairly quick return to the status quo, where progressives enjoyed tight political control over the administrative agencies and commissions that shaped municipal policy. As Coonerty explained:

> One of my concerns was to get out of Vision Santa Cruz and back to a normal process, to get back to the planning department process and all the rest of that stuff. . . . There were some in Vision Santa Cruz that wanted us to become sort of a first approval for [redevelopment] projects, to sort of play what the planning commission and the city council did. And my feeling was, once we got the recovery plan done, we had to axe this thing right away because I do feel that's exactly what happens, it creates a larger voice for business and it creates a pre-approved project. I think that given these extraordinary circumstances, [Vision Santa Cruz] was appropriate here, but then we got the recovery plan done, then, boom, we had to axe it. And we were pretty effective at that. I mean, it went on for another year and a half, but it was a skeleton group that really did nothing. There were a few people who were sort of watch-guarding it to make sure it didn't do anything more. (Interview with Neal Coonerty, February 19, 1993)

INSIDE THE VISION SANTA CRUZ PROCESS

After lengthy discussion and bargaining behind the scenes, in early January 1990 the city council finally announced a new thirty-six-member Agency for Rebuilding Downtown Santa Cruz, eventually to be known as Vision Santa Cruz, to much fanfare in the press. Perhaps emboldened by their success in convincing the city council to establish such a board, with nearly half of the appointees being property or business owners, key leaders in the growth coalition wasted no time in bringing their most ambitious plans to the table. The discussions focused on the proposals that had been resuscitated in Rittenhouse's living room, which would expand the downtown from the Pacific

Garden Mall to the beach area. The idea was to enhance tourism and at the same time try to attract major department stores so that the downtown could compete with the Capitola Mall as a regional commercial center. Several urban design experts, including one from the Urban Land Institute (yet another national-level think tank for growth coalitions), had recommended that the city not try to emulate and compete with the Capitola Mall. Ignoring that recommendation, Rittenhouse, Charles Canfield of the Seaside Company, and other large landholders believed that the extension of the redevelopment area would allow for the construction of a varied mix of housing types, small shops, large chain stores, and office buildings, as well as for provision of public gathering places, without confronting the problem of incompatible uses of space. It would also provide a long-sought link between the downtown and the beach area. As Rittenhouse put it, in effect harking back to the general plan of 1964:

> The Center City Project was Ocean Street to Chestnut [Street], and the freeway to the sea. Everything should be replanned and organized to function. The in-and-out [traffic routing] of the waterfront related to connecting into the business district, the housing element should be designed through there so you had urban housing, yet you still have retail, you still have commercial cores, you have the ability to move traffic and to make things function as far as pedestrians, bring the river elements in. (Interview with Louis Rittenhouse, August 23, 1993)

As might be expected, this plan was strongly opposed by the progressives on the panel because it threatened neighborhoods and would have met with organized protest from residents in and around Chestnut Street, the boundary of the new downtown in Rittenhouse's scheme of things. They were led in this rejection by Wormhoudt, a former vice president of the Downtown Neighbors Association, who knew from her successful activism as an "outsider" in the past that neighborhoods had the capacity to delay or block redevelopment plans. As she explained, "Because the power to block things from happening is a very substantial power, and people have become very sophisticated about stopping projects, occasionally that really worries me in terms of whether we have the potential to do any project anywhere. And frankly, that was a very real concern to me at the time of the earthquake, and after the earthquake" (Interview with Mardi Wormhoudt, August 9, 1993).

While the progressives opposed the substance of the growth coalition's proposal because it would have encroached upon neighborhood use values, they highlighted the claim that Rittenhouse's proposal would detract from the urgency of rebuilding the downtown, which was of concern to progressives because they needed tax revenues for the programs they had developed. Once it was clear that the progressives would not accept the landowners' biggest plans, language was adopted that stated a kind of compromise. The official document that laid out the purposes and bylaws of Vision Santa Cruz, the "Articles of Incorporation," stated that one of its chief purposes was "to create community-wide educational opportunities for planning, focused on the downtown core, with consideration of the needs of the beach, river, and downtown residential areas" (Vision Santa Cruz n.d., 1). The operative terms here were "focus on the downtown core" and "consideration of . . . downtown residential areas."

Limiting the post-quake planning to rebuilding the downtown core was a significant victory for the progressive political leaders, but for Rittenhouse and his colleagues this decision, which he blamed on the most vocal progressive on this issue, Wormhoudt, was the major mistake of the process, making it impossible to realize everyone's goals at the same time:

> I mean, all of these things should have been looked at as one comprehensive plan. Which is still, I think, the best way to go. And we really proved that in the whole process of Vision Santa Cruz, because what transpired in Vision Santa Cruz is you had thirty-six people sitting around a four-by-four canvas and trying to get their color on. Now the canvas should have been fifty feet by fifty feet. Because everyone sitting at the table had five gallons of paint and a six-inch brush. And everyone wanted their color on the canvas. So when Mardi brought it down [limited the size of the redevelopment area to the downtown only], she created the problem. (Interview with Louis Rittenhouse, August 23, 1993)

With downtown expansion off the agenda, Vision Santa Cruz now faced a complex set of dilemmas involving the design of the "streetscape" (that is, the layout of the streets and the provision of amenities such as benches, green space, and plazas) as well as the "mix" of uses (i.e., retail, commercial office space, and housing). The overarching goal was to make the downtown a lively, vibrant setting, while also meeting the circulation and parking needs of larger retail and commercial businesses. But underneath that general agreement there was in fact a conflict between exchange values and use values that not only pitted the growth coalition against the progressives but soon divided progressives as well. Environmental and neighborhood activists viewed the downtown as "place" (primarily as a use value), but the growth coalition saw it as "space" (primarily as a source of exchange value). The problem began with the fact that many of the environmental and pro-neighborhood activists—most of whom were even more critical of business than the elected progressives—wanted to use the rebuilding process to extend their use-value orientation into the downtown. In their view, the central business district should not simply serve the interests of developers, downtown property owners, and local business owners. They saw the downtown as the "heart and soul" of the city, as the city's "civic living room," as a place to browse, visit, and congregate as well as shop.

This tension between use values and exchange values was most evident in the debate over including large public gathering places and urban parks on the redeveloped downtown mall, with the grassroots activists naturally wanting more plazas and open space. They wanted to foster an eclectic, exciting street life, which urbanist and social critic William H. Whyte (1988) argues is essential to the success of any downtown. In this view, the downtown functions as an agora, a place of assembly and civic association, as well as a marketplace, a site of commerce. However, contrary to the most ardent use-value advocates, the progressive leadership did not think that very much, or even any, enhancing of use values in the downtown was a good idea in terms of the conflicts and delays it would bring. They had already debated this issue in private meetings in the weeks after the earthquake and decided that property owners had the stronger hand. They felt they had to cooperate with the growth coalition on issues of downtown rebuilding in order to protect their social programs and their political power. As Van Allen put it, using the leftist framework he favored, "Through a series of discussions, and meetings, and phone calls, there was a fairly explicit decision that, in a sense, we would set aside the class struggle for the rebuilding of downtown Santa Cruz. And we would not attempt to make new gains against property for democracy" (Interview with Bruce Van Allen, August 19, 1993).

This decision created a major problem for progressive leaders because most rank-and-file members of the broad progressive coalition were obviously not part of the private strategy sessions in which the progressive leaders had made their decisions regarding their approach to rebuilding. They therefore could not understand why those they had worked so hard to elect were conceding to business interests, but in a grudging manner and combative style that left many business representatives on the Vision Santa Cruz board uncertain as to whether they had just won a victory or were still engaged in heated battle. One such grassroots critic, who traced his involvement in progressive politics back to the early-1970s struggle over the development of Lighthouse Field, attended virtually every one of the Vision Santa Cruz meetings:

> My take on it is that either for relatively benign reasons like that they figured that they needed to have the goodwill of the business community, otherwise downtown would fall apart, or that they simply wanted to get out from under for their own political reasons, their strategy was to let the busi-

ness people do whatever they wanted . . . At one point, Mike Rotkin said, you know, because the business people did not understand what was going on, he just said, "Would you please just tell us what you want so we can accede to it?"

Rotkin offered the following explanation for his oft-repeated—and often misinterpreted—comment:

> That was a constant issue, how do we get them [business representatives in Vision Santa Cruz] to be players, to get into this thing, to make them realize they have a voice. I mean we had a facilitator who came and asked us to fill out little cards, "What's the one thing we wanted to have happen?" Put it on the card. I just said, "I'd like the business people to figure out what they want and tell us what to do." What do they want, and I was prepared to basically try to find a way to make that happen. Within limits. I'm not going to let Louis Rittenhouse have this idea of a closed mall. That would be bad for business. (Interview with Mike Rotkin, August 26, 1992)

Council member Katherine Beiers, who became a replacement member of Vision Santa Cruz when it was a month or two into the process, was among those who were puzzled by this overly conciliatory rhetoric and willingness to make considerable concessions. In addition to her important role in the controversy over Lighthouse Field, she had worked for progressive candidates in all subsequent local elections. Despite her many years of involvement in Santa Cruz politics at the grassroots, she reported she was thoroughly confused by the proceedings at her first meeting with Vision Santa Cruz. Progressives were in firm control of the meeting, but they conceded virtually every major substantive issue about the redesign of the downtown to business interests on the board:

> I was unhappy with the direction in which it was going. I would meet with different people, and I would ask why we weren't looking at parks, why we were doing this or that. I was finally taken out for breakfast and was told, blatantly, "You need to understand. We realize you weren't in the loop and part of the early meetings of the group. It's decided. We sold out to business; we did it intentionally. That's the direction we're going to go, and so it's a done deal." (Interview with Katherine Beiers, August 26, 1993)

Small wonder, then, that many progressive activists expressed disillusionment with the process because of these attempts to enlist business cooperation and avoid further confrontations. As Van Allen candidly explained:

What it set up was a dynamic in which the progressive political elite actually ended up not on the left position, but in the middle position, and attempted to hold the center . . . So there were a lot of people who were part of our coalition, our broad coalition, who came from neighborhood groups or from environmental groups, who became disaffected because we weren't getting a major park in the middle of downtown or a plaza that would be for noncommercial activity. (Interview with Bruce Van Allen, August 19, 1993)

In theory, public-private partnerships seek to include all stakeholders—including nonelite interests—so that their views may be heard and incorporated (Browning, Marshall, and Tabb 1984). But as Van Allen's comments show, decision making within Vision Santa Cruz actually exemplified what Jones and Bachelor (1984) refer to as "peak bargaining" over high-stakes issues. When an issue critical to the economic health of the local economy and the political legitimacy of elected officials is at stake, elected officials are not as open to influence from citizen groups, neighborhood organizations, or other activist groups, even if these same groups provided crucial electoral support in the past.

The conflict between the growth coalition and grassroots progressives over exchange and use values in the downtown, with progressive leaders in the middle, surfaced dramatically in questionnaires collected by an outside consulting firm from over three hundred business owners and citizens who attended a special town meeting in March 1990 to provide public input about how the downtown should be rebuilt. The consultants reported in their draft proposal that "the social function of downtown" and its "outdoor/garden atmosphere" were the two features of the "old" downtown that respondents valued most highly; they therefore wanted the downtown to be rebuilt in such a way that these critical functions were preserved (Lyndon/Buchanan Associates 1990, 53).

The consultants' summary of the survey responses indicated that the citizens motivated enough to attend a town meeting viewed the downtown primarily in terms of use values. For most of them, the "old" downtown was missed as "a place to go, to run into friends, to hang out . . . walk, browse, relax, visit, shop, listen to street music." It is not surprising, therefore, that when asked to name their "primary goals for a revitalized downtown," most respondents identified enhancing outdoor spaces, creating public gathering places, and making the downtown "garden-like" as their top priorities (Lyndon/Buchanan Associates 1990, 56). The survey found that Santa Cruz citizens heartily embraced the concept of a "human-scale" built environment delineated in the work of noted urbanists such as Jane Jacobs (1961) and Lewis Mumford (1961), which had been adopted by progressive planners and the political leadership of progressive cities (Clavel 1986; Capek and Gilderbloom 1992).

While some progressive advocates were singularly focused on the provision of use-value amenities and seemed far less concerned about the commercial function of the downtown, most thought an urban landscape that emphasized use values would also enhance the commercial potential of the downtown. This perspective was expressed in an opinion piece in the local newspaper by a longtime Santa Cruz resident and Lighthouse Field activist:

> The downtown should be planned not around big department stores or office buildings, but around "gathering places," restaurants, small plazas, cafes, where people feel comfortable. A downtown should be an attraction in itself, built around attractive places. If customers come directly to your store, park right in front and then go home, you only get your own customers, not anyone else's, and you encourage the traffic that is already threatening to choke us out of existence . . . The downtown should be designed not for the comfort and convenience of real estate speculators and landlords or even for the business community, but for the comfort and convenience of the customers. (Rosato 1990, A-19)

Surprisingly, the survey results also revealed that the differences in the general sentiments of downtown merchants, property owners, and ordinary citizens were often more a matter of degree than of kind. The consultants reported that "generally merchants and landowners share the public vision of Downtown Santa Cruz being a unique social center, sunny, human-scale, mixed-use" (Lyndon/Buchanan Associates 1990, 53). But our interviews with business representatives on Vision Santa Cruz showed that their greatest emphasis was on exchange values. Larry Pearson, the owner of the Cookie Company, a favorite stopping point on the mall before and after the earthquake, who was well known for being a participant in many community activities, put it this way:

> I was included in the group as a businessperson . . . So I represented a constituency that was concerned with the economic vitality of downtown, the attractiveness of the business environment, and the sustainability of the business environment. As a citizen of Santa Cruz, I brought similar concerns to everyone of Vision Santa Cruz, in that we found downtown to be a unique place that served many more functions than simply commercial. It was very much of a social center; it was the heart of downtown . . . And then, of course, my concern was that, at base, it had to be a viable commercial center. (Interview with Larry Pearson, January 8, 1993)

Despite broad-based support for the idea that the downtown should be rebuilt following a model of "mixed-use" development that enhanced both social and economic functions, deciding on the precise blend of elements in the "mix" meant making difficult choices from an array of possibilities. At this point, shared visions of redeveloping the new downtown so as to meet both use and exchange value goals began to melt away. While the idea that there could be a synergy between use and exchange values enjoyed a wide appeal, it proved to be elusive when it came time to decide exactly what should be done with regard to designing the street, setting building heights, locating parking facilities, and laying out the traffic pattern.

There was also a deeper issue apparent to most people: the growth coalition's long-standing distaste for the presence of homeless people in the downtown. They especially disliked the fact that there was a soup kitchen on a side street just off the mall. In effect, they would have tolerated far more use values if they could have been assured that the people who gathered in the downtown would not drive away business. This problem was seen as critical because local commercial lenders and representatives of larger businesses on the mall (especially department stores) insisted that dealing with downtown "social problems" was imperative for the city to attract outside investment. Within days of the earthquake, articles began to appear in the *Sentinel* on a regular basis insisting that redevelopment had to make the downtown a "safe place to be" (e.g., *Sentinel,* October 27, 1989, A-1). People were for a lively mall, the newspaper argued, but they had come to see too many of the young homeless population as dangerous. One Vision Santa Cruz member described the board's discussion of the issue in the following way:

> That was a big issue. That was a big fear by the business community . . . They wanted police—"let's police the area," security, you know. Let's make it a private enterprise kind of thing, where it's like publicly owned but privately run so they could legitimize having security guards down there so they could run people off . . . The main thing was that they kept saying that if we didn't clean up the street, people would not come down there, and it would be a waste of time, money, and investment. And we didn't buy into that. We said, "No, the mall is a very good place to invest. It's a great place to go . . ."

Still, this informant in effect admitted that there was some truth to what the merchants said, then brushed it off as a minor issue: "You know, I've been going down there since, I was raised here, and I moved back in 1980. And I love going to the mall. Yeah, people ask you for money. I mean, if you've got it, you've got it. If you don't, you don't. I've never gotten hassled. Sure, I've been approached, but I'd say, 'Sorry, I don't have it.' And they'd go on their way."

Although this male participant in Vision Santa Cruz did not feel threatened on the mall, the property owners and merchants were not alone in worrying about street people. People trying to stop violence against women were concerned, too, led by the Committee for the Prevention of Violence Against Women, an advisory group that was listened to very carefully by the elected progressives who had created it. This committee, along with feminist organizations and individual activists, called attention to the problem of routine verbal sexual harassment of women in the downtown and compellingly framed this harassment as creating a situation where women's rights to public space were constricted. Many of the most persuasive arguments advanced by feminist groups supported conclusions drawn by Bowman (1993) in her study of how street harassment of women leads to the "informal ghettoization of women." Marouli (1995) and Spain (1992) also have shown how the architecture of the built environment and the structuring of urban space reflects and reproduces inequalities of gender and power.

This complicated argument involving use values and social problems came to a head when the consultants offered their design recommendations, based on their surveys, which revolved around the theme of the mall being a "garden" (*Sentinel*, April 17, 1990, A1, A12). Their recommendations—for more public gathering places, urban green space, and pocket parks—were seen by business leaders as moving the mall more in the direction of a full pedestrian mall even though they had been advocating precisely the opposite course of action. It was no surprise, then, when Rittenhouse reacted very negatively to the new plan: "It's a nice cartoon. I don't see any way that the majority of this is economically feasible. There is just no way for the business community or the city to pay for it or support it" (*Sentinel*, April 17, 1990, A-1, A-12).

But concern about the economic viability of the plan was only one prong of the attack on this particular redesign concept. Business leaders also rejected the "garden" concept as contributing to the problem of loitering and panhandling because it would create even more spaces that were conducive to congregation by street people and difficult to monitor for "undesirable uses." In fact, one of their greatest complaints about the pre-earthquake mall was that the massive amount of foliage made it too dark and shadowy, with too many places for street people to loiter in relative invisibility.

One Vision Santa Cruz board member, Jim Pepper, a professor of environmental studies at the university as well as a professional planner and landscape architect, remembered how business leaders greeted the consultant's recommendations with derision because they did not want to see the downtown defined primarily as a social gathering place: "They were also beat up pretty badly by some bankers who challenged them at their formal presentation, demanding to know how much it was going to cost the bottom line. This made us back off their proposal. They were afraid that embracing the [consultant's] proposals would make us too likely to pick up the 'social agenda'" (Interview with Jim Pepper, November 24, 1992).

The objections to the consultant's plan united those merchants who had long called for the city to address its "social problems" with other business interests that had not been directly affected by these problems in the past. The criticisms also caused most of the progressives on the board to back away from the garden-oriented plan. Interviews with board members indicate that the threat of disinvestment or the inability to attract capital into the downtown was raised directly during Vision Santa Cruz meetings. Moreover, it was explicitly linked with the need to address the "social problems" on the mall. One progressive board member frankly stated, "Damn straight. We took that threat very seriously. It was not seen as just a scare tactic."

As virtually every informant recounted, the debate within the board over how to redesign the streetscape to address the problems of loitering, panhandling, and sexual harassment was resolved by a process of "consensus." Extreme viewpoints were eliminated from serious consideration, and a "middle ground" was reached. It is at this point in the process that learning and consensus began to develop, partly as a result of a series of lectures set up by Pepper, the environmental studies professor on Vision Santa Cruz. One key lecture came from the famous urbanist William H. Whyte himself, who said that a thriving economy was essential to a downtown that was going to fulfill the civic functions he championed. As Rotkin explained, once the extremes on both sides were "knocked out," and the message from experts on how the downtown could be successful began to sink in, a meeting of the minds was possible in a way that regime theory would suggest. From Rotkin's point of view, however, most of the give was by the commercial interests:

> But my sense of what happened to the business people, I think Jim Pepper played a key role in this. He did this series of lectures where guests came and talked about what makes urban America work, or what makes downtown succeed; it was about cities and downtowns. I think the business people began—they fell away from this, from time to time, but they really did, in their best moments—get a really good sense of what made the [downtown] mall work financially, and a lot of it was seeing [themselves] against Capitola Mall—most downtowns have not been able to compete against outlying malls—was the fact that [the downtown mall] was unique, that it had a kind of cultural vitality to it, that it was something different than just a

Main Street shopping center. That those [Main Street shopping centers] were going under in relation to outside shopping malls, along with parking and security. We couldn't compete by being a junior plastic mall; nobody would come there. (Interview with Mike Rotkin, August 26, 1992)

The hard-liners in the growth coalition, still insisting that most street people were homeless by choice, originally called for laws that would in effect drive the homeless out of town. But enacting ordinances designed to discourage loitering by targeting undesirable persons was legally problematic. As noted by an investigator who did pre-quake interviews with Santa Cruz leaders about street people on the mall, there is a "civil-liberties argument that malls are public places in which everyone has an equal right to spend time" (Robertson 1990, 270). Progressives, on the other hand, said they wanted to do as much as they could within the limits of the city budget to ensure that such people had shelter and necessary social services. Whatever their failings, the progressives repeatedly challenged the hard-liners' characterological explanation for homelessness, pointing to systematic studies showing that cutbacks in spending for mental health facilities and subsidized housing had created the problem. Leaders within the growth coalition came to agree that there should be more social services for the homeless, but only for the "truly needy" and only if the shelters and social services were located well outside the central business district.

A willingness to compromise on homeless shelters by business leaders on Vision Santa Cruz opened up some space for further compromise by the progressives. Former city council member Joe Ghio, who served on Vision Santa Cruz, provided an insightful analysis of how this contentious issue illustrated the real dynamic behind the "consensus" process that ostensibly guided decision making in the public-private partnership. According to Ghio, progressives who opposed the streetscape redesign did not raise objections to it, and as a quid pro quo (what Ghio referred to as the "trade-off"), business leaders did not challenge the city's plan to provide shelters and increased social services for the homeless (Interview with Joe Ghio, December 29, 1992). However, business leaders assented to shelters only when they were assured they would be in an isolated building near a major highway intersection, 1.2 miles from the downtown core. In the end, then, the Vision Santa Cruz board neither approved the creation of a "cordon sanitaire," as some homeless advocates feared, nor did they embrace the idea of rebuilding Pacific Avenue in the style of the old mall, with its verdant landscaping and winding streets.

Once it was agreed that shelters would be away from the downtown, the growth coalition went to work on changes in the streetscape that were meant to discourage loitering. Quite literally, the problem was addressed "concretely."

By widening the sidewalks and clearing them of planter boxes and shrubbery, and by ignoring the consultants' proposal for large plazas and open green-space areas, the overwhelming majority on Vision Santa Cruz decided to seek solutions to the street people problem through designing streets to have a social control function.

Even seemingly minor aspects of the streetscape design were meant to discourage homeless and transient people from lingering downtown. Initially, there were to be no benches on the mall because of the fear that street people would use them for sleeping. Later, after what one Vision Santa Cruz board member recalled as a "huge battle," the city council voted to have benches installed. But they were shorter than usual in order to make full reclining impossible; furthermore, they were placed perpendicular to the sidewalk and toward the curb to eliminate what one informant referred to as the "gauntlet" effect: pedestrians no longer had to walk directly in front of anyone sitting on a bench, which was seen as a way to avoid sexual harassment and panhandling. The final sidewalk plan also allowed for paid table areas just outside cafés, some with small wrought iron fences around them, to cut down on open space for standing around. One Vision Santa Cruz board member suggested that virtually every element of the streetscape plan was designed with social control of street people as an overarching consideration.

With much wider sidewalks, fewer planters, and improved visibility of storefronts, the redesigned Pacific Avenue enhanced pedestrian circulation and made it easier to shop. But simply sitting and watching the street scene was next to impossible without also making another purchase at a cafe or restaurant with outdoor seating, and such seating was very limited. In short, as one of the critics of the streetscape lamented, "We lost virtually every place that there was to sit down." (The first author also learned this lesson firsthand. When he took a break from his downtown field observations to lean against one of the few remaining planter boxes, with a cup of coffee in his hand, he was told firmly to "move along" by a police officer driving down the street.)

But none of these attempts to build social control functions into the built environment really worked. As a dissenting member of Vision Santa Cruz, one of the landscape architects who designed the original Pacific Garden Mall, had warned, "They blamed the fact that there were street people on the mall to the design of the mall. They were going to find out in actuality with the new design of the mall, that the design had nothing to do with it" (Interview with Roy Rydell, January 27, 1993).

His statement proved accurate. The continuing congregation of street people on the mall quietly led to the hiring of "hospitality hosts," persons employed to assist tourists with directions and answer questions but also to function as a form of private security. When subtle forms of social control proved largely unsuccessful, the ultimate means of enforcing social control—through the law—was adopted: the city council enacted an anti-loitering ordinance and supplemented the hospitality hosts with an increasing number of police officers.

At this point, "cleaning up" the mall focused on the relatively few people that the pre-earthquake Social Problems Task Force claimed to be causing most of the problems (Interview with John Laird, February 19, 1993). While targeting the individuals allegedly responsible for the most serious offenses might make sense from a practical standpoint, it did little to allay fears about the presence of street people in the downtown. Whether or not they engaged in any criminal or antisocial behavior, they were seen as a threat to redevelopment because their presence raised concerns about their potential for engaging in deviant behavior. Nor could any casual shopper have any way of knowing for sure who was dangerous and who was not.

Although designing the mall in a way that discouraged street people was far and away the biggest concern for the downtown growth coalition, its leaders on Vision Santa Cruz raised similar issues in relation to replacement housing for the dozens of displaced residents of single-room occupancy housing (SROs). Many of them were elderly or had lived and worked in the downtown area for years. In effect, they were lumped in with the homeless as people to be kept out of the downtown even though they were no more likely than other citizens to engage in crime. Despite some protests, including those from a displaced SRO occupant who served on the Vision Santa Cruz board, the redevelopment plan originally responded to business leaders' concerns by recommending that lost SRO housing be replaced in a dispersed fashion to prevent the concentration of SRO residents in the downtown. One Vision Santa Cruz board member recounted:

> Oh, there was just horror about the SROs. We were getting feedback from the [owners of two department stores located in the downtown] that they would never consider reestablishing a department store in downtown if we were even going to be looking at replacement of lost SROs. They had considered the vagrant population of Santa Cruz such an inhibition, they had seen that as so inhibiting people's desire to shop downtown, that it was anathema that we were talking about replacing lost SROs . . . Arguments were being made that if we were going to see a healthy downtown, they wanted to have a resident population that felt like it was their backyard. (Interview with Laura Perry, March 1, 1993)

Although most downtown property owners said they supported the concept of mixed housing in the downtown—that is, a combination of both market-rate and subsidized housing—their comments at Vision Santa Cruz meetings and in the *Sentinel* revealed a strong preference for less housing in general and a higher percentage of market-rate units in the housing that remained. They expressed the hope that market-rate housing might attract people with discretionary income who would patronize downtown businesses. People in market-rate housing also might have a greater stake in the "community," an assumption grounded in the belief that residents of mall-area housing would exhibit the same concerns for their "neighborhood"—and exercise the same vigilance toward activities on their street—as residents of more traditional neighborhoods do. In any event, most of the relatively few middle-class people who moved into downtown apartments ended up protesting the shouting and loud music that went on late into the night. They especially objected to the incessant drumming, which led to the threat of a curfew and an eventual informal agreement with the drumming community in 1996 that it would shut down by ten PM.

In the end, the progressive members of Vision Santa Cruz were successful in replacing the lost SRO units despite the opposition of the downtown business leaders. They were bolstered in their efforts by the fact that the rebuilding funds available immediately after the quake were almost exclusively from the public sector and could only be used for infrastructure improvements and replacement of lost housing. They also were successful in demanding affordable housing above the first floor of several retail buildings. In fact, the rebuilding effort actually provided an opportunity to create more apartments and rooms in the downtown area, since the upper stories of some buildings before the quake had not been useable because of their failure to meet seismic standards.

TENSIONS WITHIN THE GROWTH COALITION

Once issues concerning the homeless and SRO housing were dealt with in a way that the growth coalition thought would be satisfactory, tensions began to emerge between property owners and store owners. Several participants in the Vision Santa Cruz deliberations reported that disagreements between retailers and property owners over the direction of rebuilding were among the most heated debates that took place during the planning process. For example, Pearson, the owner of the Cookie Company, described retailers and property owners as "natural enemies" (Interview with Larry Pearson, January 8, 1993). Or, as Coonerty bluntly said, "A lot of property owners aren't business owners," which called attention to a series of related problems that he and other retailers who leased space from downtown property owners feared would become a reality (Interview with Neal Coonerty, February 19, 1993). To begin with, merchants might be forced to leave the downtown because property owners would lack the financial resources to rebuild, thus drastically limiting available rental space. Or owners who were unable or unwilling to rebuild might sell their parcels outright to developers, who might plan other uses for particular sites. Even if owners did rebuild, the costs might lead to greatly increased rental rates. Concern over this last scenario was especially pronounced. Local merchants and citizens worried that only national chain stores would be able to afford the doubling of rents in the redeveloped downtown that was predicted in early April 1990 on the basis of analyses conducted for Vision Santa Cruz (*Sentinel*, April 10, 1990, A-1, A-14).

There were also reasons for large landowners to wait to rebuild in order to command even higher prices. In effect, they were speculating against the city. Coonerty leveled just such a charge against Rittenhouse and his family in October 1991, after they filed a lawsuit against the city alleging negligence on the part of the local construction company hired by the city to demolish one of their buildings: "I think the Rittenhouse family has the means and ability to provide leadership among the property owners downtown . . . It's almost adding insult to injury to not rebuild, and then sue the city and Granite Construction in a frivolous lawsuit . . . While other people are struggling to build, they're speculating on the value of the land. . . . Then they're going to reap more value for their property. To me that's not providing leadership; it's speculating on the future of the downtown" (*Sentinel*, October 24, 1991, A-1, A-10).

As this kind of charge persisted, the *Sentinel* weighed in, albeit indirectly, when an editorial stated, "Downtown property owners also must show leadership. There is a tendency to hold out for the 'magic tenant' who will sign a long-term lease for an entire building . . . It takes a brave and staunchly committed business person to rebuild early or to lease space in the basement-pocked downtown that exists today" (*Sentinel*, January 2, 1992, A-9).

The reason landowners and storeowners did not always see eye-to-eye was their different relationship to property. For property owners, exchange values are realized as rent (Logan and Molotch 1987, 23–26). Quite obviously, the maximization of their exchange value goals depends on deriving as much rent from their holdings as possible. Conversely, and equally apparent, higher rents can mean a squeeze on profit margins for retailers who rent space (Feagin and Parker 1990, 34). This potentially divisive relationship within the growth coalition was exacerbated in the post-quake context. Retailers were under pressure to open up shop or risk losing their businesses, but the lack of available rental space in the quake-damaged downtown meant that they were faced with the prospect of relocating to suburban sites. To relocate not only meant the likelihood of facing higher rents but, more important, losing the benefit of the ambience of the downtown. Thus, most of them decided to stick it out in the temporary pavilions for as long as they could, even though business had been declining.

Meanwhile, property owners were not without their own problems. Their rental income had ceased, but those who had liens still faced mortgage payments on destroyed buildings and property taxes on unproductive land. They felt economic pressure either to sell their property outright or lease it to developers with the financial resources to rebuild. The haunting threat looming behind the widespread fear of large outside developers—on the part of small property owners, local retailers, and the broader citizenry for whom the "old" downtown was a beloved place—was the potential transformation of the downtown into a standardized, sanitized shopping destination. In short, they feared the possibility of the mall being redeveloped to resemble an open-air version of the Capitola Mall, with locally owned small businesses driven out by large national chains.

Political leaders also expressed fears about the possible displacement of small businesses, first because they embraced the progressive ideal of supporting locally owned enterprises, but also because they were concerned about the political and economic ramifications of the concentration of capital. In discussing his concerns about post-quake redevelopment, for example, Laird admitted:

> And that's the fear that I can recall having in the weeks and months following the earthquake: that all the independents in the downtown, business people who had one holding and lost the building, would be very vulnerable to somebody coming in and buying them out. And there was really a chance that we could have a complete consolidation of holdings in the downtown among three or four or five businesses or interests. That a Canfield, for example, who had financial ability, could come in and just pick off people who couldn't hang onto their mortgages . . . And that we could actually have a consolidation of power, basically. (Interview with John Laird, February 19, 1993)

LIMITING PARTICIPATION: THE TECHNICAL ADVISORY GROUP

After a four-hour meeting on April 23, 1990, about four months into the Vision Santa Cruz process, the board finally agreed to a set of "First Principles" to guide the redevelopment effort. These principles were then approved by the city council two weeks later. Now the growth coalition leaders felt it was time for action. They seemed as eager to deep-six Vision Santa Cruz as the progressives secretly were. So they made a motion at the next meeting, on May 21, to radically modify the structure and function of the public-private partnership by giving responsibility for actually implementing the rebuilding plans to a subcommittee of the board.

Pearson of the Cookie Company, who made the motion to create the subcommittee, acknowledged the importance of the consensus on "First Principles" developed by the full Vision Santa Cruz board, but then argued that "we now need an infusion of expertise" to move into the implementation stage of the rebuilding process (*Sentinel,* May 22, 1990, A-1). He therefore proposed that a small group of "experts"—the city manager, downtown property owners, local bankers, developers, and realtors—be assembled into a formal subcommittee to develop and implement a specific "downtown recovery plan" (Vision Santa Cruz Board of Directors 1990, 5a-2). According to Pearson, the proposal was made because of business concerns that the Vision Santa Cruz process was bogging down, despite the best efforts of progressive political leaders to control the meeting agendas:

> At the time we felt a very pressing need to move on and make some decisions. We did not feel that we had the benefit of an unlimited amount of time to deliberate these things. And we were beginning to get frustrated with re-discussing issues that we felt had been covered already . . . There was no way we were going to accomplish what we wanted to accomplish unless we got this into the hands of a very few stakeholders . . . That's what we wanted to do; I just feel that fewer people was more efficient. (Interview with Larry Pearson, January 8, 1993)

Progressive political leaders endorsed the idea, but many progressive board members nonetheless objected, claiming that this move would effectively put an end to the process and turn decision-making power over to a narrow range of business interests. Several of them later reported that they saw this move as further evidence that elected progressives endorsed this proposal precisely because they wished to "kill" the public-private partnership. From the point of view of key planners and more centrist observers, however, the new direction was necessary because the city needed some specific plans that less politicized members of the community could understand and buy into.

The issue of who would serve on this small expert subcommittee, which came to be called the Technical Advisory Group, also sparked debate among board members. Strikingly, Pearson's original proposal made no mention of including progressive political leaders, nor did he suggest that any Vision

Santa Cruz members should be appointed to this subcommittee. Some critics saw the fact that there was no provision for formal participation by any board members as further evidence that the partnership was being disempowered. Because of the confusion and outright disagreement over the details of this proposal, the board moved quickly to designate a seven-member task force to work with the city manager, the redevelopment director, and two city planners to determine who should serve on the Technical Advisory Group.

But that move did not work either because the task force became mired in debate about the composition of the Technical Advisory Group, a debate that continued during the full meeting of the Vision Santa Cruz board in June, with progressives pushing for more "community members" and leaders within the growth coalition advocating for more property owners. This stalemate prompted one of the most powerful business representatives on the board, the chief executive officer of a major bank, to urge in the strongest possible terms that the task force and the board should proceed quickly to come to agreement about the membership of the Technical Advisory Group. His words carried a lot of weight because, as one informant put it, "the city did not want to lose the confidence of the investment community." The loss of investor confidence was specifically invoked and warned against by the banker:

> We're sending a message with our lack of a decision that is terribly detrimental to this community. The reality is, if we can't make a decision, we can't put a plan together and we can't proceed with anything . . . I'm telling you that I have met with enough investment people that if you don't get on with it, you'll continue getting what you have now, piecemeal development downtown. It's not that they're bad or good plans. But until an environmental impact report is done, no investment person in his right mind is going to get involved, and investment cycles are such that it might be another year before they can commit money again. (*Sentinel,* June 12, 1990, A-4)

Shortly after the banker made his pointed remarks, the task force agreed to follow a recommendation by Wormhoudt that the Technical Advisory Group would consist of twelve members: four downtown property owners, one downtown merchant, four city staffers, one city council member, one vision Santa Cruz member, and the major banker who had spoken out so forcefully. This configuration of appointees was designed to achieve equal representation between the public and private sectors, but some rank-and-file progressives on Vision Santa Cruz did not see it that way. Although they acknowledged that the city staffers and the city council member were all "public" representatives in a legal sense, they did not see them as truly representing the public at large during the rebuilding process. More generally, as the Vision Santa Cruz process became increasingly narrowed by instituting other task forces and subcommittees, the appointees to the board who were there to represent neighborhoods and displaced residents of single-occupancy dwellings came to feel marginalized, as did many of the activists who attended meetings and spoke for friends and neighbors. In their eyes, the more deliberative and open Vision Santa Cruz process had been steered in the direction of elite decision making.

But why would progressive political leaders, who originally were wary of the public-private partnership because it might provide an organizational vehicle for greater business power in the city, agree to the creation of a subcommittee that was proposed by and primarily made up of business interests? Notwithstanding their espousal of opening up government decision making to wider citizen involvement, progressive politicians on Vision Santa Cruz shared the business leaders' frustration with long drawn-out discussions that might delay planning for earthquake redevelopment. Wormhoudt later explained, "I had a fear, that's for sure. I had a fear. The fear was that every, I mean I can tell you that every wacko had a great idea about what to do, and some of them were interesting, but clearly impossible, others were just plain nuts, others were interesting and maybe possible if we had twenty years to spend millions and millions of dollars to do it . . . And we tried very hard to balance that need for movement with the need for process" (Interview with Mardi Wormhoudt, August 9, 1993).

Clearly, then, there was an affinity between the growth coalition's interest in "efficiency" and the progressive leadership's interest in keeping public participation in Vision Santa Cruz to a minimum, an example of the kind of collaboration that is emphasized in regime theory. This convergence was a good part of the reason why some progressive leaders saw the process as leading to a greater understanding between the two sides. The decision to streamline the process by entrusting more of the specific decision-making power to subcommittees exemplifies what Jezierski (1990) identifies as the tension between "efficiency and equity" in public-private partnerships. Creating subcommittees composed mostly of property interests, political leaders, and technical experts undermines citizen involvement and focuses almost exclusively on addressing the concerns of economic and political leaders.

In addition, those members of the partnership controlling capital, or possessing special technical skills, can draw upon widely held societal beliefs about the special status of "professionals" and the importance of "private efficiency" to argue that they should be the key decision makers (De Neufville and Barton 1987). As for the Vision Santa Cruz members who were appointed to represent neighborhood organizations, nonprofit agencies, and various secondary interests, they were not in a position to mobilize resources to bring to the partnership, nor could they seriously threaten to delegitimize the Vision Santa Cruz partnership if their particular interests were not realized in the redevelopment plans. Their opinions were therefore less compelling, which relegated their ideas to the dustbin of decisional outcomes (Pateman 1970). Thus, the creation of the Technical Advisory Group was a critical moment in the history of Vision Santa Cruz when appeals to "expertise," "efficiency," and the need to "implement" plans were contrasted to the supposedly endless "deliberations" and the "unwieldiness" of the thirty-six-member Vision Santa Cruz board.

Moreover, the planning process was turned over to the small elite group because at least some of the elected progressives worried that they might pay a political price with voters if they were perceived as delaying the rebuilding process. According to several of our progressive informants, these elected officials were disconcerted by the constant refrain from the growth coalition that they were responsible for the delays, even though they claimed they had adopted every recommendation made by Vision Santa Cruz that supported the commercial function of the downtown. In fact, they had approved the plans for rebuilding five buildings at the first council meeting at which the proposals appeared on the docket, a point repeatedly mentioned by elected progressives in interviews with the media and talks to local groups. But according to one Vision Santa Cruz board member, who identified himself as a staunch progressive supporter, the leadership remained fearful of the power of the major business figures: "They were worried, the people in power, the people elected to city council. They were worried that come the elections, nothing was going to be going on. They didn't want that to happen so it would be used against them politically. Louis Rittenhouse, who sat on Vision Santa Cruz, used to pound away, you know, 'Let's get going.' So I think there was a real fear."

Still, it may seem surprising that the elected progressives would risk alienating activist members of the broader progressive coalition by short-circuiting the rebuilding discussions. Losing activist support could hurt at the ballot box and, more critical, in grassroots campaign work. Nevertheless, they were only one part of the electoral coalition. The political calculus for elected progressives involved weighing the costs of alienating some key members of the electoral coalition against the benefits of holding on to the support of the less ideologically aligned "median voter" (Hoffman 1976). The support of this electoral middle, which had shown its independence by turning Van Allen out of office in 1983 and by rejecting a SCAN-endorsed candidate in 1985, might be jeopardized if responsibility for delays in rebuilding could be blamed on progressives. As the November 1990 elections approached, with few overt signs of progress in the rebuilding process, and with members of the growth coalition and some activists in the progressive coalition highly critical of their leadership, the elected progressives were about to find out if they had suffered any damage to their electoral coalition.

SURVIVING THE QUAKE: THE 1990 ELECTIONS

The 1990 elections provided the first opportunity to see if the progressives had lost any ground with centrist voters or if the activists who previously supported progressive elected officials had become alienated from them because of the compromises they had made. Although Vision Santa Cruz had indeed moved slowly, with constant wrangling and much bad press, it needs to be kept in mind as we think about the voting public that the progressives had killed the big landowners' hopes for enlarging the downtown and linking it with the beach and boardwalk complex. This point often passed unnoticed in the rush of local politics, but it mattered greatly because it eliminated the concerns of neighborhood activists in the downtown area that their neighborhoods would be at risk for development once again. It also served as a testament to the power the progressives had developed.

To convince city voters that they were working hard to restore the downtown, and at the same time encourage university students to vote in large numbers, the progressives selected two candidates who could project the needed image for that historical moment. The first was Neal Coonerty, by now as well-known for his service on Vision Santa Cruz as for his bookstore and likely to be acceptable to at least some downtown business leaders as well as most progressives. He was seen as a bridge between progressives and members of the growth coalition and was soon to become one of the rare progressives to be endorsed for office by the *Sentinel*. The second candidate was Scott Kennedy, a 1969 graduate of UC Santa Cruz and one of the founders of the local Resource Center for Nonviolence, a highly visible and popular organization in the eyes of all progressives and university students because of its international efforts on behalf of peace and conflict resolution. Although Kennedy was known more for his advocacy and educational work on these broader issues, and for his involvement in civil disobedience campaigns, he had strong ties to the campus community.

The fact that neither Coonerty nor Kennedy came out of a neighborhood or environmental organization was not a strong concern at the time, and both were enthusiastically endorsed by SCAN. Nevertheless, they gained SCAN's endorsement partly because neighborhood activists were reassured by the fact

that Beiers, the one progressive incumbent on the ballot, who seemed certain
to win the election to fulfill the remaining two years of her appointed term,
was a strong neighborhood advocate going back to her Lighthouse Field efforts. Then, too, it mattered that the possibility of downtown expansion was
off the table and there seemed to be no major neighborhood issues on the
horizon.

Pro-growth interests had good reason to believe that the creation of Vision
Santa Cruz, and then the Technical Advisory Group, had opened up a new institutional avenue through which they could influence local policymaking.
They nonetheless sought elected office in order to have a stronger hand in
shaping the direction of municipal policies, both those affecting downtown
redevelopment and others bearing on overall development and land use in the
city. They understood that final authority over land-use, zoning, and development issues still rested with the city council, which meant that winning direct
representation of their interests was essential if they were ever going to realize
their most ambitious plans.

As expected, Rittenhouse threw his hat in the ring as the leader of the informal growth coalition ticket. He was joined by Joe Ghio, running as an
incumbent after his victory in 1985. The third pro-growth candidate was a
loan officer for Nickelson's Coast Commercial Bank.

Understandably, rebuilding the downtown was identified by candidates
across the political spectrum as the most critical issue in the campaign. And
despite continuing substantive disagreements over exactly how downtown redevelopment should proceed, the existence of Vision Santa Cruz helped to
blunt open conflict between candidates aligned with either side of the political divide because it established "cooperation" as the key to rebuilding. Conse-
quently, no candidate wanted to be perceived as contrarian or identified with
classic Santa Cruz partisan politics.

The focus on rebuilding also meant that relatively little attention would be
given to land-use and development issues affecting other parts of the city,
such as open-space growth control measures and the routine updating of the
city's general plan. Even the greenbelt provision adopted by the voters in 1979,
which was due to expire at the end of 1990, was extended by the city council
without fanfare for another two years, because the necessary land-use planning had been delayed by the earthquake. Predictably, this decision angered
property owners whose holdings were within the compass of designated
greenbelt areas, but it did not become a campaign issue.

Although there was consensus between the opposing slates on the importance of rebuilding the downtown, clear differences remained on some issues.
Rittenhouse, a caustic conservative, with views on most social issues that were

upsetting to moderate and liberal voters, and perhaps especially student voters, seemed to be an ideal person for the progressives to run against. In addition, the loan officer at Coast Commercial Bank raised an issue that was a red flag to progressive voters, the construction of a new campus access road that would link the campus to Highway 17. It would do so by cutting through the hillsides saved from development by the greenbelt measure, which were considered untouchable by environmentalists and students. He also called for the construction of another dam in the Santa Cruz Mountains to augment the city's water supply, a proposal that had been defeated by progressives several years earlier as being unnecessary and labeled for what it was, an opening for large-scale growth. Ghio's campaign also invoked older, divisive issues that easily could have been mistaken for the campaign platform of a pro-growth candidate during the first several years of the 1980s.

When the votes were counted, the electoral inroads the growth coalition hoped for and progressives feared did not materialize. Coonerty and Kennedy won two of the three open contests easily, and with Beiers's victory over a write-in candidate in a separate election for her appointed seat assuring that she would serve for two more years, progressives maintained the 5–2 margin they first gained in 1988. On the other side of the divide, Rittenhouse unexpectedly beat Ghio by six votes for the final seat. And for the second election in a row, the progressives would have won even without their strong majorities in the campus precincts, where Kennedy and Coonerty received 1,304 and 1,066 votes respectively, compared with a mere 135 for Rittenhouse. The progressive electoral coalition, now reinforced by an electoral machine based in community nonprofit agencies, and by the increasing numbers of UC Santa Cruz alumni living within the city limits, proved it was solidly entrenched even when there were policy disagreements within it.

THEORETICAL IMPLICATIONS:
A REVIEW AND PREVIEW

The battles over rebuilding after the earthquake clearly demonstrate several key points in relation to the theoretical issues of concern in this book. First, the main disagreements arose from the conflict between exchange values and use values, as growth coalition theory would predict; this finding is contrary to what public choice theory would expect because it emphasizes the lack of conflict within cities over growth issues. Second, there were divisions within both the growth coalition and the progressive coalition, which explains why organizational structures and leaders—that is, power structures—develop within each coalition to create the consensus and maintain the discipline that is needed to defeat the other side and take control of government. Third, the growth coalition had considerable help from the nationwide urban policy-planning network in forging its plans and insisting on a public-private partnership to maximize its impact, which is in keeping with what has been found in studies of power structures in other cities (e.g., Domhoff 1983, Chapter 6; Dreier, Mollenkopf, and Swanstrom 2004; Hartman 2002). Fourth, and contrary to regime theory, the progressives had once again demonstrated that an electoral coalition can indeed be an effective governing coalition, even in the face of major adversity.

Fifth, and perhaps most important for our purposes, the dynamics of the Vision Santa Cruz process do not fit with the expectations of regime theory. Although compromises between the growth coalition and the elected progressives eventually emerged from this public-private partnership, they provide only limited support for regime theory's emphasis on the ability of rival groups to find common ground. Compromises did not occur until the growth coalition had been defeated on its primary objective, the expansion of the downtown. Put another way, there was little or no fluidity when it came to the main preferences of the two sides. While the conceptual distinction between "social production" and "social control" models is a plausible one, it is not possible to distinguish between them empirically, to the extent that regime theory does, because collective and distributive power are always intertwined and operating simultaneously (Gendron 2006). We elaborate on these issues in a more extensive critique of regime theory in the final chapter, which includes our own analysis of how the relationship between collective and distributive power evolved in the course of human history.

But first it is necessary to see if several unexpected conflicts within the progressive coalition provide further insight into a key tenet of growth coalition theory: the primacy of neighborhood use values in any struggle over urban development.

6

$\sim\sim\sim\sim\sim\sim\sim\sim\sim\sim\sim\sim\sim\sim\sim\sim\sim\sim\sim\sim\sim\sim\sim\sim\sim\sim\sim\sim\sim\sim\sim\sim\sim\sim\sim\sim\sim\sim\sim\sim$

PROGRESSIVES VERSUS PROGRESSIVES OVER GROWTH AND NEIGHBORHOODS

With electoral issues out of the way for another two years, and with many of the major downtown rebuilding issues more or less settled, the battles over growth and development shifted momentarily to other parts of the city. Progressives now faced the difficult question of whether they could develop a viable progressive economic development strategy while continuing to ensure that the use values of neighborhoods would be protected. Working within the context of the fiscal crunch caused by the combination of the earthquake, a recession, and a decrease in intergovernmental transfers of funds, their first new test came in January 1991, just one month after they assumed office. The result was bitter acrimony within the progressive majority, some of which had not abated when we did follow-up interviews in 2007.

This era of progressive policy disagreement began when a local developer announced plans to build a twenty-seven-thousand-square-foot building on Mission Street that would be rented to the Longs Drug Stores Corporation, a sundry store and pharmacy chain with over four hundred stores throughout the western United States. The corporation, with headquarters a few miles to the east of Berkeley, already had a large store in downtown Santa Cruz, just a

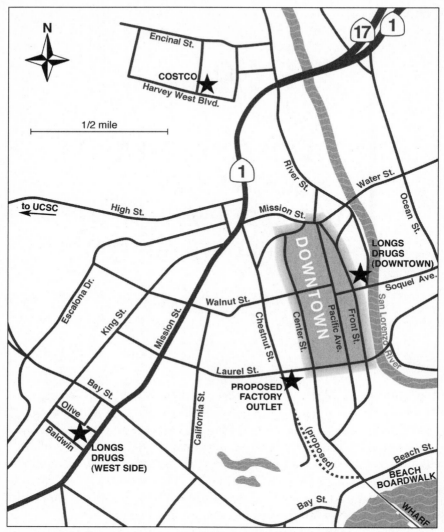

MAP 6.1 The area within Santa Cruz that encompasses Longs Drugs (West Side), the proposed Factory Outlet, Longs Drugs (Downtown), and Costco

block from Pacific Avenue, which had survived the earthquake intact. The proposed new store on Mission Street would be on the site that had housed the Santa Cruz Medical Center until it moved to the other side of town in 1978. Then the site became the home for the West Side Health Clinic, which was triumphantly opened by the progressive coalition in 1982. Although the land had been the site of a one-story medical building for decades, most of it was in fact zoned as residential land. According to pro-neighborhood activists, this meant that the owners had purchased the land at residential land prices and stood to make a considerable gain if they could convince the city council to rezone it as commercial property. Moreover, two houses in the adjoining neighborhood would have to be torn down and a rezoning of the land under them also would be required. Since Louis Rittenhouse and the one pro-growth holdover on the council, John Mahaney, were sure to vote for the project, the question was whether the landowner/developer could find two votes within the progressive majority.

Although the inclination of the progressives might have been to deny such a project as an encroachment on neighborhood use values and as the kind of retail store that might detract from the efforts to draw customers into the struggling downtown, there were several countervailing factors. First, most of the land around the site was already commercial, with stores on either side of it and a small strip mall and a gas station across the street. Second, there never had been a neighborhood group in the area near the site. Finally, and most intriguing, the landowner/developer did not fit any of the Santa Cruz stereotypes of a "developer" and was a long-time friend and supporter of progressive causes.

The landowner/developer behind the project, George Ow Jr., was the son of financially successful Chinese-American immigrants who developed a flourishing grocery store business in Monterey in the 1940s and 1950s. In the 1960s they bought open farmland near Santa Cruz that was later developed right next to the Capitola Mall. Ow and his wife, Gail Michaelis-Ow, a graduate of UC Santa Cruz, were active supporters of many cultural, civic, and liberal advocacy groups, including Planned Parenthood, where Michaelis-Ow had a major role, and the NAACP. As the landlords of the West Side Health Clinic, the Ows made clear that they would help relocate the clinic to a new site.

The Ows immediately announced they had hired what they referred to as an "All Neighborhood Team" ("To Our Westside Neighbors," bulk-rate mailing, August 14, 1991). It began with a local construction firm to carry out the project, which in turn emphasized that it would use local workers (and thereby gained the support of the local building trade unions). The Ows also employed a local environmental consultant, Jim Pepper, the UC Santa Cruz environmental studies professor who served on Vision Santa Cruz. Finally, they hired local architects to design the building and a media and public relations consultant, who was also a highly visible progressive supporter, to write pamphlets and help develop a media strategy. Soon after announcing their development team, they pledged to the local NAACP that they would insist that the Longs Drug Stores Corporation have a diversified work force in the store itself. With all these local connections and credentials, no one could charge that Ow fit the image of the vilified "outside developer," an epithet that had proved effective in mobilizing grassroots opposition to development in the Santa Cruz area in the past (Gendron 1996).

Despite the massive efforts by the Ows to forestall any protest, including a petition drive that led to nine thousand signatures in support of the new store, and despite the lack of any previous neighborhood organization in the area near the proposed store, some residents soon mobilized against the proposal, sending letters and petitions to the city council that claimed their quality of life was in jeopardy (*Sentinel*, February 8, 1991, A-3). With an active core of twenty to twenty-five residents who lived within a mile or two of the proposed store, they then started a full-fledged neighborhood organization—Westside Neighborhood Alliance, a name reminiscent of the defunct Westside Neighbors. By July 1991 they were putting out a newsletter, soliciting assistance for their own petition drive, urging residents of the area and other concerned citizens to attend public hearings on the project, and identifying their specific concerns about the proposed development.

The nature of these concerns—and the rhetoric that was employed in the *Westside Neighborhood Alliance Newsletter*—were exemplary appeals for the protection of use values. The newsletter emphasized the residential nature of the area just behind the site, talked about threats to the "integrity of our family-oriented community," and pointed out the dangers for children from increased traffic volume. The newsletter also pointed out that the development would require zoning changes and amendments to the city's general plan and claimed that it posed a threat to two small pharmacies located within two blocks of the proposed building. The newsletter further suggested that the new Longs would compete with the existing Longs in the downtown, only 1.5 miles away. By framing the conflict as involving more than the protection of one neighborhood, the Westside Neighbors Association attempted to fend off charges of NIMBYism, enlist support from other neighborhood organizations, and draw support from the downtown business community.

In particular, the new neighborhood association sought the endorsement of the Downtown Neighbors Association through a letter to its president. But most members of the Downtown Neighbors Association did not find the argument compelling, so they did not offer any support. As one of the downtown group's leaders found out to his dismay, his appeals to other members to rally behind the Westside Neighborhood Alliance, by arguing "that a threat to one neighborhood was a threat to all," did not meet with a positive reception:

> I was involved with Longs long before it began to surface. At that time, I was speaking to [then-mayor] Jane Yokoyama and Scott [council member

Kennedy], and saying, "You know, if this comes, that is terrible for the neighborhood, for what's going to happen on Mission Street. We've got to watch this." . . . I was surprised that certain people [here several members of Downtown Neighbors are identified by name] that were neighborhood activists sort of considered that someone else's turf. But I didn't. I felt, as I feel right now, that a lot of [neighborhood] problems are endemic. You deal with them no matter where they happen. (Interview with Ralph Meyberg, August 15, 1993)

Despite this rejection, the Westside Neighborhood Alliance was able to win the attention of individual neighborhood activists, including several in the Downtown Neighbors Association, who brought the issue to SCAN. The group thereby triggered a broader public debate, especially after a SCAN member who was part of the Westside Neighborhood Alliance wrote a well-crafted article in the August 1991 SCAN newsletter. Her analysis went beyond the specific issues of traffic increases, children's safety, and noise to frame the new Longs as a challenge to progressive values because it required a special zoning change— a "spot" zoning for an individual project—and amendments to the general plan that threatened the loss of housing in general, which in turn could "increase the pressure to develop our greenbelt." After linking the proposed Longs development to many of the long-standing concerns of the progressive movement, the author concluded, "This is a classic neighborhood issue" (Arnold 1991, 8).

The Ows themselves may have helped to galvanize more residents against them when they distributed a signed letter door-to-door, claiming that the new store was good for the neighborhood. They said that traffic actually would be reduced in the neighborhood because people would not have to drive through it to go to the downtown Longs, and that customers might even bike or walk to the store, claims that did not seem credible to the neighborhood activists who lived on the three or four residential streets that would be most affected. The Ows said the store was especially convenient for elderly residents, which drew criticism in letters to the *Sentinel* pointing out that elderly citizens were unlikely candidates to be walking home from the store with bags of purchases. They may have overreached when they reminded readers that the Longs Drug Stores Corporation supported projects in the community, especially when the one they singled out was the university's marine lab. Other neighborhood activists took it as an annoying threat when the Ows' letter mentioned that the land might be used for high-density housing if their project was not approved.

The Ows' handouts to residents also addressed the rezoning issue, which was seen as crucial by the opponents because it allegedly provided a windfall profit to the Ows and set a precedent for converting residentially zoned land into commercial land for an individual developer. Their handout said "85% of the property had been in commercial use since the early 1950s," so the "rezoning we are applying for is only to make official what has been true for over 40 years." But the activists said that this statement downplayed the key issues.

To further complicate the picture, both proponents and opponents attempted to use the issue of downtown rebuilding to bolster their arguments. Proponents argued that the new Longs should be built because the city needed all of the tax revenues it could realize while the downtown recovered, but opponents countered that all new projects should be targeted for the downtown to aid its recovery. Even the Downtown Association was divided on the issue, with its board voting 8–5 to send a "letter of concern" to the city about the proposal, reflecting a compromise between those who ardently opposed the project and others who strongly supported it (*Sentinel*, December 11, 1991, A-3).

The issue of downtown rebuilding entered into the debate on another level as well, one that went beyond strictly economic considerations. For example, a *Sentinel* editorial acknowledged that a "Westside Longs would reduce some anticipated income from its downtown sister store," but then went on to claim that "Santa Cruz needs some good business news, an example that respected private developers can work with the city to build something here" (*Sentinel*, December 8, 1991, A-16). This argument played into the same concerns that arose among progressive political leaders immediately after the earthquake. Even after their recent electoral victory, progressives feared the ramifications of being labeled "anti-business" and did everything they could to avoid it.

Although most of the momentum appeared to be on the pro-development side, the efforts of the neighborhood forces were rewarded with a first-round victory in late 1991, when the zoning and planning commissions, dominated by progressive appointees, voted to deny the zoning and general plan changes that were needed for the project to move forward. That was not the end of the matter, however. The newly elected progressives, Neal Coonerty and Kennedy, had made it clear at council meetings and in an exchange in the SCAN newsletter with opponents of the project that they did not think local government should protect what they called the "special interests" of neighborhoods at the expense of fostering economic development that would benefit the city as a whole. When the council met to decide the issue in January 1992, they joined Rittenhouse and Mahaney in a 4–2 majority, with Don Lane and Katherine Beiers voting against the project. Lane expressed concerns about increased traffic on Mission Street and the need to take out residential housing. Beiers discussed the problems of violating the general plan to benefit one landowner at the expense of local homeowners, who might see a decline in their property values as well as their use values. (Yokoyama was absent because of illness and did not cast a vote on the issue.)

The vote by Coonerty was expected by many progressives—even though he was advised to oppose it by his closest advisors, including Wormhoudt—because he was a business owner who had never made strong statements in favor of protecting neighborhoods. On the other hand, the vote by Kennedy was extremely upsetting to many neighborhood-oriented progressives because his campaign literature said that he supported "neighborhood integrity," a statement he was reminded of many times by critics in the course of the approval process. He also voted for the project against the advice of many of his closest informal advisors, which led some of them to break with him shortly thereafter. For their part, Coonerty and Kennedy were not hesitant to discuss their reasoning after the vote was taken. They said it was a good project and that Ow deserved the benefit of any doubt because of his reputation as a quality developer (*Sentinel,* January 30, 1992, A-9).

Members of the Westside Neighborhood Alliance then considered the possibility of suing the city, but according to one member we spoke with, they could not find a local lawyer who was willing to oppose the project. They finally retained a lawyer in Monterey, who advised them to seek the best mitigations they could obtain. Deciding they could not win in the long run because the Ows were likely to appeal any unfavorable decisions, their primary demand became strong neighborhood traffic controls, which were agreed to by the city council. The residential side street adjacent to the new building was blocked 150 feet from Mission Street, which allowed customers to enter the Longs parking lot from a side entrance but eliminated through traffic on the residential part of the street. Turns off of Mission Street to two other side streets northwest of the new building were also prohibited. In addition, truck deliveries to the store were restricted to certain hours of the day, and large glaring floodlights in the parking lot were prohibited.

The battle over Longs generated hard feelings, serious divisions within the progressive coalition, and personal animosities that still persist, further complicating the problem of developing unity within the progressive coalition. The final decision was not compelling evidence of a rejection of neighborhood use values, however, because it could be argued, as the Ows and their supporters had argued, that Mission Street was a commercial zone and that most of the Longs site had not been used for residential purposes since the 1950s. For others, though, it was the beginning of a worrisome trend. The stage was thus set for the next, and much bigger, development battle that would put the neighborhood use-value basis of the progressive coalition to a critical test.

THE FACTORY OUTLET

As divisive as the Longs project was for progressives, conflict over an even larger development proposal just a few blocks from the downtown core proved to be far more protracted, acrimonious, and revealing as far as the divisions within the coalition are concerned. It involved a huge Factory Outlet center (4.5 times the size of the new Longs) that was likely to affect nearby neighborhoods, including the turf defended by the Downtown Neighbors Association. It even held out the possibility of providing a rationale for realizing Rittenhouse's dream of linking the downtown and the boardwalk by turning Chestnut Street into a four-lane road to the beach (see the map at the start of this chapter). However, Rittenhouse would not be able to vote on the proposal if it came before the city council because his family owned land near it; this meant that pro-growth advocates would have to find three progressive votes to join the remaining conservative in order to win. To add further spice to the drama, the developer, Maynard Manson, although by then a moderate who gave financial support to nonprofit social welfare agencies, was the one-time ultraconservative who became a red flag for progressives as far back as 1973, when he made the claim, as part of his failed campaign for city council, that leftist activists and students would turn Santa Cruz into "Berkeley-by-the-Sea."

The project was made all the more suspect for progressives because it had the support of Charles Canfield, a longtime proponent of direct roads to the beach, and an ultraconservative who consistently tangled with the progressives over his anti-union policies at the amusement park and the Holiday Inn. In addition, the project was supported and partly owned by the headstrong founder and CEO of a highly successful local software company, the Santa Cruz Operation, which marketed a version of the open-source UNIX operating system that it had purchased from Microsoft. He inflamed passions by sending an e-mail to his employees urging them to attend public hearings to voice their support for the project. He also attended public hearings at which he derided project opponents, sarcastically commenting that the hearings were dominated by "a city of experts" (Gendron's Field Notes, September 29, 1992).

The proposed Factory Outlet would be situated on land that housed a long-abandoned ice plant, which was serving as a temporary home for a thriving used bookstore displaced from the downtown core by the earthquake. An earlier, more modest proposal for the area, brought to the city council by Manson, then serving as an agent for a previous owner, had been approved in late September 1989, just a month before the earthquake. It called for a small (sixty-one thousand square feet) retail sales complex, to be known as the "Ice House Factory Outlet Center," and a three-acre parcel zoned for medium-density housing, which was increasingly in short supply and there-fore an attractive carrot for pro-neighborhood progressives.

But then the plot thickened. Hoping to capitalize on the city's need for rev-enue, and the sentiment that seemed to be running in favor of development after the Longs proposal passed, Manson, by then the owner of the land, re-submitted a much more ambitious plan to the city in July 1991, that would double the size of the project. He argued that this expansion, which came to be known as "Phase II" to distinguish it from the earlier proposal, could only be carried out if the city would rezone the three-acre housing component for commercial usage. This meant a major intensification of land use that would be certain to detract from the quality of life in the neighborhoods near the site. But Manson insisted that the financial viability of the entire Factory Out-let complex required that the square footage devoted to retail had to be dou-bled, which could only be accomplished by dropping all the housing.

Perhaps as a result of everyone's focus on the downtown mall, the new plan did not receive a great deal of attention until it came to a planning commis-sion hearing in February 1992. At that point the Downtown Neighbors Asso-ciation, other neighborhood activists, and some members of Vision Santa Cruz protested mightily because the enlarged plan would eliminate the op-portunity to provide much-needed residential housing and encroach on two recently completed housing projects adjacent to the site. The expanded pro-posal also raised the possibility of wider access roads (in effect, a revival of the plan to widen Chestnut Street, but with a new rationale). Despite the strong protest by neighborhood activists, a planning commission long dominated by progressive appointees sent the proposal to the city council by a vote of 4–2. The battle was now fully joined.

The leaders of the Downtown Neighbors Association and their allies quickly met with several downtown storeowners who were nervous about the project cutting into their own sales. They soon formed an organization to spearhead the opposition, Friends of the Downtown, a name that could encompass the downtown neighborhoods as well as businesses on Pacific Avenue. Together they argued that the enlarged plan was precisely the type of threat that numer-ous consultants warned against when they cautioned the city not to allow a competing base of retail activity to develop before downtown rebuilding was well underway.

Supporters of the Factory Outlet advanced the standard litany of argu-ments used by growth coalitions everywhere: increased tax revenues and more jobs for city residents. Manson claimed that his retail complex would generate $558,000 a year in sales tax revenue and provide four hundred jobs for area residents. Addressing the critical issue of the impact of the Factory Outlet on downtown economic recovery, he said of himself and his proposal: "The city has somebody who is able and willing to provide the economic engine to really bring back the economic basis to downtown. This is a real project, with real dollars" (*Sentinel,* March 10, 1992, A-2). In his view, the Factory Outlet would draw more shoppers to Santa Cruz, who would then also patronize the downtown.

Starting with Coonerty and Kennedy, the standard pro-growth arguments were embraced by some progressive city council members. In their view, it was precisely because downtown redevelopment lagged that the Factory Outlet was needed. They positioned this argument within a progressive framework by maintaining that the revenues from the Factory Outlet were essential if progressives were to continue to fund social services. Not only would the entire city benefit from the Factory Outlet, the downtown would enjoy "spillover" patronage as well, thus facilitating downtown recovery.

The progressives and business owners in Friends of the Downtown responded with the concern expressed to Vision Santa Cruz by a number of consultants: commercial development should be discouraged outside of the downtown core until redevelopment was well under way. Opponents of the Factory Outlet also relied heavily on the advice of the director of the California Main Street Program, an advisory body organized under the auspices of the California Department of Commerce and dedicated to providing cities with information on downtown revitalization. The director's assessment of the likely effects of the Factory Outlet on downtown business was stated bluntly in a letter she wrote to the president of the Santa Cruz Downtown Association: "Downtown Santa Cruz, in its current condition, is not in a position to complement a nearby shopping center offering a volume of shopping opportunities. A new, comprehensive shopping district becomes absolutely overwhelming competition to the existing uses in downtown—at least the way the current project is being proposed" (Letter dated April 3, 1992; received by, and on file with, Santa Cruz city clerk, April 9, 1992).

Hesitant to make a decision in the face of competing claims about the project's effects on downtown redevelopment, the city council directed the Redevelopment Agency to commission an independent evaluation of the Factory Outlet's economic impact on downtown business. One month later, an "opportunity evaluation" prepared by an outside consulting team recommended that the city council approve the zoning changes requested by the developer. The report claimed that the Factory Outlet would help to recapture monies spent by Santa Cruz residents outside of the county, attract more shoppers to the city, and produce "a net gain of $8 million or more in added downtown sales annually" (Nudelman/Hovee 1992, 1). The consulting team did leave the opponents with an opening when it cautioned that it was unable to fully assess the "project's financial feasibility or probability of success" because certain of its characteristics (most notably its distance from a freeway) made comparisons with other locations problematic (Nudelman/Hovee 1992, 14). Not surprisingly then, the bottom-line conclusion about a net gain to the downtown of $8 million annually (and a total net benefit of $39 million citywide) was greeted with considerable skepticism by opponents, especially downtown retailers. Moreover, the consultants' statement about the project's distance from a freeway raised all the old fears that a widening of Chestnut Street would be the next demand from the growth coalition.

This time the Downtown Association itself, not just the Friends of the Downtown, called for an "independent, unbiased" economic impact analysis. When the city council rejected this request for yet another report, it lent credence to the claims by the opponents that the council had not been acting as a disinterested arbiter, weighing the pros and cons of the proposal, but had been an advocate of the project from the beginning. As evidence to support their claim, critics now pointed specifically to the fact that the council, following a planning department recommendation, had not originally required an environmental impact report.

At this juncture, Friends of the Downtown retained the legal services of a San Francisco law firm to challenge the council's failure to provide an environmental impact report. Shortly thereafter, the council reversed its decision and requested an impact report after all. It also took the unprecedented step of subsidizing the report for the developer, which only added fuel to the critics' fire. The crux of their criticism now took on a new angle: the city council was being unduly influenced by the Redevelopment Agency director and the city planning staff, a criticism that ignored the fact that the city council had authorized the agency director and city planning staff to work more closely with developers because of the need to rebuild as quickly as possible.

The battle over the Factory Outlet then became the focal point of the forthcoming elections, which meant that the conflict between use values and exchange values within the progressive coalition would be decided by the voters if they elected a three-person slate of pro-neighborhood progressives who opposed the project. This progressive slate was led by Beiers, running for her first full four-year term, with her clear record as the strongest supporter of neighborhoods on the council. She was joined by Mike Rotkin, trying to return to the council after a four-year absence during which time he continued to work at the university as a field studies coordinator and lecturer in Community Studies, completed his dissertation for the History of Consciousness program, and served on Vision Santa Cruz. One of his comments to a *Sentinel* reporter revealed that the neighborhood-based progressives, even those who defined themselves as socialist-feminists and had a strong interest in class-based issues,

saw the 1992 election as a watershed: "The reason I'm running is primarily because I am concerned the accomplishments of the progressive government are
in danger of being lost" (*Sentinel*, September 27, 1992, A-1). The third member
of the slate, Cynthia Mathews, was a founder of the local Planned Parenthood,
a longtime member and onetime president of the Downtown Neighbors Association, one of the leaders in the battle against the Factory Outlet, and, not in-
cidentally in terms of how the university inadvertently provided resources for
the progressive coalition, the wife of an astronomy professor.

As might be expected, Beiers's campaign literature emphasized her extensive experience with grassroots neighborhood and environmental groups, going back to her role in the legendary struggle over Lighthouse Field. Rotkin
focused on downtown redevelopment, sustainable economic development,
the provision of social services, the need for affordable housing, and, most
important, neighborhood integrity. He underscored this last point with a
closing line in one of his campaign pieces that read: "Nobody knows the needs
of a neighborhood better than the people who live there." Mathews appealed
to three traditional goals of the progressive coalition—neighborhood integrity, environmental protection, and historic preservation.

The progressive-neighborhood slate also clearly defined itself and height-
ened its visibility by endorsing another hot-button issue, a ballot initiative
that would extend the original greenbelt ordinance passed in 1979 for two additional years in order to give the city time to develop a plan to acquire the
greenbelt lands. This measure was enormously popular with students, environmentalists, and neighborhood leaders alike, and was therefore likely to ensure a high voter turnout even among constituencies not interested in the
Factory Outlet proposal.

The pro-growth forces endorsed two relatively unknown candidates, the
first of whom described himself as a business-oriented supporter of the Factory Outlet; he went on to raise the most money for his campaign, $24,249, far
surpassing the best-financed progressive, Mathews, who raised $14,381. The
second pro-growth candidate referred to himself as a "Third Force" candidate,
neither progressive nor conservative, a centrist who argued that it was necessary to do away with the "polarized politics" that had "led the city into stagna-
tion and a plunging quality of life" (*Sentinel*, January 23, 1992, A-2). He, too,
supported the Factory Outlet. The third member of the informal growth
coalition slate was Ghio, back for another try even though he had lost the last
time out, hoping that his recent service on Vision Santa Cruz would remind
voters of his long record of government involvement.

As the election campaign gained momentum after Labor Day, criticism of
the city council by neighborhood and environmentally oriented progressives

reached a crescendo just prior to its September 29 meeting, when it was to hear public testimony on the Factory Outlet proposal. Shortly before the meeting, Friends of Downtown circulated a letter that bore the signatures of five former progressive mayors—Muhly, Rotkin, Wormhoudt, Laird, and Weed. It began with a reference to earlier efforts that blocked the growth coalition's numerous plans to bring "generic commercial development" to the city, "sacrifice a whole neighborhood for a massive 'beach loop plan,'" and transform Santa Cruz into little more than a container and a conduit for the Seaside Company's arcade and amusement park. By emphasizing the current proposal's link to the growth coalition's broader development plans, the letter raised the specter of precisely the type of wholesale development that earlier progressive city councils had successfully opposed.

Even more important, the letter launched a direct broadside against the incumbent progressive council members for their support of the Factory Outlet. It did so using language and allusions suggesting that progressives on the city council had abandoned the progressive agenda. The battle lines for and against development were starkly drawn in this controversy, but this time the fight was not between progressives and the growth coalition. It was more like a civil war within the progressive coalition.

Many of the strong charges in the letter were openly voiced during the September 29 council meeting, which was preliminary to a meeting set for three weeks after the elections, when a decision would be made on Manson's request for rezoning. Supporters and opponents took turns voicing their opinions, and, as was typically the case, most of the arguments came down to more jobs and higher tax revenues versus protecting neighborhood integrity. Because of the opposition expressed by many downtown merchants, however, this was not simply an exchange-value versus use-value debate. The executive vice president of the Downtown Association testified that its members had held a special early-morning meeting just the day before, at which they decided to shift their official position from one of "neutrality" to one of "contesting" the proposal. This disagreement between downtown retailers and developers created the opening for an even stronger alliance of neighborhood organizations and downtown business leaders, suggesting that divisions within a growth coalition can make it more vulnerable to defeat.

But disagreements within the local growth coalition were not the most striking or unusual aspect of this public hearing. More remarkable was the way in which several well-known progressive leaders blistered the progressives on the city council and questioned the integrity of the city's planning process. Mathews, coming to the podium as a mainstay of the Downtown Neighbors Association and the Friends of the Downtown, as well as a candidate in the

November elections, argued that the testimony presented by the planning department and the Redevelopment Agency ignored some problematic issues that were raised in the environmental impact report. Another Friends of Downtown member, a local architect who had once served on the planning commission and generally took a centrist position, also questioned the "credibility" of the city planning process.

Perhaps the most pointed claim that the city's planning department had overstepped its bounds came from Muhly, the former county planner and city mayor, by then a venerated progressive spokesperson. Muhly, whose primary commitment as a planner was to the integrity of the planning process, did not mince words, charging that the relationship between the planning department and the Redevelopment Agency was "too close," with the latter pursuing speculative development projects and the former all too willing to find reasons to support them. "Since the earthquake," he continued, "the city has not been pursuing redevelopment; speculators have." Then a member of the Friends of the Downtown, who was both a property and bookstore owner on Pacific Avenue, put the fine point on what most of the other critics had been intimating, claiming that the proposal had only moved as far along in the planning process as it had because after the earthquake there had been a "shift from progressive to business control" of city land use (Gendron's Field Notes, September 29, 1992).

Members of the city staff were taken aback by these strong criticisms. As the city manager pointed out, the city council had instructed them to work more closely with developers to facilitate the rebuilding process: "We have a new job. Our job used to be to receive applications from people who wanted to do projects, and then run those applications through the process and have the city council make a decision. Now, our job is to help produce the applications" (Interview with Richard Wilson, August 19, 1993). He denied that he and his staff had in any way usurped the council's decision-making role:

> I mean, after the applications have been produced, after they have been created, and they are put in a process, we step back. We're not advocates; we don't get up in front of the city council and say, "You ought to vote for this project because we've put a lot of hours into putting it together." It's perfectly appropriate for the council to say, "No, we don't think it's in the city's interest to do this project." But we are playing a different role in developing the proposals and helping to put them together. (Interview with Richard Wilson, August 19, 1993)

In fact, grassroots progressives had accepted the need for greater cooperation between city staff and developers when it came to rebuilding the downtown because such an arrangement posed few, if any, threats to established neighborhoods. Nor did rebuilding, as narrowly circumscribed by the progressive majority on Vision Santa Cruz, affect greenbelts or open space. But when the pro-development progressives on the city council supported the Factory Outlet, a project that would shift the focus from downtown redevelopment and have an impact on neighborhoods, the basic issues that led to the original defeat of the growth coalition in the 1970s and early 1980s came to the fore once again for many of the neighborhood and environmental activists as well as grassroots voters. From their point of view, it was one thing to have the planning staff work closely with developers to speed up approval for downtown redevelopment, but it was another when development projects were proposed for sites outside of the downtown core near residential neighborhoods. The strength of the use-value wing of the progressive coalition was now the core power issue in this conflict.

Following the dissemination of the Friends of the Downtown letter and the contentious council meeting, the fissure within the progressive ranks split wide open. Criticizing those who made neighborhood integrity their primary goal, Coonerty and Kennedy stated, "We find it increasingly impossible to put street traffic counts ahead of the poor in our own community" (*Sentinel*, October 22, 1992, A-9). Kennedy also attempted to counter the accusation that the current city council had sold out the progressive agenda by arguing that the five former progressive mayors who were signatories to the Friends of the Downtown letter were mired in "nostalgia politics." He continued in this vein by stating: "There's a kind of harkening back to the days before the earthquake that I think is totally unrealistic . . . The progressive community more broadly has not come to terms with the financial reality of Santa Cruz in 1992" (*San Jose Mercury News*, October 7, 1992, 1B).

However, Rotkin and other neighborhood-oriented progressives did not simply argue in favor of the use values of neighborhoods. Drawing on what they had learned from meetings and publications of the Conference on Alternative State and Local Policies, they also spoke for a different kind of development, a community-based development, which assesses the quality of new jobs in terms of wage rates, examines the effects of increased employment on housing supply, and looks for the hidden costs for the community (Schramm 1987). In that context, they pointed out that the Factory Outlet would create minimum-wage jobs, eliminate opportunities to build affordable housing, and at the same time have a negative impact on both downtown neighborhoods and businesses. They concluded that the city could do better in terms of the kind of retail firms it could attract.

Still another factor related to the local economy, but certainly not reducible to strictly economic issues, entered the conflict over the Factory Outlet: a challenge to the progressive leadership on the issue of increasing job opportunities for persons of color. This issue had surfaced to some degree in the battle over Longs, but this time it played a much bigger role, primarily through the testimony and writings of a longtime African American activist, Tony Hill, the leader of the Alliance for Improving Race Relations and an active member of the NAACP. Working with five major local developers whom he had approached as part of his concern for jobs for young people of color, Hill said he had decided to seek an alliance with the developers because the local progressive leaders "hadn't been very sensitive and welcoming to diversity." Then he added: "The progressive agenda has basically ignored the needs of minorities, so now I'm going to private industry and asking them to take the leadership role . . . Although they are 'progressive,' they actually haven't been very progressive. They champion diversity in the greenbelt, the Monterey Bay sanctuary, the salamanders in Elkhorn Slough, but when it comes to people, there is very little concern about diversity" (*Sentinel,* October 10, 1992, A-1, A-14).

A few days later, Hill wrote a guest column in the *Sentinel* (October 22, 1992, A-9) that addressed the impending decision, arguing that the city council should support the development as an economic boost to the city and as a way to provide jobs for persons of color. Launching a renewed and even more pointed attack on progressives, Hill denigrated the opponents in language that reveals their vulnerability to charges that they are predominantly white members of the middle class who really don't care much about communities of color. Focusing on the subject of how the Factory Outlet would bring jobs to the city, Hill said, "Perhaps for those who have high-paying jobs at the university or elsewhere, such jobs may not mean much. But for those who are unemployed or for those young people who are looking to secure employment for the first time, these jobs can mean a world of difference."

Hill's criticism of progressives became even more acerbic when he took aim at the letter from the former mayors and claimed that "neighborhood integrity . . . has been used as a politically correct catch-phrase for maintaining the status quo and denying people of color their fair share of the Santa Cruz Dream." Ignoring the socialist-feminist roots of many progressives and their attempt to articulate a community-based approach to economic development, Hill called their approach "elitist."

REBUILD SANTA CRUZ NOW

With the election about two weeks away, and the Factory Outlet project riding on its outcome, a new organization made its public debut. Rebuild Santa Cruz Now, which had been drawn together by the Downtown Property Owners

Committee, a subcommittee of the Downtown Association, held out the potential to assume a key role in downtown redevelopment now that Vision Santa Cruz was due to go out of business at the end of the year. Unlike Vision Santa Cruz, it did not have an official status, but it included some of the same property owners, developers, and bankers. Its stated goal was to "jump-start" the rebuilding of the downtown by securing "letters of intent" from firms interested in relocating in the downtown, but its arrival in the midst of the debate over the Factory Outlet was not lost on those who wanted to create an atmosphere in which everyone agreed that something must be done. Strikingly, and perhaps with the recent vote on the Longs project in mind, none of the Rebuild Santa Cruz literature blamed the progressives for the delays. The group also signaled a less antagonistic stance toward local elected progressives, who were invited to attend the meeting and made positive remarks about the new group in return.

In addition, the opening remarks by the chair of Rebuild Santa Cruz Now frankly acknowledged the contribution of the public sector (some $30 million in infrastructure improvements), although he also insisted that only private capital could "lead the way," based on "enlightened self-interest" (Gendron's Field Notes, October 15, 1992). Instead of criticizing the progressives, the group now identified the main obstacle to rebuilding as a "credit crunch that had stalled several large retail and office projects worth more than $20 million." The group's informational brochure went on to note:

It's a "Catch-22" situation. Builders can't get construction loans from banks because of new state and federal bank loan mandates that have arisen in the wake of the Savings and Loan scandal and current banking crisis. One rule in particular—requiring developers to secure lease agreements for at least 70 percent of their project before any loan is issued—is choking off rebuilding in Santa Cruz. The Catch-22 comes because many space users will not sign leases until developers have secured loans and are undertaking reconstruction. Without the leases in hand, developers can't get a penny in loans. Without the loans, space users won't sign up for leases. ("Questions and Answers about Rebuild Santa Cruz Now," October 15, 1992)

Having adopted a structural explanation for the redevelopment delay, Rebuild Santa Cruz Now sought to break the impasse by undertaking aggressive tenant recruitment to "help developers meet pre-lease loan requirements and 'prime the pump' for future building." Although the original idea had been that the new mall would grow from the many businesses previously housed there, Rebuild Santa Cruz Now had decided there was a need to attract new and larger businesses. As Ceil Cirillo, the redevelopment director, explained at the inaugural meeting, it was not enough to "recycle" existing businesses. She added that it was critical to expand the business base throughout the city, which of course could be interpreted as an endorsement of the Factory Outlet proposal.

In actuality, for reasons that went beyond a tight credit market and stricter banking regulations, not all individual property owners were in a position to begin rebuilding. As Harvey Nickelson, the president and CEO of Coast Commercial Bank, later explained, many property owners had no development experience or expertise and were thus uncertain as to how to proceed. He also made a point discussed in the previous chapter: some property owners had carried heavy debt on their buildings, which were now destroyed and hence unable to generate revenue, thus forcing foreclosure (Interview with Harvey Nickelson, January 20, 1993).

All this seemingly minor finger pointing reveals a key point about urban power structures. Even within a group whose members share economic interests as landlords, there is the potential for division and conflict if some owners do not join in the common cause—in this case, reconstruction. Thus, a few individuals acting in their self-interest can hamper overall development, thereby undercutting the growth coalition's claim that the best policy is simply to allow individual choice. Contrary to this usual appeal to the "market-knows-best theory," the strong forces in urban development are business coalitions and organizations, which have to shape the behavior of self-serving individual owners (Feagin and Parker 1990, 4–9). Furthermore, the fact that these organizations have to seek alliances with elected officials shows that leaders in the growth coalition need the visible hand of government to help them realize their exchange-value goals (Logan and Molotch 1987, 9). We return to this point when we critique public choice theory in the final chapter.

CRUNCH TIME

With the council due to make a final decision on the Factory Outlet rezoning at its October 27 meeting, the impending decision was frequently linked in *Sentinel* editorials and everyday politicking to the forthcoming third anniversary of the earthquake and the slow pace of downtown redevelopment. Only four of twenty-nine demolished buildings had been rebuilt, with eight more under construction or about to begin (*San Jose Mercury News*, October 17, 1992, 1B). The clear intent of the editorials was to make a pitch for the Factory Outlet, both for its promised fiscal benefits and as a sign that the city leadership welcomed development.

Because the November city council election was to occur one week after the October 27 council vote, it is not surprising that the *Sentinel*, the alternative newspapers, and the candidates for council viewed the election as a referendum on the Factory Outlet decision. The *Sentinel* labeled the council race "a crucial turning point," and the four candidates it endorsed—progressive Yokoyama, the two new pro-growth challengers, and one-time council member Ghio—all supported the Factory Outlet proposal. The editors said they endorsed these four because they "understand the importance of welcoming economic revitalization" (*Sentinel*, October 18, 1992, A-14) and were "realists" who understood that a commitment to providing social services required support for economic development in order to fund them (*Sentinel*, October 20, 1992, A-14). By implication, most progressives were idealists whose economic naïveté would lead the city to ruin. The editorial suggested that the upcoming election could result in regime realignment and a more pro-development position by the city's political leadership.

Beiers could not attend the crucial council vote because of illness, and Rittenhouse could not vote because of the conflict of interest created by his nearby property holdings, but none of that made any difference. The five remaining members, four progressives and one conservative, voted unanimously to grant the necessary zoning. Supporters of the project were elated that the progressives on the council had ignored the arguments of the neighborhood activists, but they knew the project could still be halted if Beiers, Rotkin, and Mathews won in the upcoming elections, thereby creating a 3–3 stalemate on the council.

And that is exactly what happened. As it had in the previous thirteen years, the pro-neighborhood base in the progressive movement demonstrated its ability to mobilize electoral support for its candidates and beat back challenges by moderate and conservative candidates. In the process, the pro-neighborhood progressives also sent a message to those progressives who were more sympathetic to standard-issue, growth-coalition development projects. Beiers, Rotkin, and Mathews finished first, second, and third, and incumbent Yokoyama took the fourth seat, leaving Rittenhouse, perhaps the wealthiest real estate owner in the city, as the only conservative on the council. The fact that the initiative to extend the greenbelt passed by an overwhelming 70 percent to 30 percent also showed that the great majority of voters opposed a return to growth-inducing developments (*Sentinel*, November 4, 1992, A-9).

The pro-neighborhood mandate signaled the end for the Factory Outlet project. As Rotkin announced shortly after he was elected, "Phase II of the Factory Outlet is dead in the water" (*Sentinel*, November 5, 1992, A-1). The following year, Manson submitted a proposal to build a large condominium project and a small neighborhood shopping center on the site; the new city council approved it unanimously.

But it was not only Rotkin and other pro-neighborhood progressives who interpreted the defeat of the Factory Outlet as a victory for neighborhood-based politics. So did leaders within the growth coalition. As Nickelson of Coast Commercial Bank later said:

> The only issue that should [have been] germane in that thing is the fact that because of neighborhood politics, we screwed up our street scene. The problem is, Chestnut Street ought to be four lanes. Not restricted half-lanes. And that's one of the easiest accesses. One time the [*San Jose Mercury News*] put it out: "What's the greatest way to get to the big beach in Santa Cruz? Go right down Chestnut. Avoid all the traffic on Ocean Street." Of course, that just pissed off Mardi and all the people who lived near Chestnut Street, and Cynthia Mathews, and Ralph Meyberg [active member of Downtown Neighbors]. (Interview with Harvey Nickelson, January 20, 1993)

Rittenhouse shared Nickelson's view: "The Factory Outlet had nothing to do with business, in my opinion. It had all to do with the fact the Downtown Neighbors, Cynthia Mathews, and that whole group, for years, have considered that their private street" (Interview with Louis Rittenhouse, August 23, 1993).

Although the election results, and thereby the defeat of the Outlet project, were a triumph for the neighborhood-oriented progressives, their victory was not as neighborhood-based as they made it out to be. Without the four campus precincts, Rotkin would have finished fifth, and Ghio would have been on the council. While the student vote had mattered greatly in several previous elections, in 1992 its consequences were particularly dramatic: if Ghio had been elected to the council, the vote would have been 4–2 in favor of the Factory Outlet rezoning and expansion. The importance of the student vote to one side, the election nonetheless established for the foreseeable future that any future development projects would not be successful if they posed any threats to neighborhoods.

Following this clash, there was a tendency for pro-neighborhood progressives to play down the depth of the disagreements between them and those who favored the Longs and Factory Outlet proposals. For example, one of Coonerty's closest advisors, Denise Holbert, a longtime aide to Gary Patton at the board of supervisors who had played a key role in his early electoral campaigns, continued to be a supporter of Coonerty's even though she and Patton had advised him to vote against the Longs project. At the time of our interview she was serving as a member of Vision Santa Cruz:

I was the treasurer for Neal Coonerty's campaign. I'm a big supporter of Neal's. I just happen to disagree with him on this issue . . . They [Neal and Scott Kennedy] are not neighborhood people, and you've seen a big shift in the council in terms of people who are on this council are no longer springing from neighborhood groups with neighborhood kinds of concerns. They don't even have it in their consciousness. So Mike Rotkin, for instance, came out of the Westside Neighbors group. Mardi came out of a neighborhood group. I've come out of a neighborhood group. Jane [Yokoyama] doesn't come out of a neighborhood group . . . It's just a different focus than the previous council, really. (Interview with Denise Holbert, February 17, 1993)

Coonerty, on the other hand, thought that there was a "real split" on the council, and that he and Kennedy stood for "traditional liberal and progressive issues—jobs and housing," which to our way of thinking is a classic expression of the division within the progressive coalition between an emphasis on neighborhood use values and class-oriented issues (Interview with Neal Coonerty, February 19, 1993). Still, he expressed surprise at the vehemence of the reaction by his progressive critics: "It's one thing when the *Sentinel* opposes you, and that's your natural enemy, and who cares. It's another thing when a group of progressives feels like you've been a traitor, and they react much more strongly and react much nastier. And that's really what happened [over the Factory Outlet]."

After mentioning, as Holbert did, that he, Kennedy, and Yokoyama came out of different perspectives from that of the three pro-neighborhood progressives elected to the council in 1992, and that progressives had become entrenched in a "neighborhood political power base" with the potential to be very conservative, Coonerty softened his stance slightly by saying that there was a need to find a balance: "If you say that neighborhoods are the 'only issue,' you end up with suburban single-family dwellings. If you take economic issues as the only issue, then you end up doing anything that business wants. And I think that's the sort of political dialogue that is useless and destructive" (Interview with Neal Coonerty, February 19, 1993).

With his independent bookstore facing a major challenge from the chain bookstores that wanted to come into downtown Santa Cruz, and ultimately did so with the enthusiastic support of some of the "moderate" business owners on Vision Santa Cruz, Coonerty decided that one term on the city council was enough and did not run in 1994. He was replaced by a pro-neighborhood progressive.

On the other hand, the willingness of the neighborhood-based progressives to join with Coonerty, Kennedy, and Yokoyama in taking a proactive stance toward community-based development, meaning projects that are compatible with neighborhood use values and create jobs with at least living wages and good health benefits, was demonstrated within the next year. After learning through a survey that 42,000 people in the county had Costco cards, which they used in stores in San Jose and near Monterey, city officials informally invited Costco to build a store in the large business park 1.5 miles north of the downtown. When Costco's plan was opposed by the zoning board out of fear of possible negative effects on downtown businesses, progressive proponents of the plan were able to convince 500 Costco cardholders, including many small business owners who testified that they bought their supplies at Costco, to attend the council meeting where a final decision would be made. Opened in 1995, the store soon became one of the largest private taxpayers in the city and employs 250 people.

CONTINUING RIFTS IN
THE PROGRESSIVE COALITION

Although our systematic research ends with the defining 1992 election that locked Santa Cruz into its pro-neighborhood path, we can show how the same trends continued through a brief look at the major political events in the city since that time. We do so based on interviews and newspaper accounts.

By 1999, on the tenth anniversary of the earthquake, and then again in 2005, nostalgic stories about the rebuilding process appeared in the local press, romanticizing the Vision Santa Cruz process in a way favorable to business interests (*Sentinel*, October 17, 1999, 1; Connor 2005). According to this new narrative, the downtown was a seedy and declining place when the earthquake struck. (In fact, as Rotkin explained to us in our interview with him in 1992, its percentage of county consumer spending had remained just about constant from the late 1970s until 1989, despite more population growth outside the city limits.) Thanks to the harmony created through Vision Santa Cruz, the revisionist history continues, the quake turned out to be a blessing in disguise because the downtown is now booming. Many (in fact most) of the persons who were key players in that process, including many progressive leaders, now emphasize the effectiveness of the consensus-based deliberations and the successful policy outcomes they brought about. The often tense—and sometimes outright contentious—interactions between the public and the private sector representatives on the Vision Santa Cruz board tend to be downplayed.

Despite an occasional lament for the "world we have lost"—that is, for the old Pacific Garden Mall—few would deny that the redesign and reconstruction of downtown Santa Cruz have been extremely successful. Anchored by the nine-screen movie complex, Pacific Avenue is both a lively street scene and a successful commercial core, with new cafés, gay and lesbian bars, restaurants, brew pubs, and other businesses keeping the downtown buzzing long into the evening. The pro-neighborhood and use-value forces remain annoyed that they were not able to create a plaza on the ground near the cinema complex, where a four-story Rittenhouse building now stands, but they take satisfaction in the fact that they have been able to keep national franchise businesses to a minimum. They also can rightly note that the downtown is still a place to visit with friends in a slow-paced atmosphere. In a statement that may summarize the standoff between the growth coalition and the progressives in the down-town area, one city staff member told us, "It's a social center with adequate sales." This outcome confirms the foresight of those leaders who argued that the downtown should focus on niche marketing and serve as the area's hub for entertainment, dining, and cultural activities, but it also attests to the power of those progressives who insisted on incorporating more use-value amenities in the downtown area in the aftermath of the earthquake.

Still, all is not perfect in the downtown area. Conflicts between street people and shoppers still flare up frequently, leading the city council to defend and enforce a ban on overnight camping originally passed in 1967 as well as anti-panhandling ordinances. This stance has generated considerable tension between homeless advocates, who are supported by many civil libertarians, and progressive elected officials, who feel they must preserve the climate for investment in the downtown in order to protect their revenue base. And as progressive political leaders point out to their critics, their continued control of the city has allowed for budget allocations to human and social services at levels not likely to be continued by a pro-growth regime such as the one that dominated city politics and set city policies prior to 1981. While the com-bined local efforts by progressive politicians at the city and county levels of government cannot eradicate poverty and homelessness in Santa Cruz, they have improved the quality of life for low-income and less powerful residents. In this sense, it is surely once again the case that "politics matters" in shaping policy, contrary to what public choice theory would expect.

Just outside the downtown core, business is doing even better and pro-viding the bulk of city sales tax revenues. The most dramatic example is the success of Costco and other enterprises in the business park, but business is also good in the beach area, although the long-standing battles between neighborhood-oriented progressives and Canfield of the Seaside Company over expansion of its tourist-serving facilities continue unabated. Canfield and the social-welfare progressives on the city council entered into negotiations in 1998 that would have made possible an expansion of the company's facilities, which by then included motels, apartment buildings, and a bowling alley. But they were blocked by three new council members, who ran on a strong neighborhood and environmentalist platform that emphasized the negative effects the plan might have on the low-income residents in the nearby Beach Flats neighborhood and on the quality of life in the city generally.

By 2007, the year in which the Seaside Company celebrated the hundredth year of its amusement facilities, touting them as the last remaining amusement park of any size on the entire Pacific Coast, Canfield seemed philosophical about such setbacks. "You don't always get what you want in this town," he said. "But you try to negotiate and work within those parameters" (McCord 2007a, 1). He added that everything has to be done on a piecemeal basis. Strikingly, Canfield was not the only one disappointed by the defeat of the expansion plans. So too was his longtime critic, Rotkin, who had favored at least some expansion of the amusement area as a way to generate new revenues for social programs. Still, the boardwalk area in general, which includes several other tourist-oriented businesses in addition to the many facilities owned by the Seaside Company, remains the largest private taxpayer in the city and the third largest nongovernment employer, after UC Santa Cruz and the local private hospital.

Despite the successes of the city's retail businesses and its considerable locational advantages as a place to live, it has been hurt by the same forces of deindustrialization that have hit cities everywhere in the country, as manufacturers move to China and other low-wage/slave labor sites across the globe. The city lost seventeen hundred manufacturing jobs between 1996 and 2006, and the county as a whole lost over thirty-seven hundred such jobs, a 40 percent decline. The result has been a steady decline in city revenues from property taxes and utility taxes as manufacturing plants have closed. That constraint, along with a diminishing allocation of funds from state and federal governments, and the rising costs of health insurance for municipal workers, has led the city to eliminate eighty city jobs—a fair number of which were added during the boom years in the late 1990s. It also has reduced the budget by an estimated $8 million and counting, which has meant cutting back on municipal services such as recreation programs for city residents and their children (*Sentinel,* June 23, 2007 [online archives, retrieved July 16, 2007]).

In an attempt to make up for these lost revenues, progressives tried to increase the transient occupancy tax (i.e., "bed tax"), which is paid by visitors who stay in the city's motels and hotels. As mentioned earlier, such a tax is painless for local residents and not likely to hurt tourism to any significant degree (the tax is 10 percent in Santa Cruz and 15 percent in San Francisco), so the progressives raised it several times during the 1980s, thanks to loopholes in Proposition 13. However, in 1996 yet another successful statewide antitax provision, Proposition 218, was passed, requiring majority voter approval for all local general taxes and two-thirds voter approval for all local special taxes, such as the bed tax. This makes it all but impossible to increase taxes if any organized group is opposed.

Thus, when the progressives tried in 2000 to raise the bed tax to 12 percent, with a mere 1 percent going directly to services for the homeless, the tourist industry opposed it because the money did not go into the general fund, where it could be used to support city infrastructure, and the majority support did not reach the two-thirds level. In 2002, progressives tried again to raise the tax to 12 percent, this time with 1 percent going to the Conference and Visitors Bureau to promote tourism. But the idea of money being dedicated to tourism was opposed by grassroots progressives, including the liberal People's Democratic Club, who argued that the city should not commit money to supporting local businesses. The elected progressives were perceived as caving in to business, and the result was another majority vote that did not reach the two-thirds level. The combined effect of these defeats has led the city council to increase taxes on various utility bills, to the great annoyance of many city residents. From their point of view, an allegedly progressive city council is charging them a significant amount of money for what they expect to be a normal part of basic urban service delivery.

It was in this context that in 2005 Santa Cruz progressives repeated the conflicts over development that had divided them on the Longs Drug Store and Factory Outlet projects over a decade earlier. The battle began when the new owners of the Dream Inn, a ten-story hotel on the beach a stone's throw from the boardwalk, wanted to make renovations. (It's the tall building on the far right-hand side of the photograph on this book's cover.) However, Scott Kennedy, one of the social-welfare progressives on the city council, working in conjunction with city planners, urged the owners to expand their plans to include more rooms and a conference center, complete with a twelve-hundred-seat auditorium. (In the parlance of city development, "conference centers" provide seating for up to twelve hundred people, whereas "convention centers" provide rooms with seating for as many as ten thousand people.) It would be a "green building" that met the latest energy-efficiency standards. This planned expansion of the hotel would help to bring visitors to the city during the slower winter months. Projected city revenues were estimated at $2.7 million per year from a combination of increased property taxes, bed taxes, and sales and parking taxes (Rotkin 2005).

Serving his fifth term on the council, Rotkin spoke for the socialist-feminist and liberal supporters of the project, who by then had no differences between them on economic issues in the complete absence of any hope for a socialist movement. He argued that without a new revenue stream, such as the one from the hotel complex, Santa Cruz citizens would surely face more reductions in urban service delivery in the future, as proved to be the case by 2008 (Rotkin 2005). Virtually all of the city's major business organizations and their leaders then joined the Community Coalition for a Hotel Conference Center to support this project. This coalition included the Locally Owned Business Alliance, the Beach Area Business Association, the Santa Cruz Chamber of Commerce, and major landowners and developers such as George Ow Jr. In addition, since the agreement involved a promise by the hotel owner to employ union labor, the Service Employees International Union and HERE/UNITE Local 483, which already represented the hotel's employees, offered their support, as did the building trades unions that tend to favor any new development project. On the political side, ten former mayors from across the ideological spectrum came out in support of the project.

But the plan did not satisfy the neighborhood-oriented and environmentalist members of the progressive coalition, who were led by five former progressive mayors. They opposed it through Santa Cruzans for Responsible Planning (SCRP, pronounced "scrap"), which they had created the year before to keep Home Depot and Lowe's from opening retail outlets in abandoned manufacturing buildings on the west side. These use-value activists first questioned the $2.7 million enhanced revenue projection as just that: an estimate, with no guarantee of its realization. Moreover, they criticized the city's $30 million contribution to the project as a mere subsidy for business (*Sentinel,* January 20, 2005, 1). They were incensed by the idea that the project included a four-story parking structure on the parking lot across the street, which would cast shadows over the long-standing trailer park next to it and eliminate the residents' view of the bay. They argued that the project would generate too much traffic on nearby neighborhood streets and that it was out of compliance with the general plan, zoning ordinances, the city's beach area redevelopment plan, and the local coastal plan (Porter 2005).

The pro-expansion forces thought they had five or six sure votes on the city council for the project, but they won only four, including Kennedy, Rotkin, and Cynthia Mathews of the Downtown Neighbors Association. Heartened by their near success, SCRP immediately announced that the council's vote would not be the final word. It then collected eighty-four hundred signatures to put the question on the ballot for voters to decide. Faced with another landmark development battle, the owner of the hotel abandoned his plans for the project rather than be drawn into a political conflict that likely would be followed by ongoing legal challenges (*Sentinel,* March 26, 2005 [online archives, retrieved July 16, 2007]).

The disagreement over the hotel and conference center project once again highlights the tensions within the progressive coalition between the social-welfare liberals and socialist-feminists on the one hand, who want some development so they can provide jobs at good wages, and pro-neighborhood and environmentalist advocates on the other, whose primary focus is on use values. More important, it shows that the use-value advocates have the tenacity to win even when they seem to be in the minority within the progressive coalition itself. In fact, they now see themselves as the "true progressives," questioning the credentials of the four progressives who voted for the project. They are formidable enough that two developers who hoped to start projects on the west side of Santa Cruz in the future met with SCRP in 2005 and 2006 to see if they could reach an accommodation with the use-value coalition before they entered the formal governmental planning process. SCRP's success in shaping the progressive coalition on development issues is once again strong support for growth coalition theory.

The tensions between the competing tendencies within the progressive coalition also raise an important political question: Is there such a thing as progressive economic development? The question suggests that developing a community-based economic development program is the biggest challenge faced by the progressive movement in Santa Cruz—and in cities throughout the country. We return to this issue at the end of the concluding chapter.

Although the anti-growth/pro-neighborhood members of the progressive coalition succeeded in blocking the Dream Inn expansion, the two most visible progressives on the city council who supported the project, Rotkin and Mathews, were nonetheless the top two vote getters in the 2006 election. This outcome came as a surprise to those who expected that Mathews and Rotkin might pay a price at the polls for their support of the development. Based on our analyses of the rifts within the progressive movement, we believe there are several reasons why Mathews and Rotkin were able to win reelection in 2006. First, their vote for the hotel expansion likely attracted political support from the "electoral middle," which approved of their stance in favor of the project because of the revenues it would bring to the city. For the same reason, persons who worked for, or depended on, local social service organizations and nonprofits would be favorably inclined to vote for those who had supported the development. Third, both Mathews and Rotkin are, without a doubt, two of the city's most experienced and savvy political leaders. At the end of his current term, Rotkin will have served on the council for twenty-five years (1980–1988, 1993–2000, and 2003–2010), and Mathews for sixteen (1993–2000 and 2003–2010).

The windswept stretch of weeds and dry grasses called Lighthouse Field, which is also home to a few venerable Monterey cypress, returned to the political spotlight in 2007, when the city's thirty-year management contract with the state came up for renegotiation. Seeing an opportunity, local dog owners pressured the city to buy the land from the state so they could run their dogs without a leash, something that is prohibited in state parks. (The city of Santa Cruz, to the annoyance of state park officials, had allowed local dog owners to ignore this law during certain hours of the day from 1993 through 2007). Long mobilized by their annoyance with leash laws, many dog owners already displayed bumper stickers and plaques saying "I love dogs and I vote." Optimistic city officials, with the aid of former council member John Laird, by this point a member of the state assembly who served on several important committees, believed they could obtain the land—one of the last headlands in any California urban area—at a bargain price of $1 or $2 million because it cannot be developed. Local critics pointed out that such a purchase would create the world's most expensive dog run. "The city is catering to a special interest group by keeping it as a dog park," one leading opponent said. "It's a waste of money unless the city is just looking for ways to throw money down the drain" (McCord 2007b, 1). When the purchase effort failed, the city responded to the "dog people," as they call themselves, by building dog runs in several city parks and allowing dogs to run free on one city beach north of Lighthouse Field.

The Frederick Street saga also reappeared in 2007, when dozens of residents, now part of a larger neighborhood group, the Seabright Neighborhood Association, responded to a proposal for luxury units on a small parcel near the end of the street by demanding that the land be added to the popular park the Frederick Street Irregulars had won in the 1970s. The proposal was all the more galling to the neighbors because the city council seemed willing to deed away an easement owned by the public so the developers could have more units. Carole DePalma and Sally DiGirolamo from the old Frederick Street Irregulars were among those who testified, but the council voted 6–1 in favor of the project after several concessions were made to ease neighborhood concerns. Members of the Seabright Neighborhood Association noted that every member of the council was from the west side and wondered why the city council would put up money to buy Lighthouse Field from the state ("We already own that park," they noted) instead of adding to the city park on Frederick Street.

In the aftermath of all this conflict, two major development projects passed with relative ease in the summer of 2008, one for a new 150-room hotel in the beach and boardwalk area, the other for the construction of a large live-work development of up to 250 units to be built over a fifteen-year period. The live-work development will feature a combination of affordable housing and work spaces for businesses on twenty acres of open land on the far west side at the corner of Delaware and Swift streets (see Map 3.1). The hotel proposal, which

Santa Cruz publicists see as a major addition to the tourist industry, caused little controversy because it simply replaces three small motels owned by the same landowner who is building the new hotel. The development at Delaware and Swift, touted as an environmentally friendly incubator for new design offices, engineering companies, and software firms, encountered no organized opposition in good part because the owners had discussed the plans with leaders in SCRP beforehand, but also because it abuts an industrial park that lost several businesses in recent years.

Far overshadowing any other issues, however, is the fact of unrelenting university growth, with the UC Santa Cruz campus reaching 14,894 in the 2006–2007 academic year. This growth occurred with slightly less contentiousness than in the previous decade because university officials had assured one and all that there were no plans for further growth beyond 15,000. Nevertheless, in 2005 the campus administration appointed a faculty-staff committee that soon proposed adding another 6,500 students by 2020. The city sued, only to have its lawsuit thrown out of court on a technicality. Two anti-university initiatives on the local ballot in 2006 received 76 percent and 80 percent of the vote, making clear that university growth is still deeply resented, even by those who work there, and even by those, the progressives, who have been able to take power in Santa Cruz in good part because of it. The university reacted to the ballot initiatives by suing the city and saying it would settle for an increase to 19,500 students.

Aside from the pressures that university growth puts on traffic, the water supply, and local housing markets, progressives resisted university growth because it often involves buying buildings in the city and using them as office and research space without having to pay taxes on them. Nor did the money the university remits to the city for water and other services help to pay for infrastructure (Marshall 2007). The university is a boon to the growth coalition because it brings potential customers to the city, but it created a heavy burden for the city government because it did not pay its fair share of the expenses generated by its presence. This is the case with university campuses in many other cities in the United States, except for those few that make large payments to their host cities. In effect, city governments provide a subsidy to universities that leads to lower tuition and fees for students, courtesy of local taxpayers.

But suddenly, after eight months of behind-the-scenes negotiations that began in late 2007, some of the local antagonism disappeared. In August 2008, the university entered into what was publicized as an historic model agreement with the city, county, and a citywide neighborhood coalition that had filed a lawsuit against it. As part of this agreement, the university said it would pay the usual city fees for new water hookups, honor any city moratoriums if the water supply runs low, and pay the standard city fees to offset expected traffic increases from new development projects it undertakes. The university also agreed to limit the size of the campus to 19,500 students until the year 2020 and to submit its plans for expansion into forested lands north of the current campus to local government agencies. In exchange, all lawsuits against it were dropped (*Sentinel*, August 9, 2008 [online, retrieved August 9, 2008]). If the agreement sets a statewide precedent, it will mean that Santa Cruz progressives have spearheaded the effort to protect neighborhoods and support city services in several cities where university campuses are expanding.

While all these events were unfolding, the city gradually became unaffordable for most working families that were first-time homebuyers. The median price of homes rose from $236,000 in May 1996, the first year for which figures are available for Santa Cruz, to $749,500 in May 2006, a 218 percent rise that was far beyond the inflation rate, which would have taken the median price to $303,200. Newly arriving faculty members, most of them making from $55,000 to $95,000, were priced out of the market as well, leading the university to buy two apartment complexes for faculty rentals and to build more faculty housing on the campus. Although critics of the progressive regime blamed allegedly onerous growth-control policies for the steep climb, the increase was not any greater than what happened in California as a whole in the same time period ($177,270 to $556,640, a 214 percent increase). Nor was the decline any less after the housing bubble burst in July 2006, to the great surprise of the many Santa Cruzans who were sure that homes would hold their value because of the city's many unique features. Placing the blame for increased housing prices on progressives is also contradicted by the fact that in the 1980s housing prices increased at the same rate in Southern California cities with and without growth controls (Warner and Molotch 1995; Warner and Molotch 2000).

Meanwhile, the involvement of university students in the progressive coalition as either voters or activists has greatly declined. The students remain more liberal than those at other University of California campuses, as shown earlier in Table 3.2, but they are not focused on local issues.

As of late 2008, there was no sign that the growth coalition could regroup politically, but there was not much forward motion on the part of the progressives after several years of declining city revenues.

LESSONS FROM SANTA CRUZ

As this and the preceding chapter show, progressive elected officials in Santa Cruz have been afforded considerable political autonomy in dealing with the growth coalition and its allies because of their strong base of electoral support in both key neighborhoods and the campus community. They have been able to forge and maintain a progressive coalition without including commercial real estate owners, bankers, or merchants in the governing coalition, as evidenced by their success in defeating new growth initiatives and in winning complete control of city government. As Rotkin put it, "this is a situation where the city council is very, very powerful in setting policy for the city and had effectively beaten back the business community on a whole range of different kinds of conservative issues" (Interview with Mike Rotkin, August 26, 1992). Stated in other terms, progressives in Santa Cruz are able to cooperate with business (for example, by approving development projects and modifying zoning ordinances) from a position of such political strength that they can set the terms of the cooperation, even under circumstances of considerable economic pressure and constraint. This finding does not fit well with the doubts raised by regime theory about the ability of an electoral coalition to be a governing coalition. Nor is it an outcome that accords with Marxist theory or public choice theory.

As was quite evident after the earthquake, not only did the city council approve every project that came before it, it used public resources to subsidize rebuilding and redevelopment by spending millions of dollars on infrastructure improvements. It also provided a new parking structure just off Pacific Avenue that made the multiscreen movie complex economically feasible and a magnet for drawing customers to all nearby stores. In addition, the council introduced changes in the city planning bureaucracy and used the Redevelopment Agency to provide the growth coalition with an avenue to influence political decision making. In this sense, the progressives demonstrated that they could operate as a "facilitator regime" when the pressing matter at hand was downtown revitalization (Kantor, Savitch, and Haddock 1997, 348). Then, too, the inability of the neighborhood-based mobilization to influence the city council's decision on the Factory Outlet just before the elections in 1992, despite the progressive majority, illustrates that Browning, Marshall, and Tabb (1984) are right to conclude that "protest is not enough" for insurgent groups at the local level; it is also necessary to have elected officials in the government who are sympathetic to the cause.

Nevertheless, as our history of Santa Cruz politics makes clear, the political autonomy enjoyed by progressive elected officials in Santa Cruz is the result of an unusual mix of political and economic factors that does not appear in most cities. To begin with, the mild weather and beach location make it an attractive place to live and vacation, putting it high in the hierarchy of places. Tourism, the university, and the increasing presence of well-paid technical experts and executives from Silicon Valley all but ensure that the growth coalition's downtown properties will remain valuable. Then, too, the development of a liberal university campus that was formed in the turbulent 1960s provided the neighborhood-oriented use-value coalition with activists, expertise, financial support, and sympathetic student voters, who joined together to create a community that, somewhat ironically, became even more attractive to highly paid employees from Silicon Valley because of its enhanced use values.

Although the success of the progressive coalition in Santa Cruz provides an object lesson in how the dominance of a growth coalition can be successfully challenged, the atypical convergence of factors that made a challenge possible also makes it doubtful that what progressives did in Santa Cruz could serve as an exact blueprint for progressive forces in other cities. There seem to be only two general political lessons. First, highly committed activists on a range of issues have to find ways to work together to create the widest possible coalition based on the mix of issues that are salient in their city. But they have to do so without becoming so vague and bland as to lose their focus and zeal, as also shown by the victories for progressives in other cities in the 1970s and 1980s (Capek and Gilderbloom 1992; Clavel 1986; Conroy 1990). Walking this tightrope is easier said than done. It is almost a contradiction in terms to expect those who have the necessary moral fervor to become activists to turn around and engage in compromises that water down their demands and allow the injustices that moved them into action to continue into the foreseeable future.

Second, activists have to be able to develop the patience and trust to make their presence felt in the electoral arena, which is, once again, easier said than done. Elected officials, even those who originally came from the activist ranks, are always under suspicion from activists as mere "liberals" who have their eye on higher offices and are too eager to compromise. Contrary to this belief, we think progressive politics in Santa Cruz were in good part successful because a handful of social movement activists, and especially Patton, Rotkin, and Wormhoudt, were able to adapt to electoral politics and still maintain the respect of their fellow activists, thereby giving them a key role in working out compromises with liberals and moderates.

We return to these and others issues relating to the problems of creating a progressive social movement in the final chapter.

7

~~~~~~

FAULT LINES OF POWER
Assessing Theories of Urban Power

In this chapter we draw on the findings in our case study of Santa Cruz and other empirical studies to show the limitations of the three alternative theories discussed in Chapter 2, as well as to suggest new emphases within growth coalition theory. We also discuss the challenges activists face in transforming local progressive coalitions into a nationwide movement.

As we explained in Chapter 1, there are four main issues that tend to divide the four theories of urban power. First, there is the question of the degree to which power is seen as "collective," that is, as a common effort that generates new capacities for the city or country as a whole, as contrasted with "distributive" power, where the emphasis is on the efforts of one group or class to dominate other groups or classes for its own profit or benefit. Second, there are differences over the degree to which the preferences of the various competing power groups are said to be fixed by the nature of the economy or their position within the overall socioeconomic system. Third, theories differ on the degree to which they think local citizens, whether as members of growth coalitions or residents of neighborhoods, can have much influence on local political decision making. Finally, the theories differ on the degree to which local government can have an independent role in shaping the city in the face of outside economic forces. Using these four issues as a starting point, we turn to a critique of Marxist urban theory, public choice theory, and regime theory, and then discuss the additions that we think are needed to growth coalition theory based on our case study. Such a discussion prepares the way for seeing if growth coalition theory provides any insights as to how progressive coalitions might go beyond what they accomplished in Santa Cruz and other progressive cities.

MARXIST URBAN THEORY

The primary Marxist emphasis when it comes to the local level—the essential determinative role of the larger economic structure that surrounds the local economy—receives ample support in this study. The growth of Santa Cruz in the late 1840s and early 1850s was stimulated by the Gold Rush and then by the growth of San Francisco and other Northern California cities, making Santa Cruz County the second largest industrial county in the young state for a brief time until its timber and tanning bark played out, its limestone lost out when better mixes of concrete were developed, and its small manufacturers were surpassed by rivals in San Francisco, Oakland, and San Jose with larger markets and lower transportation costs. Then, too, capital investment from San Francisco–based railroad companies greatly shaped local land-use and development patterns in the city after 1870, making it possible for Santa Cruz to become a major tourist destination.

Fast forwarding to the post-earthquake era, the structure of the outside economy mattered greatly in how rebuilding unfolded in 1990 and 1991 because the tight money markets arising from the national economic recession and the fallout from the national savings and loan collapse meant that it was more difficult for developers to obtain loans at good interest rates than it had been just a few years before. In addition, as Marxist theory would stress, progressive political leaders in Santa Cruz found themselves operating within an economic context that they understood to favor the interests of the growth coalition because it owned the land and stores that could bring needed revenues to the city. The main landowners made clear that they would fight to realize their interests, and that they could afford to wait longer than progressive city officials in terms of how much time to take to rebuild the downtown. Both the way in which Vision Santa Cruz was constituted and the specific policy outcomes that emerged from it are examples of how progressive political leaders had to deal with the constraints owners can create when they make use of the potential power created by ownership of private property.

However, Marxist theory misstates the relationship between outside capital and local real estate capital when it says that the latter is merely part of a secondary circuit into which leftover capital flows when the primary circuit is overflowing. The actual relationship is more complex and fraught with tensions for several reasons, beginning with the fact that the original local landowners in the late nineteenth century were able to amass capital of their own through a variety of means, including making use of their timber to develop a residential housing industry. On the other hand, we do see that the decline of extractive industries and the closing down of long-standing manufacturing plants, such as the loss of the gunpowder company in 1914, can force local landowners to adopt new strategies.

We also note that it is not just the outside economic structure that matters. So, too, do the state and federal governmental structures, as first seen when the little unincorporated town of Santa Cruz, with fewer than 650 residents, became a county seat in 1850, giving it state government money via rents for a county building, salaries for state employees located in Santa Cruz, and revenues for the local newspapers that printed government notices. Recall, too, that the federal urban renewal program gave Santa Cruz the unexpected wherewithal to use the 1955 flood as a way to buy out those who owned the land in the faltering Chinatown and create new opportunities—protected by new levies constructed by the Corps of Engineers—for the expansion of the downtown.

Conversely, Proposition 13, the state initiative that slashed property taxes in 1978, along with the decision by the Reagan administration in the early 1980s to make drastic cuts in grants to county and city governments for housing and other infrastructure, increased homelessness and forced major changes in the local budget. As a result, it became necessary for the progressives to make a deal with the ultraconservative owners of the Seaside Company and other local tourist-oriented businesses to ensure that they would not face a challenge in their efforts to capture sufficient tax revenues for their social programs.

Most crucially in terms of outside government, it was the decision by the state of California to expand higher education in the 1950s, and the subsequent placement of a University of California campus in Santa Cruz, that ensured that local land values would grow for decades to come. This particular government "investment" had a far larger impact than anything outside private capital provided to the local growth coalition in the twentieth century.

Generally speaking, then, we think our case study shows that a local growth coalition has far more room to maneuver than is allowed for in Marxist theory. At every turn, property entrepreneurs and pro-growth politicians in Santa Cruz were the intermediaries that encouraged the flow of outside capital and decided where in the city it would touch ground and become a "sunken investment." This is nicely demonstrated by the way in which Frederick Hihn maneuvered to bring railroad lines into the city in the 1870s and 1880s, and also in the case of Fred Swanton's relationship with San Francisco capitalists in building an early version of the boardwalk and amusement park in the beach area at the beginning of the twentieth century. Later, the local growth coalition worked diligently to make sure that the new campus came to its area, continuing its lobbying effort even after an initial decision had been made to locate it on the other side of the mountains. Thus, we see the external economic and political structures as both a constraint and an opportunity when it comes to local growth coalitions.

We also think our study shows that the basic conflict in Santa Cruz was not a mere reflection of the class struggle. It was growth coalitions versus neighborhoods, with upscale as well as low-income neighborhoods opposing the established growth coalition at one juncture or another on the basis of their shared use values. True, they were aided by environmentalists and many other social activists, but the battle was fought in terms of neighborhood use values when it came to the voting booth. More often than not, construction workers and their unions, the most coherent embodiments of the working class on these issues, sided with their seeming class enemies in the growth coalition. Faced with these conflicts, local elected officials had to attend to the needs of capital, particularly in times of economic constraint, but they also had to pay attention to the demands made by neighborhoods, making city government into "the main battlefield" for urban politics, with elected officials becoming the "clear and visible target against which to express discontent" (Smith 1988, 68).

Then, too, Marxist theory underestimates the ability of opponents of local growth coalitions to shape the built environment. The use values attributed to neighborhoods by those who live in them, and by environmentalists concerned with the overall quality of life in the city and county, were strong enough in Santa Cruz to generate long-lasting, high-energy coalitions in a context in which their leaders knew they had a real chance for success if they could win the allegiance of university students as activists and voters. For reasons we analyzed earlier, the progressive electoral coalition was both secure and reliable in Santa Cruz, continually returning progressive politicians to elected office as long as they kept neighborhood and environmental issues in the foreground. As a result of this political power base, progressives were able to bargain with the growth coalition on favorable terms. In short, politics in Santa Cruz has been "relatively autonomous" from economics, contrary to the arguments advanced by those Marxists who argue that local politics are largely irrelevant (e.g., Gottdiener 1987) or that a municipality necessarily becomes a "dependent city" (Kantor 1995; Kantor and David 1988).

In summary, Marxist theory makes the national economy more determinative than it is when it comes to the local economy and government. It downplays the active role of members of local growth coalitions in crafting urban development and redevelopment policies, focusing instead on the operation of abstract forces such as the secondary circuit of capital. It ignores the room to maneuver that elected officials have and misses the degree of important political conflict that can occur at the local level. To the extent that Marxist theory sees any political conflict at the local level, it reduces conflict to class struggle, mistaking the conflict over the exchange and use values of land and the built environment for class conflict over profits, wages, and control of the productive process (c.f. Logan and Molotch 2007, viii).

PUBLIC CHOICE THEORY

The most glaring shortcoming of public choice theory is its main point: growth policies and economic development are supposedly noncontroversial because the city has a "unitary interest" in attracting capital investment (Peterson 1981). While it is certainly true that all cities, however they may be governed, require an economic base to support municipal service delivery, maintain urban infrastructure, and meet the needs of their citizens, public choice theory ignores the fact that the costs of development—and its benefits—are not borne equally by the residents of the city (Logan and Molotch 1987, 33; Stone and Sanders 1987). As a result, growth policies and development proposals give rise to conflict, not consensus, as seen again and again, and in great detail, in Santa Cruz. Once progressives won control of the city council in 1981, they were able to set development policy in ways which show that local government need not be the "able servant" or the "inefficient slave" of business, the only two roles that public choice theory deems possible for local elected officials (Peterson 1981, 143–146). The fact that the progressive coalition was able to divert some of the city's tax monies to various "redistributive" social welfare programs without losing support also contradicts a basic claim of public choice theory.

The theoretical insistence that there is no conflict over economic development or redistribution at the local level also has been refuted by a large body of empirical research that precedes our study. As one urban political scientist put it, the main proponent of the theory, Paul Peterson, "made the blooper of the decade in claiming that developmental politics were quiet and rational" (Jones 1989, 36). Blooper or no blooper, the fact that citizens often oppose growth projects, or vote against bonds for convention centers and stadiums, has not stemmed the ardor for public choice theory among those who start with the assumptions of neoclassical economics. The theory is still a cornerstone in the subfields of urban economics and urban politics.

City politicians fit into public choice theory as the people who respond to the messages sent by the market and the ballot box. They are therefore assumed to be responsive to the general will, not to growth elites. This analysis is contradicted by the empirical fact that most politicians in most cities soon become enmeshed in growth coalitions if they do not emerge directly from them, or else they represent neighborhood interests, as seen in the case of Santa Cruz.

Public choice theory not only denies the conflict that is everywhere seen at the urban level; in effect, it says that the concerns of neighborhoods are irrational because the residents do not understand their "true" interests. But interests are supposed to be well understood according to this theory. It thus ends up contradicting itself unless it is altered to assume that neighborhoods understand their self-interest and are being rational in opposing the growth coalition. (For a free-market economist who breaks with orthodoxy and argues that voters are indeed irrational in opposing free-market economic policies, and therefore should be discouraged from voting by a variety of methods, see Caplan 2007.)

Most egregiously, the idea that the "greater good" can be realized through the aggregation of individuals pursuing their "self-interest"—a foundational premise of neoclassical economic theory—ignores the fact that interests are in fundamental conflict because of resource inequalities. Although the form and function of the built environment of cities are in general shaped by the actions of individuals pursuing their interests, as market-oriented explanations assume, these actions are not guided to a socially optimal outcome through the "invisible hand" of the market. Instead, all markets (and perhaps especially urban land markets) are intertwined with and thus shaped by human interests in wealth, power, and sentiments about place. As Logan and Molotch argue, "markets *work through* such interests and the institutions that derive from and sustain them" (1987, 9; emphasis in original). Given the fact of systemic inequalities in precisely those "human interests" that individuals seek to maximize through the market, especially in wealth and power, a "win-win" outcome for all participants cannot be expected. The belief that a socially optimal result will be obtained through market forces is not warranted.

When Logan and Molotch criticize highly abstract "market-driven" explanations of how and why cities come to be built the way they are, they summarize their critique with a sentence that might well serve as the defining instance of how growth coalition theory differs from public choice theory: "In brief, *price is sociological* and sociology is needed to analyze its determination as well as it consequence" (1987, 9; emphasis in original). Thus, even though it is necessary to take account of the underlying motivations behind the social actions of individuals, it is analytically inadequate to posit the pursuit of self-interest as the prime motivation and let it go at that. Purposive social action is both enabled and constrained by social constructions such as the market. It is therefore essential to examine how "interests" are socially constructed and how some actors come to enjoy systemic advantages that give them the ability to realize their particular interests over and against competing interests.

Moreover, it goes too far to say that the shape of cities is determined exclusively by individuals acting in their self-interest. In fact, as seen in the case of Santa Cruz, it is almost always necessary for individuals to organize and accept the decisions of the organization as a whole in order to make it possible for projects to go forward. For example, for the downtown to be fully rebuilt in a way that benefited all landowners and the city government, individual owners who wanted to hold off on their rebuilding plans had to be pressured by their fellow landowners, embarrassed by newspaper accounts, or even coerced by government. Put another way, all interest groups, classes, and cities have power structures within them.

Based on our study of Santa Cruz and the community power structure literature, we do not think there is anything that is right about public choice theory. It denies the importance of distributive power in the name of purportedly fair and rational economic and political markets that naturally check and tame power. It thereby attributes power to individual citizens through their consumer purchases that in fact belongs to the growth coalitions that own the land and buildings. It rightly says that the participants in urban politics have relatively fixed preferences, but it misunderstands those preferences, especially when it comes to neighborhoods. It ignores the active role of local growth coalitions and instead attributes the push for growth to market forces and sensible citizens. It denies the agency of local government officials on both economic development and social welfare issues, turning them into simply sensitive responders to the signals from economic markets and voters. It mistakenly says that policy drives politics. It reduces conflict to mere allocative issues even while it marginalizes what are in fact vital issues from the point of view of neighborhood use values. As Smith (1988) cogently argues, public choice theory does not adequately address the role of politics at the local level, dismissing local politics as analytically irrelevant and relegating city governments to serving the interests of capital.

THE LIMITATIONS OF REGIME THEORY

Although regime theory has many advantages over Marxist theory and public choice theory, and shares some similarities with growth coalition theory, we think it also suffers from severe limitations. First, and most generally, the relationship between collective and distributive power is not well theorized.

Although regime theory notes that the two types of power are usually inter-twined (Stone 2006), it does not provide an account of their origin and rela-tionship that explains why they always operate simultaneously. Further, it does not explain why distributive power is always at the forefront in studying the power relationships in any large-scale society.

Historically, we believe an understanding of power that transcends the lim-its of regime theory begins with the fact that collective power originally grew out of cooperation in pursuing common goals, as most theorists, including regime theorists, would agree. This point can be seen most clearly in small hunting and gathering societies when hunting parties are organized, when communal gatherings are called in an attempt to defuse interpersonal dis-putes that threaten to rip apart the whole group, when the men band together to do battle with rival groups or clans, and when rituals of religious solidarity are performed to deal with anxiety, guilt, and the fear of death. The claim that these four main forms of collective power—economic, political, militaristic, and religious—can become the basis for distributive power is supported by the fact that even in small-scale societies they are often used to exclude or sub-jugate women. The secretive men's huts in which religion is practiced often exclude women on pain of gang rape or death, and men will band together to kill women who resist changes in the social order (Gregor 1985; Sanday 1990).

Generally speaking, however, these collectivities do not become the basis for distributive power in hunting and gathering or tribal-level societies. Collective power is still ascendant because the members of those societies are able to be surprisingly and subtly vigilant against would-be power seekers, who are con-trolled through gossip, chastisement, shunning, and, if necessary, assassination. Contrary to the image of these societies as lacking a power structure, it seems more plausible that they have an "inverted power structure" in which the "rank-and-file" are able to maintain an egalitarian social structure through col-lective actions against potential dominators (Boehm 1999).

When the level of organization reaches a large enough scale over a long enough period of time within the context of accumulating material abun-dance, a division of labor develops that can further increase an organization's collective power, based on a specialization of function at all of its levels. Yet this division of labor is "deceptive," as Michael Mann puts it, because "those who occupy supervisory and coordinating positions have an immense organiza-tional superiority over the others" (1986b, 6–7). As many theorists of varying persuasions have noted, those at the top can then turn the organization into a power base for themselves because of the information and material resources they control, their ability to reshape the structure of the organization, their power to hire and fire underlings, and their opportunities to make alliances with other organizational leaders. They then use these resources to develop barriers that make it harder for people outside the organization to participate in the governance of the society in general (see Gaventa 1980 for an excellent synthesis of how these various processes are carried out).

At this point, the followers are organizationally outflanked, no longer able to maintain the more informal inverted power structures that kept pre-civilized societies largely egalitarian (Boehm 1999). They become trapped in the form of society called "civilization." The gradual process by which civilization develops can be seen at about its midpoint through the ways tribal chiefs come to power by using a variety of strategies to create chiefdoms, weaving together the growing economic, military, and religious power bases in unique ways (Earle 1997). Indeed, sociologists sometimes use the image of a "caged" population as part of their definition of civilization, which starts with a network of economic activities that generate large surpluses coordinated and stored in religious institutions (Mann 1986b; Weber 1904/1958, 181). These religious centers soon evolve into city-states that have somewhat separate religious and "state" institutions—and then into empires of domination that have large armies.

Once these power bases are intertwined, they have even more potential to greatly increase collective power in the way emphasized by regime theory. This is most directly observed in the case of state and military organizations, which can increase the collective power of economic organizations through activities as varied as protecting trade routes and making it possible to employ coerced or slave labor. In other words, because of the collective power that can be generated by hierarchical organizations, there is going to be a power structure of some shape or form once societies reach the level of a civilization. That is—and this is where regime theory is too sanguine—the mobilization of greater collective power comes to depend on the resolution of prior questions about distributive power arrangements. Who has power over whom has to be settled within organizations, cities, and nation-states before collective power can be exercised in any useful way, as the collapse of ruling classes, armies, and states over the centuries amply demonstrates.

The emergent necessity of resolving distributive power conflicts before co-operative power can be effective leads to the conclusion that, contrary to regime theory, it is not possible to distinguish between "social production" and "social conflict" models in either urban political governance or at the level of modern nation-states. Nor does the ongoing development of the two types of power lead to any firm generalizations about the relationship between them. Although distributive and collective power usually increased hand-in-hand in the first several thousand years of Western civilization, this is not always the case. According to Mann (1993), for example, the economic transformations of the eighteenth and nineteenth centuries had a large impact on collective economic power, but none on distributive power, whereas the increased collective power of states during the same time period actually helped to decrease the distributive power of political elites. More generally, Mann (1993, 16) finds a "surprising continuity of distributive power" in Western Europe and the United States between 1760 and 1914 despite the vast increases in collective power, except that women began to gain power in relation to men (Mann 1986a).

Based on our analysis of how hierarchical organizations and nation-states develop, we believe regime theory is also incorrect when it concludes that the difference between a social production model and a social control model involves the degree to which the consent of the rest of the population can be manipulated. Instead, we believe that most people go along with the prevailing power arrangements because they lack an organizational base from which they could reasonably contest them. Mann speaks for many power analysts when he says that the issue is not primarily one of "values" or even force: "The masses comply because they lack collective organization to do otherwise, because they are embedded within collective and distributive power organizations controlled by others" (1986b, 7). This is a domination theory, but it allows for the fact that ordinary people will act in what they understand as their interests when they have the opportunity. For much of Western history in the past thousand years, this has meant mob actions, riots, and social movement challenges to authority that sometimes lead to small improvements (Piven 2007). Contrary to theorists who believe that powerless people usually do not understand their true interests, we argue that people are not ideologically dominated or hoodwinked. Although powerless people may sometimes underestimate their ability to resist because of cultural memories of past defeats, or a misdiagnosis of current trends, they generally understand the situation they are in and the odds they face (Gaventa 1980).

Recalling our analysis of the reconstruction in Santa Cruz after the 1989 earthquake, our general point about the simultaneous operation of collective and distributive power is supported in great detail by the way in which events unfolded there. From the outset, leaders within the downtown business community were plotting to use the catastrophe as a way to regain political power, while the progressives quickly began to meet informally to thwart those aims. But the two sides were nevertheless able to work together just enough, after the delays caused in part by their power conflicts, to rebuild the downtown. The size and shape of downtown Santa Cruz after the earthquake should first and most centrally be understood as the outcome of a power struggle.

General theoretical differences on the concept of power aside, regime theory's most central specific claim in terms of constructing governing coalitions is that preferences are not necessarily fixed beforehand. Instead, it suggests that they arise and evolve as the potential coalition partners interact, educate each other about their interdependence, and make compromises. This argument is called into question because there is little evidence that preferences changed on either side during earthquake construction. Instead, fixed preferences were temporarily set aside when it became clear to the antagonists that neither side could take advantage of the crisis to gain greater power. However, no new preferences arose from the ongoing interactions between leaders of the growth coalition and the progressives as they did battle over specific issues within the public-private partnership called Vision Santa Cruz. Taken to its extreme, regime theory's emphasis on fluid preferences would mean that rents and profits are optional for developers and capitalists, and that people's attachment to their homes and neighborhoods aren't very deep after all.

Because regime theory denies fixed preferences and instead focuses on the fluid processes through which institutional cooperation is brought about, it does not have any underlying dynamism and lacks insight into the inherent tension between exchange values and use values that is fully demonstrated in Stone's (1976, 1989) own research on Atlanta. A similar point is made in another recent comparison of competing urban theories. Altshuler and Luberoff note that Stone's 1989 study of Atlanta shows that "the business partners are clearly dominant" despite his "disclaimer of interest in whether some groups have more power than others" (2003, 68–69). Thus, regime theory's emphasis on collective power, even though the theory retains a distributive dimension within it, does not leave it with a way to recognize dominance on the many occasions when it does occur. It is therefore best described as an institutional analysis because it focuses on "an institutional form rather than making a substantive statement of who holds power and what they do with it" (Molotch 1999, 249).

The conflict over preferences that are fixed and enduring points to another weakness in regime theory. Although it recognizes the limits of an argument claiming that business has a privileged position in a capitalist economy because it has the near-exclusive right to invest resources in new productive facilities, it nonetheless overstates the importance of the "systemic power" that business thereby enjoys. As this account of Santa Cruz, along with the history of many other cities, shows business does have to fight to hold on to its preferences, and it sometimes loses. Even in the case of the rebuilding process after the earthquake, it is doubtful whether the Vision Santa Cruz partnership would have been created if local business leaders had not acted in ways that indicated that they believed they occupied a privileged position based on the systemic power created by virtue of ownership and control of the investment function. It is even less likely that progressive political leaders would have deferred to the growth coalition in the rebuilding process to the extent that they did if business leaders had not mobilized almost immediately after the earthquake.

We therefore agree with Imbroscio when he argues in a critique of regime theory that "the determinants of urban economic development policy are largely political," and that it is "ideology and raw political power, not the need to respond to economic constraints, that shapes development policy" (2004, 23). He is suggesting that challenging the distributive power exercised by growth coalitions is more critical to achieving policy justice than trying to enhance civic cooperation and governing capacity. The organized efforts of business inside and outside the electoral arena are much more essential than regime theory allows. While it acknowledges that business is not a "passive partner in governance, simply resting on its structural laurels," it mainly views business elites as promoting "civic cooperation" through creating business organizations and supporting nonprofit organizations (Stone 1989, 231–233). Regime theory thereby underemphasizes the degree to which instrumental political actions by organized business do matter, although not to nearly the degree that Marxist theory and public choice theory do. This point is best shown by the way in which the Santa Cruz growth coalition reshaped both local election rules and local government twice in the first half of the twentieth century.

The final major problem in regime theory is that it does not explain what it takes as a given: the relative weakness of American urban governments. The theory does not incorporate the fact that local governments are weak and in need of coalition partners in good part because growth coalitions have worked very hard to keep them that way, as the history of the nationwide municipal reform movement and the charter reforms in Santa Cruz in 1911 and 1948 graphically illustrate. Working within an electoral system designed during the Progressive Era by urban policy planners to favor business interests, elected officials in most American cities are first of all faced with a minimum tax base as a result of the antitax ideology of both the corporate community and the growth coalitions. Next they have to turn to corporate-funded urban think tanks for policy suggestions and expert staffing, and then they have to deal with a parallel structure of nonprofit organizations that provides many social services with the help of yearly grants from foundations.

Nor is control of city government all that matters. State governments provide the charters for cities and can change the laws under which they operate (Frug 1999, Chapter 1). On some of the occasions when growth coalitions have been stymied at the local level by their opponents, they have been able to go to the state level to obtain the local changes or resources they desire. For example, historian Samuel Hays (1964) shows how the elites of Pittsburgh went to the state government during the Progressive Era when they lost at the local level on city charter reform. We also saw examples in Santa Cruz when the insurance lobby pushed for state-level legislation that made it impossible for cities to sell home insurance to their citizens and when the cable television industry obtained federal legislation in 1984 that made it much more difficult for local governments to take possession of cable TV franchises. Faced with the strong rent control laws in Berkeley and Santa Monica, which saved renters tens of millions of dollars each year in both cities, the growth coalitions went to the state government and finally succeeded, after fifteen years, in passing legislation stipulating that rents had to be allowed to rise to the market level every time a rental property was vacated, which essentially gutted the local ordinances (Barton 1998; Gilderbloom 2008, Chapter 4).

The weaknesses of regime theory are also apparent when it is compared with growth coalition theory on the four possible types of urban regimes it recognizes (Stone 1993, 21):

- developmental regimes
- middle-class progressive regimes
- lower-class opportunity expansion regimes
- maintenance regimes.

Development regimes, as the name implies, try to expand and develop the city. They need large amounts of resources and therefore usually involve the local business community because of its systemic power. This is the kind of regime that flourished in the years between 1945 and 1980 in most cities, including Atlanta, where city officials and the local growth coalition entered into an alliance that benefited both of them (Dreier, Mollenkopf, and Swanstrom 2004; Stone 1976, 1989). For these cities, then, there is little difference between regime theory and growth coalition theory as to who governs and why (Logan, Whaley, and Crowder 1997).

Middle-class progressive regimes are "slow-growth" administrations that seek "such measures as environmental protection, historic preservation, affordable housing, quality of architectural design, affirmative action, and linkage funds for various social purposes"; to achieve such ends, they require "a more complex form of regulation" than do development regimes, and also an element of coercion (Stone 1993, 19). There is a need for the exercise of "power over," at least to some degree, in order to advance the agenda of progressive regimes over and against the interests of business leaders. The relative strength of the political sector in progressive regimes derives from the ability of political leaders to forge an electoral coalition of nonbusiness elements, that is, the same neighborhood groups, environmental activists, and other use-value proponents that growth coalition theory identifies. These progressive-environmental-neighborhood coalitions are most successful in small or middle-size cities, or in university towns where faculty families and students are willing to mobilize to oppose one or another noxious encroachment. That is, they take a form that makes more sense within the framework of growth coalition theory because it predicts their political goals.

Lower-class opportunity expansion regimes, which require even more mass mobilization and electoral vigilance than middle-class progressive regimes, turn out to be "largely hypothetical" (Stone 1993, 20). That is, they do not exist, which fits better with growth coalition theory than regime theory. Stone (1993, 20) says there have been "hints of such regimes," for example, during the mayoralty of Harold Washington in Chicago, but that these hints have occurred only "from time to time" and have not been sustained. In the Chicago case, it is also noteworthy that this coalition depended in good part on one person's vision, experience, energy, and personality, and that it could not be sustained when he died unexpectedly in 1987. Nevertheless, some of his supporters were able to carry the ideas he championed for economic development into the Democratic Party machine—embedded in the city growth coalition—that has governed the city ever since (Rast 1999).

Regime theory also allows for the possibility of developing lower-class opportunity expansion regimes through community-based organizations, but this does not fit with the fact that most of these organizations are part of an urban social control network that was developed in the 1950s and 1960s. They were created by corporate and foundation leaders when inner-city residents began to resist the wholesale destruction of their neighborhoods caused by the massive urban renewal program that local growth coalitions instigated in order to clear land for the expansion of downtowns, universities, and cultural institutions (Domhoff 2005a). With the Ford Foundation taking the lead, this new network evolved in a step-by-step fashion through reaching out first to African American activists who were trying to stop urban renewal and then to white neighborhoods that were agitated by the influx of African American migrants from the South. Most of these organizations took the form of nonprofit community-based organizations, which employed local activists and social workers to provide social services, job training, affordable housing, support for neighborhood groups, or advocacy for tenant's rights.

More generally, the Ford Foundation and its allies, including dozens of corporate foundations, used grants and tax breaks to create a parallel government of nonprofit organizations controlled by private interests to provide social services to the inner city. It is an arrangement that can deliver needed resources to the inner city and at the same time minimize a direct role by local government agencies. Then, too, this privately funded network is less expensive for property owners than paying local taxes because nonprofits pay their employees lower wages than do city governments. Since most of these organizations have to apply for funding every year or two, they also can be eliminated more easily than government agencies (Domhoff 2005a; Funicello 1993).

In addition, many community-based organizations are by now as much demobilizers as mobilizers from the perspective of local activists. They draw would-be activists into helping individuals with their day-to-day problems and into writing grants to raise money to keep the organization going, which leave little time for organizing and protesting (Shaw 1999, Chapter 5). "School compacts," in which those who graduate from high school are guaranteed a job or are assured financial support for college, are also mentioned by regime theorists as the kind of program that might be part of a lower-class opportunity regime (Stone 1993, 21). But such programs are few and far between, and are just as likely to come from corporations and their affiliated foundations as from the community or local government (Zweigenhaft and Domhoff 2003, especially 164–173).

Lower-class opportunity regimes also seem unlikely for a reason emphasized within regime theory: a group has to have some resources of interest to city officials if it is to have a chance of becoming part of a regime. Low-income groups are thus likely to be ignored and to have no choice but to protest in some way when their neighborhoods are slated for redevelopment for commercial purposes or high-income housing. In fact, the history of the power struggles in cities where insurgents have had some success stands as a refutation of regime theory's claims about the prime importance of thinking in terms of collective power when strategizing about progressive social change for low-income groups. Those who oppose a growth coalition's incursions into neighborhoods via freeways and high-rises have little or nothing to offer the local government and are faced with a power structure that wants the land they live on for the purpose of gaining enormous wealth without providing anywhere close to the amount of economic compensation that would be included in a more cooperative or partnership strategy. Low-income and inner-city neighborhoods therefore come to believe that they have to resist with litigation, demonstrations, civil disobedience, and ballot initiatives. A growth coalition does not give an inch until the activists raise the costs of compliance and win set-asides, payment of moving costs for renters, linkages, and other mitigations.

Even electing liberal officials and having a vigilant electorate usually is not enough because people who don't own property are readily dominated in the economic and political spheres by those with greater economic resources and direct access to elected and appointed government officials. For example, people without income-producing property or home ownership are in real trouble if they lose jobs or economic support from the government. They are also hurt badly if they lose their neighborhood networks, which are vital for job information, moral support, and even material support in tough times (e.g., Venkatesh 2006).

In addition, the same property-owning people who want to push low-income people out of their neighborhoods very often support those politicians in Washington who resist any increase in the minimum wage and are out to cut welfare benefits, including any rent supplements for poor people. As we noted in our discussion of Santa Cruz in the 1980s, local growth coalitions are quite literally helping to create homelessness through the combination of policies they advocate at the local, state, and national levels. In a country that has seen millions of people forced from their homes in the inner cities since the 1950s, and massive increases in homelessness since the Reagan Republicans took over in 1980, the issue of distributive power is far more fundamental than collective power.

These points are demonstrated in the case of San Francisco, which regime theory (Stone 2006) sees as an example of the right kind of progressive change based on a book on the successes of activists in that city between 1965 and 1992 (DeLeon 1992). But the story of what happened in San Francisco actually shows that it is not a mistake for those with few resources to respond by trying to raise the costs of compliance (Beitel 2004; Domhoff 2005c). Only after the San Francisco growth coalition was battled to a near standstill on several issues—thanks to marches, disruption, lawsuits, and ballot initiatives—did it enter into a coalition of sorts with the neighborhood, environmental, and progressive activists on some issues (Hartman 2002). In that sense, it had been "educated" by the successes of the activists. It then agreed to allow the activists to build affordable housing through nonprofit community development corporations, and it met with the activists before projects were underway in order to bargain over mitigations and exactions (Beitel 2004). But to create this quasi-coalition, the activists had to decrease the growth coalition's ability to intensify land use at will. And even after all this effort, the San Francisco growth coalition has been able to build new projects at a record pace ever since DeLeon's 1992 book appeared (Beitel 2004; Domhoff 2005c).

Regime theory's final category, maintenance regimes, is labeled as the least dynamic and interesting because such regimes are not trying to bring about expansion or change. Since they simply carry out the routine functions of city government, they need fewer resources from the private sector. Regime theorists believe that such regimes were frequent occurrences in the past, but it is doubtful that very many have existed for very long, if they exist at all. There are always new ways to intensify land use, starting with new and taller buildings that replace old structures, or else new tourism and entertainment gimmicks. Moreover, contrary to the idea that they are mere maintenance regimes, local leaders of seemingly dead cities spring into action when they see what they think might be a growth opportunity they could actually compete for, such as a prison or a waste disposal facility. In so doing, they express little or no concern for the actual benefits or the fiscal or ecological consequences of such projects. When cities fail in the pursuit of even the most noxious and objectionable of growth opportunities, they may be slated for the status of ghost towns, the ultimate evidence of failure by a growth coalition.

In summary, regime theory downplays the large degree to which distributive power shapes and directs collective power. Although regime theorists fully understand that growth coalitions are out to make money, they do not stress that profits and rents are a necessity for capitalists and growth entrepreneurs, who can lose market share, suffer major financial losses, or go bankrupt if they do not constantly compete for the most that can be gotten. Regime theory agrees that neighborhoods often protest, but the theory does not build on the depth of neighborhood sentiments or start with the deep conflict between exchange values and use values. It agrees that growth coalitions have to play an active role, but because of its emphasis on systemic power, it does not fully appreciate how essential it is for them to exert power constantly in political and policy arenas to maintain their dominant position. Regime theory agrees that insurgent politics can matter, but it is too optimistic about the likelihood that growth coalitions or government officials will enter into alliances with neighborhoods and progressives without a sustained demonstration of disruptive and/or electoral power by their opponents. The theory lacks precisely what growth coalition theory provides: a substantive grounding of urban political conflict in the commodified nature of land in the United States and a larger historical context that explains why local governments are weak.

EXTENDING GROWTH COALITION THEORY

Although we think that growth coalition theory provides the best starting point for understanding urban power structures and urban conflict, we also believe that a study such as ours shows how the theory can be further developed on both the exchange-value and the use-value sides of the equation. It also can be strengthened by incorporating the insights of power structure research.

First, even though growth coalition theory recognizes that there can be disagreements and divisions within the growth coalition, it tends to argue that these differences typically involve disputes over where new developments will be sited within a given locale. Such disputes are usually portrayed as relatively minor matters compared to the broad consensus within the growth coalition on the fact that all its members benefit from growth, which signals that the city is "on the move," raises everyone's land values, and leads to increased spending on infrastructure for attracting more outside investments. But as our case study suggests, the idea that the growth coalition is more cohesive than schismatic can be problematic.

This is first shown by the long-standing tensions in Santa Cruz between the pro-tourism and balanced growth forces in the forty years between 1890 and 1930, which led to policy and political disagreements that were only suspended in the face of seeming threats such as those posed by the Union Labor ticket in 1904 and the Socialists in 1911. Arguments over rebuilding after the earthquake also make this point, whether it was tensions between landowners and store owners in the downtown area, the annoyance with Rittenhouse for delays in rebuilding his properties, or the conflict within the growth coalition over the Factory Outlet proposal. All of these examples suggest that cohesion has to be created and enforced through organizations to a greater degree than growth coalition theory tends to emphasize, as nicely demonstrated in work on transportation issues in California in the 1970s (Whitt 1982). It is our view that the cohesive front presented to city government and the general public is often enforced by the faction within the growth coalition that wins control of local government and imposes its will. Once such a faction has won the day, it is rare for the losing side to make an alliance with neighborhood or environmental groups because it has so little in common with them. Instead, it accepts its secondary status within the growth coalition. In short, there will inevitably be a power structure to enforce internal discipline and fend off opponents. In that regard, Hunter (1953) and Mills (1956) remain as relevant today as they were in the 1950s.

Turning to the use-value part of the equation, it first needs to be noted that in recent decades homeowners in some neighborhoods have not always focused exclusively on use values. With the increase in housing prices after World War II and the booms in California and the Northeast in the late 1970s and late 1990s, many homeowners rightly came to realize that their property can be a significant source of financial wealth if they can hold on to it long enough, not least because of various tax advantages accorded to homeowners and the ability to obtain equity-based loans from banks (Gilderbloom 2008, Chapter 9). By the 1980s, two-thirds of what the great majority of Americans have by way of wealth, over and beyond consumer durables, consisted of the equity in their homes, so it is not surprising that many homeowners now talk about their homes in terms of exchange values as well as use values (Domhoff 2006a, Figures 2b and 3; Wolff 2000, 2004).

For the most part, of course, there is little conflict between these two goals for homeowners: as we noted in the first chapter and underscore here, the exchange value of a house is in good part related to the use values of the neighborhood in which it is located. In a city like Santa Cruz, where the growth of the university and the attractiveness of the locale for well-paid employees in Silicon Valley led to a steady increase in home values from the mid-1970s to mid-2006, many longtime homeowners can look forward to "cashing out" and retiring to less expensive areas, where they are able to buy a house or condo at a lower price and put several hundred thousand dollars into other investments.

Still, the idea that housing always and everywhere generates increasing exchange values for homeowners has to be taken with a grain of salt because it is part of the hype and propaganda from one part of the growth coalition, real estate salespeople. Whatever the actual case may be in any given region or era, the National Association of Realtors always claims that buying a home is an ideal investment. Even in 2007 and 2008, when housing prices were falling precipitously almost everywhere, the Realtors insisted that it was a perfect time to buy a house, adding the claim that the value of houses doubled every ten years in the United States (Leonhardt 2007; Story 2008). However, when inflation, the real estate broker's fee, inspection costs, and other costs are factored into the equation, it is not at all certain that home purchases are the extraordinary investment that the National Association of Realtors makes them out to be. Between 2005 and 2007, for example, new buyers lost money, and by 2008 many of them started to lose their houses; they would have been better off to pay rent and invest the money that went into the down payment and closing costs in stocks and bonds. More generally, if housing prices are rising at 5 percent a year, buying makes more sense than renting after five years. But if the rate of increase is only 2.5 percent a year, buying is not a better deal for twenty-five years (Leonhardt 2007). Such calculations come as a surprise to people because they usually do not take the rate of inflation into account when they think about housing values (Shiller 2005, Chapter 2).

The questionable nature of claims about the exceptional exchange values available through owning a home also can be seen in studies of housing prices over decades. Based on an index that is a composite of housing prices in ten major metropolitan areas, including Boston, New York, Miami, Chicago, Las Vegas, San Diego, and San Francisco, which were all hot growth areas in the last two decades of the twentieth century, homes purchased in January 1989, a peak year, could not be sold at a break-even price until January 1998, which was a long time to wait for those homeowners who were interested in exchange values (Norris 2007). Taking an even longer perspective, housing values declined for most of the years between 1895 and 1945, followed by a postwar boom that leveled off by 1950. The rapid increases in home prices in the mid-1970s and mid-1980s were followed by declines to the baseline levels for the 1960s when inflation is taken into account (Shiller 2005, Chapter 2 and 120–125).

Generally speaking, a decline of about 10 percent in the value of a home wipes out most of the equity for most people, which is now well understood after the decline of 15 to 20 percent in prices in the housing market in major cities from its peak in July 2006 to June 2008 (e.g., Bernasek 2007; Baker 2008b). When inflation is factored into the equation, there was a 23 percent loss for homeowners in twenty major cities during this time period, which is nearly $5 trillion ($70,000 per homeowner) (Baker 2008a). Thus, growth coalition theory seems to be on the right track in claiming that over the long run use values are the primary issue when it comes to homes and neighborhoods.

Turning to the role of neighborhoods in urban governance, we think growth coalition theory is correct in arguing that they are usually too narrowly focused or divided among themselves to play a sustained role unless they include many upscale homeowners. Nevertheless, the theory needs to be expanded to include the fact that middle-income and low-income neighborhoods can enjoy some success, or even become part of governing coalitions, if they gain activist allies from social movements. This need for sustained leadership and coalition partners was solved in many cities in the 1970s, when neighborhood leaders were joined by veteran activists of the civil rights, environmental, and antiwar movements (e.g., Capek and Gilderbloom 1992; Whalen and Flacks 1989), a point also noted in Molotch's (1976) first statement of growth coalition theory. This was the case not only in Santa Cruz but in many other cities as well, including Berkeley, Burlington, Madison, Santa Barbara, San Francisco, and Santa Monica (Clavel 1986; DeLeon 1992). However, as we explain in the next section, it is not easy to sustain such a coalition because most social movement activists focus on class-based and social justice issues, whereas neighborhood and environmental activists have a primary if not sole concern with the use values of land.

CAN MORE BE DONE?

One of the strongest features of growth coalition theory is that it explains how use-value coalitions can sometimes defeat growth coalitions on neighborhood and environmental issues with the right mixture of strategy and leadership. In the first statement of growth coalition theory, Molotch (1976) noted that neighborhood and environmental leaders in several cities were able to stop developments through the brandishing of careful cost-benefit analyses, which show that leaving things as they are sometimes makes more sense than development. The most salient case at the time concerned Palo Alto, California, the home of Stanford University, where the development of the city's attractive foothills was stopped on the basis of a cost-benefit analysis and a faculty-based environmental and neighborhood movement.

Because of the successes in Palo Alto and several other cities in the 1970s, Logan and Molotch (1987, 293), pointing to the social costs of development that usually go unexamined, argue that there is room for activists to maneuver because there is no inevitable economic logic that justifies specific developments. The many positive outcomes for neighborhood use values institutionalized in Santa Cruz are further evidence for their point, as are the policies crafted in several other progressive cities in the 1980s (Clavel 1986). These victories are sometimes downplayed by noting that they often happen in highly desirable cities with many high-income and professional neighborhoods. But in fact such cross-class neighborhood coalitions set precedents and limits that are useful for activists in other cities as well as preserving use values for all the local neighborhoods. They set standards that strengthen the negotiating position of cities that are somewhat lower in the status hierarchy of places (Molotch 1998, 67).

These victories also point to what Logan and Molotch (2007, xxii–xxiii) advocate as the starting point for any use-value coalition at the local level: just say no from the outset. Assume that any new development is likely to have more hidden economic and environmental costs, along with nonquantifiable psychic costs, than the landowners and developers claim. And contrary to the claim that bigger is always better when it comes to cities, there may be optimum sizes for urban areas in terms of use values. In fact, most Americans say they would like to live in medium-sized cities, which suggests that growth controls in large cities would also be of use to those smaller cities that would benefit from some growth (Logan and Molotch 2007, 97).

Once a neighborhood-based coalition is able to say no to specific developments, it is in a position to enhance neighborhood use values by forcing commercial landowners and developers to include the amenities, mitigations, and exactions that would make the project acceptable if it is decided that a modified form of the project would be worth having. Such demands have the advantage that they do not require a battle in the political process over taxation that might lead to legislation at the state level that forbids some taxes or limits property taxes.

Such measures hardly add up to a program for widespread progressive social change, however. There are limits to what can be accomplished without creating new tax sources or raising tax rates. The squeeze on cities is further exacerbated by the increasing burdens they face for providing social services ever since the Reagan administration initiated cuts in federal funding for cities. And when cities try to create new taxes or start income-producing business ventures, then statewide or nationally organized business groups can override them by going to the state or federal government, as they generally did in the face of progressive initiatives in the 1970s and 1980s. It therefore becomes necessary to ask if there might be ways for local progressives to transcend the limits of local politics by creating a nationwide movement.

Based on past experience, we think it would take great ingenuity and new strategies to develop a nationwide coalition of locally based progressives, which would face strong resistance from the national corporate community as well as local growth coalitions. There are three basic challenges: (1) build a program that addresses both local-level use values and the redistributive class-based issues concerning wages, health care, and social security that are central to national politics; (2) develop political leaders who can represent the movement and its program in the electoral arena at both the local and the national levels; and (3) create a political strategy for working within the national electoral arena that supports and reinforces social movements.

We do not presume to know the specifics of a unifying program, nor would there be space here to present it if we did. But we do think there are two basic principles that should be the starting point for any progressive program. First, the challenge should not be framed in terms of classes and class conflict. Second, the program should be framed in terms of socializing markets—embedding them within an egalitarian social system and strong government oversight—rather than in terms of socialism.

Although research on social movements shows that an "us versus them" framing is crucial in mobilizing opposition to the extant power arrangements, any framing of "them" that uses categories from which individuals cannot escape—race, gender, sexual orientation, or in this instance social class—is a mistake because it creates a self-fulfilling prophecy and overlooks the possibility that people can change their political attitudes (Wright 2001). National power struggles often revolve around classes and class conflict, but it does not follow that political conflict should be framed in terms of social classes. Politics is about values, coalitions, and gaining political power, not classes, so the conflict should be framed as one between those who do and do not share the values and program put forward by the progressive coalition. The "in-group"—"us"—should be defined as all those who come to embrace the program of the progressive movement, and the out-group should be all those who oppose such changes. If the challenge is framed in this way, a progressive coalition has a chance to win over the moderates, neutrals, and independents who currently accept the power structure. This approach might even attract dissident members of the ownership class who transcend their class interests—and in the process become valuable in legitimating the progressive movement to those in the middle of the class structure who are hesitant to climb on board.

Framing politics in terms of class categories is first of all a mistake because members of the "working class" tend to take on all virtue in the minds of left activists, and those outside that class are ignored or demonized. Moreover, arguments often break out among leftist theorists as to who qualifies as a member of the working class. The small shop owners and independent craftsmen who were part of the Socialist Party in Santa Cruz in the early twentieth century, for example, would have been dismissed as "petty bourgeois" by many Marxists in the 1970s.

Conducting politics within a class conflict framework also fails because it does not appeal to most everyday working people. Average Americans want to break down class distinctions, not heighten them. They do not like to think of themselves in terms of their class identity, which immediately reminds them that they are not as well off and respected as they would like to be. Finally, a class framing for a progressive movement that includes a focus on the national level would conflict with the non-class framing that proved to be successful at the local level in Santa Cruz and other cities. One of the strengths of coalitions based on neighborhood and environmental use-values is that they are able to bypass or mute the differences in income levels—and race and ethnicity—among neighborhoods. A successful progressive movement at the national level would need to do the same.

Thus, the civil rights movement provides a better model for social movements in the United States because it was based on a more open-ended framing of the conflict by refusing to define "whites" as the enemy, but only "racists" and "bigots." Racists and bigots included most whites in the South at that time, and plenty of whites in the North as well, so there was a clear opposition, but at the same time there was room for pro-integration whites. Drawing on the Judeo-Christian religious tradition, the movement was able to incorporate the concepts of forgiveness, redemption, and conversion in the service of strategic nonviolence to forge a black-white coalition. By opening its doors to people who believed in equal rights for African Americans whatever their class, race, religion, or previous beliefs, the movement was able to use these concepts to make it permissible for people to change their attitudes without violating their self-images as sensible and decent people. In similar fashion, if the kind of "cross-class" coalitions that were necessary in Santa Cruz and other progressive cities in the 1970s and 1980s are going to be assembled at the national level in the twenty-first century, then it makes sense to begin with a political framing of the "us versus them" issue (see Domhoff 2003, 65–67, for a more complete statement of the preceding argument in support of a political framing).

In explaining the progressives' success in Santa Cruz in the late 1970s and early 1980s, we stressed the important role of socialist-feminist activists inspired by the vision of an egalitarian socialist society, that is, a society in which income-producing property is publicly owned and economic markets are replaced by a system of centralized economic planning. However, socialism no longer provides the vision of the future needed by activists because centralized planning does not work for a wide range of economic and sociological reasons and has strong authoritarian tendencies built into it that do not promote freedom.

Central planning first of all fails because no one has been able to design methods to analyze the tremendous amount of information necessary to manage a large-scale economy. It also fails because the large bureaucratic system created to obtain and utilize this information becomes inefficient and corrupt: the planning managers use their positions to feather their own nests, enter into power struggles with each other, and look out for their friends and relatives. Because of their lack of good information and uncertainty about receiving the necessary raw materials, the planning managers have to buy on the black market, cut corners, and cheat in order to meet their production quotas, which increases corruption, destroys morale, and dampens any desire to work better and harder for the sake of the collective good. Waste, corruption, lack of innovation, and environmental degradation were the hallmarks of the Soviet Union, China, and other efforts at central planning (see Domhoff 2003, 42–48, for a full statement of the preceding argument about central planning). Even if managers in centralized planned economies had had enough information to generate optimal plans, and even if there had been enough democratic pressure to keep planning bureaucracies from becoming elitist, the process would have ended up hierarchical and nonparticipatory anyhow because information goes upward in such a system while orders and commands flow downward (Hahnel 2005, 94–106).

The failure of centralized non-market planning as a plausible vision for a better future has meant that progressives have been lacking an energizing vision since at least the 1980s. Although many different progressives have set forth specific policy proposals, they have not been able to agree upon a new set of principles to inspire and guide positive changes in the economic system. The search for an alternative vision is made all the more difficult by the fact that most leftists cannot envision a solution that might involve markets, which are seen as too impersonal and too conducive to competitiveness. Nevertheless, there may be more hope than most leftists assume because it may be possible to socialize markets and use them for egalitarian ends, as suggested in the work of sociologist Diane Elson (2000).

Borrowing from political scientist Charles Lindblom (2000), who also has discussed the possibilities for greater equality and fairness through the market, this approach is best described by the idea of "planning through the market." Contrary to the claims of free-market economists who insist that the market is a self-regulating system that leads to the best possible outcomes on all but a few matters without the guidance of government, research shows that all markets need guidance from government to operate well, and that there is no inevitable trade-off between equality and efficiency or between equality and freedom (e.g., Kuttner 1997; Krugman 1994; Massey 2005; McMillan 2002). More equality might even mean more efficiency, and it can mean more freedom for more people (Bowles and Gintis 1998).

Most important for our purposes here, it may be that markets could be reconstructed by a progressive coalition to make it possible to plan for a more cooperative and egalitarian economic future. As Lindblom argues, "many of us have been on the wrong track in identifying the market system with individualism, as though it could not serve collective purposes or could do so only exceptionally and badly" (2000, 259). He goes on to suggest that the market also can be seen as the "major administrative instrument of the state," which makes progressive planning possible by using four well-known policy tools as carrots and sticks: subsidies, taxes, government purchases, and regulations. In this form of planning, the feedback information is supplied by the price system that is so central to the considerable, but far from perfect, efficiency brought about by markets. Furthermore, Congress, with relatively slight adjustments in its current procedures and goals, could function as the government's elected planning body. According to this way of thinking, then, the big issue is taking political power from the corporate community and the growth coalitions, not trying to create a whole new economy that runs on entirely different principles.

Within the context of Congressional planning through the market, it would be possible for a nationwide progressive program to give cities greater control over their own destinies by breaking the current nexus "between the local tax take and the amount available for local welfare expenditures," which adds up to a "national takeover of welfare, health, and education costs" (Molotch 1998, 65). An expansion of the Earned Income Tax Credit program to include more employees, along with more generous payments to the individuals already covered, would fit well with such a program, as would a national program for full employment and a variety of innovative ways to provide affordable housing for a far larger number of people (Gilderbloom 2008, Chapter 9).

The most important initiative in terms of a national coalition that included the enhancement of local use values as a key part of its program would be state and national laws that give cities greater power to determine their own fate in dealing with developers and corporations. This empowerment strategy could be modeled on various environmental laws, including the mandate for environmental impact reviews, which give some rights and protections to communities. According to a formulation by sociologist Richard Flacks, the "agenda would include establishing national rules requiring the inclusion of community voices in corporate decisions that affect localities, and providing major national resources to support community planning, development, ownership, and control aimed at sustainable local and regional economies" (1995, 262).

Over and beyond the question of a comprehensive progressive program, there is the issue that was solved in Santa Cruz: the blending of movement activism and electoral politics. In the case of Santa Cruz, this problem was in good part solved because several movement activists were able to function well as elected officials. Generally speaking, few activists are able to make this transition to politics because their temperament and experience have led them to believe that their effectiveness is based on taking principled stands against the established political order. Based in part on the Santa Cruz experience, however, we think that encouraging and supporting those rare individuals who can make this transition—and thereby bridge two worlds—is essential. Strong social movements are indeed built by challenging established structures and taken-for-granted ways of going about everyday routines, including the ways in which political officials go about their business, but social movements nonetheless have to produce their own politicians and then find ways to both support and pressure those politicians. It is not a contradiction in terms to vote for progressive politicians and then to picket against them when necessary (e.g., Shaw 1999, 171–177). Movement activists have to appreciate the crucial role progressive elected officials play as go-betweens, as tension reducers, as masters of timing and symbolism, and as people who know when to do battle and when to compromise—to make the most gains possible for their side at any given moment and to be back for the next round.

Developing a progressive economic program that unites a wide range of activists around a combination of use values and redistributive values, and then supporting progressive politicians who can carry the program into the political arena, is a good start. However, it is also necessary to realize that the nature of the electoral rules is a critical factor in shaping a social movement's electoral strategies. At the local level, the electoral arrangements make it possible for activists to run as independents, as part of slates (as in the case of Santa Cruz), or as members of third parties. But at the national level, the long-standing two-party system has to be taken seriously as the structural outcome of a single-member district plurality system that works inexorably toward two pre-electoral coalitions, as shown by systematic cross-national research (Rae 1971; Lipset 1963). The pull is even stronger in the case of the United States because of the importance of presidential elections (Rosenstone, Behr, and Lazarus 1996). The power that goes with the presidency means that anyone who is serious about contending for power cannot afford to allow his or her rivals to win, and third parties are therefore even smaller and more ephemeral in the United States (see Domhoff 2003, Chapter 2, for a summary of evidence).

Nevertheless, most progressives opt for third parties when it comes to electoral politics at the national level. This includes the dozens of highly visible academicians, literary figures, and artists who identify themselves with progressive causes and have an influence on young activists, as seen in the long list of famous supporters for Ralph Nader's presidential campaign on the Green Party ticket in 2000. But third-party campaigns to the left of the Democratic Party create immediate clashes with liberals and moderates while putting the interests of low-income families, feminists, religious minorities, and the environmental movement at risk by helping to elect conservatives. This strategy dooms any progressive attempt to move to the national level from the outset. The failure to take the structure of the electoral system into account, which is sadly ironic given the emphasis most of the academic leftists put on "structure" when it comes to the economy, may be the biggest single reason why the American left has never been able to have a sustained presence at the national level.

The insistence on electoral action through a third party also ignores the evidence that the American two-party party system has been changed by activist efforts, first by instituting party primaries that can be used by insurgent candidates, and then through the Voting Rights Act of 1965, which was won by the civil rights movement. In particular, the Voting Rights Act made it possible for African Americans and their handful of white liberal allies in the South to defeat the worst racists in Democratic Party primaries and drive them into the Republican Party, thereby making a nationwide liberal-labor-left party possible for the first time in American history. Moreover, there is evidence that leftists who challenged in Democratic Party primaries—and rightists who challenged in Republican Party primaries—received a far larger share of the vote than they would have as third-party candidates in regular elections (Domhoff 2006b, 143–145). In fact, all-out ideological campaigns in Republican primaries were one of the key components in the rise of a New Right. We argue that program-based campaigns in Democratic primaries would have the same effect, creating a progressive presence in national politics.

As a result of the legislative changes that created the primary system, "parties" in the usual sense of the term—with the power to accept and reject members, create a party platform, and pick their own candidates—are much weaker than in the past. Parties are in good part government-controlled pathways into elected government office because anyone can register to be a Democrat or Republican, and any party member can run in the party primaries. Winners in the primaries put their coworkers into leadership positions in the party, where they have some autonomy from government. The winners, of course, often have more financial support than the losers, but overcoming the financial odds is no less of a problem, and perhaps more so, for those who run as candidates of third parties on the left.

Moreover, there is a way for progressives to take advantage of these changes and move the Democratic Party in a progressive direction even while disagreeing with mainstream Democrats. They could form a network of clubs within the structural pathway to government labeled "the Democratic Party." In effect, these clubs would be a true party within the Democratic shell, with the ability to sign up members and collect dues from them, develop a platform, and select candidates from within their ranks to run in primaries if and when the circumstances seemed right. The goal of this network would be to transform the Democratic Party through a direct appeal for the allegiance of the party electorate on the basis of the progressive movement's program.

Such clubs would give progressives a distinctive new social identity as well as an organizational base within the electoral arena. Forming a network of clubs also makes it possible for activists to maintain their primary social identities— e.g., as community or civil rights activists, as feminists, as environmentalists— while competing within the Democratic Party. The candidates selected to run in primaries should focus on winning on the basis of the program and make no personal criticisms of their Democratic rivals. Moreover, with rare exceptions progressives should back the winners in the primaries if they lose because any Democrat is usually better than any Republican from a progressive point of view because the Republican Party is controlled by a corporate-conservative coalition that is the sworn enemy of progressivism, liberalism, feminism, the minimum wage, and organized labor. Then, too, Democratic voters are more likely to listen to what progressives have to say if they see them as faithful supporters of the party.

The approach that we recommend has never been tried in a sustained way before. Most activists who entered the Democratic Party in the past did so on a temporary basis or in an attempt to split the party so that a new third party might emerge. Both approaches ensured that the activists would never gain the trust of the party's voting base. At other times, the primary challenges by activists have been based on single issues of overwhelming importance, such as Eugene McCarthy's antiwar challenge in the 1968 primaries. These activists fell away when the issue disappeared.

In suggesting a progressive challenge by a club network operating under the Democratic Party label, we have no illusions that success is guaranteed. And even if this approach worked far better than anything that has been tried in the past by leftists and progressives, there may be limits to what can be achieved without creative new thinking about how to organize the economy. Perhaps these limits can be glimpsed in what has transpired in Canada, which is similar to the United States in its history, values, and economic system but has a parliamentary political structure that leaves room for several parties to emerge.

Because of this difference in government structure, the Canadian party system does include a left-oriented party, the New Democratic Party, that has sometimes controlled the government in one or more provinces and sometimes helped to move the country in a leftward direction by holding the balance of power in parliament. It has been most effective when it played a minority role within a coalition that put the Liberal Party into power, which is roughly akin to creating a liberal-left coalition within the Democratic Party in the United States. However, the limits of the appeal of even the New Democratic Party's mild leftist platform can be seen in the fact that the party usually receives between 12 percent and 18 percent of the national popular vote, and has never exceeded 20.4 percent, which it achieved in 1988.

The Canadian political system makes it possible for average working people to put constraints on the power of the wealthy few, in good part through a large and robust union movement that has an influence within the political arena. But the results are not as dramatic as progressives in the United States might hope. The impact is perhaps best revealed by comparing the United States and Canada on one revealing power indicator, the distribution of privately held wealth. In the United States, the top 10 percent of families now have 69.8 percent of all the privately held wealth, but in Canada the top 10 percent have 53.0 percent, which compares more favorably with two of the most egalitarian northern European countries in terms of wealth distribution, Norway (50.5 percent) and Germany (44.4 percent) (Davies, Shorrocks, and Wolff 2006, Table 9). Figures from the other end of the wealth and income ladder tell the same story: 17 percent of Americans live below the poverty line, second only to Mexico, at 22 percent, among twenty-one developed nations, compared to 11.4 percent for Canada, 8.3 percent for Germany, and 6.4 percent for Norway (Smeeding 2008).

As these wealth and poverty indicators reveal, the owners of income-producing property are far more powerful in the United States than in most other countries where organized workers and elected officials have greater power for a variety of historical and structural reasons, including the nature of the electoral system. At the national level in the United States, a corporate community dominates through several means, including major financial support for moderate and conservative political candidates in both political parties, lobbying by business associations, active opposition to union organizing, and financial and leadership support for the foundations, think tanks, and policy discussion groups that generate major government policies. At the local level, landowners and developers—the heart of the growth coalitions—usually dominate through many of the same methods.

Given the great power exercised by business elites in the United States, Santa Cruz's standing as the leftmost city in the country does not mean that its socialist-feminist, environmental, liberal, and neighborhood activists came anywhere close to realizing the goals that inspired their tireless efforts. Nevertheless, winning as much as they have for as long as they have is an unusual accomplishment, which for us has the added advantage of calling traditional theories of urban politics into question and providing guidance for future progressive activists.

REFERENCES

Alford, Robert, and Eugene Lee. 1968. Voting turnout in American cities. *American Political Science Review* 62:796–813.

Alperovitz, Gar. 2005. *America beyond capitalism: Reclaiming our wealth, our liberty, and our democracy.* New York: Wiley.

Altshuler, Alan, and David Luberoff. 2003. *Mega-projects: The changing politics of urban public investment.* Washington, DC: Brookings Institution.

Applebaum, Richard P. 1978. *Size, growth, and U.S. cities.* New York: Praeger.

Applebaum, Richard P., and John Gilderbloom. 1983. Housing supply and regulation: A study of the rental housing market. *Journal of Applied Behavioral Science* 19:1–18.

Arnold, Sally. 1991. Neighbors organize against Westside Longs. *SCAN Newsletter* (Santa Cruz Action Network), August, 1, 8.

Bach, Eve, Thomas Brom, Julia Estrella, Lenny Goldberg, and Ed Kirschner. 1976. *The cities' wealth.* Washington, DC: Conference on Alternative State and Local Policies.

Baker, Dean. 2008a. Housing market monitor: House price decline accelerates. Center for Economic and Policy Research, May 28. http://www.cepr.net (retrieved June 2, 2008).

———. 2008b. The meltdown lowdown (no. 8). *American Prospect,* May 29. http://www.prospect.org/cs/articles?article=the_meltdown_lowdown_0529 08 (retrieved June 2, 2008).

Barber, Dave. 1982. Still coasting after all these years. *Santa Cruz Express,* April 8, 11–14.

Barnhill, Mark. 1990. Thrift rescue gouges state. *Santa Cruz Sentinel,* September 4, A1, A14.

Barton, Stephen E. 1998. The success and failure of strong rent control in the city of Berkeley, 1978 to 1995. In *Rent control: Regulation and the rental housing market,* ed. W. Dennis Keating, Michael B. Teitz, and Andrejs Skaburskis, 88–109. New Brunswick, NJ: Rutgers University Press.

Beal, Chandra Moira, and Richard A. Beal. 2003. *Santa Cruz Beach Boardwalk: The early years—never a dull moment.* Austin, TX: Pacific Group.

Bean, Walton, and James Rawls. 1983. *California: An interpretive history.* 4th ed. New York: McGraw-Hill.

Beitel, Karl Eugene. 2004. Transforming San Francisco: Community, capital, and the local state in the era of globalization, 1956–2001. PhD diss., University of California, Davis.

Bernasek, Anna. 2007. When does a housing slump become a bust? *New York Times,* June 17, 6.

Boehm, Christopher. 1999. *Hierarchy in the forest: The evolution of egalitarian behavior.* Cambridge, MA: Harvard University Press.

Bowles, Samuel, and Herbert Gintis. 1998. *Recasting egalitarianism: New rules for communities, states, and markets.* New York: Verso Books.

Bowman, Cynthia Grant. 1993. Street harassment and the informal ghettoization of women. *Harvard Law Review* 106:517–580.

Browning, Rufus P., Dale Rogers Marshall, and David H. Tabb. 1984. *Protest is not enough: The struggle of blacks and Hispanics for equality in urban politics.* Berkeley: University of California Press.

Brownlow, Louis. 1958. *A passion for anonymity.* Vol. 2 of *The autobiography of Louis Brownlow.* Chicago: University of Chicago Press.

California Institute of County Government. 1966–1969, 1973, 1976–1977. The California County Fact Book. Sacramento: California Institute of County Government, in conjunction with California State Association of Counties (CSAC).

Capek, Stella, and John Gilderbloom. 1992. *Community versus commodity: Tenants and the American city.* Albany: State University of New York Press.

Caplan, Bryan. 2007. *The myth of the rational voter: Why democracies choose bad politics.* Princeton, NJ: Princeton University Press.

Carnoy, Martin, and Derek Shearer. 1980. *Economic democracy: The challenge of the 1980s.* White Plains, NY: M. E. Sharpe.

Castells, Manuel. 1977. *The urban question.* Cambridge, MA: MIT Press.

———. 1978. *City, class, and power.* New York: Macmillan.

Clavel, Pierre. 1986. *The progressive city: Planning and participation, 1969–1984.* New Brunswick, NJ: Rutgers University Press.

———. 1999. The decline of progressive government in Berkeley, California. *Plurimondi* 1:139–148.

Collins, Robert M. 1981. *The business response to Keynes, 1929–1964.* New York: Columbia University Press.

Committee for Economic Development. 1982. *Public-private partnership: An opportunity for urban communities.* New York: Research and Policy Committee, Committee for Economic Development.

Community Studies Proseminar. 1969. Santa Cruz and the freeway: A study of community attitudes. Santa Cruz: University of California, Santa Cruz.

Cone, David. 1983. How we lost rent control in Santa Cruz. Senior thesis, University of California, Santa Cruz.

Connor, Mike. 2005. Revisioning Santa Cruz. *Metro Santa Cruz,* April 27–May 4, 9, 11–12, 14, 17.

Conroy, William J. 1990. *Challenging the boundaries of reform: Socialism in Burlington.* Philadelphia: Temple University Press.

Cox, Kenneth. 1981. Capitalism and conflict around the communal living space. In *Urbanization and urban planning in capitalist society,* ed. Michael Dear and Allen J. Scott, 431–456. New York: Methuen.

Cummings, Scott, C. Theodore Koebel, and J. Allen Whitt. 1989. Redevelopment in downtown Louisville: Public investments, private profits, and shared risks. In *Unequal partnerships: The political economy of urban redevelopment in postwar America,* ed. Gregory Squires, 202–221. New Brunswick, NJ: Rutgers University Press.

Dahl, Robert A. 1961. *Who governs? Democracy and power in an American city.* New Haven, CT: Yale University Press.

Dancis, Bruce. 1979. Community and electoral politics: An interview with Mike Rotkin and Bruce Van Allen. *Socialist Review* 47:101–118.

Davies, James B., Anthony Shorrocks, and Edward Wolff. 2006. *The world distribution of household wealth.* Helsinki: The World Institute for Development Economics Research.

DeLeon, Richard L. 1992. *Left coast city: Progressive politics in San Francisco, 1975–1991.* Lawrence: University of Kansas Press.

De Neufville, Judith, and Stephen Barton. 1987. Myths and definitions of policy problems: An exploration of home ownership and public-private partnerships. *Policy Sciences* 20:181–206.

Domhoff, G. William. 1978. *Who really rules? New Haven and community power reexamined.* New Brunswick, NJ: Transaction Books.

———. 1983. *Who rules America now?* New York: Simon and Schuster.

———. 2003. *Changing the powers that be: How the left can stop losing and win.* Lanham, MD: Rowman and Littlefield.

———. 2005a. The Ford Foundation in the inner city: Forging an alliance with neighborhood activists. http://sociology.ucsc.edu/whorulesamerica/power/ford_foundation.html (retrieved June 2, 2008).

———. 2005b. The political economy of urban power structures. http://sociology.ucsc.edu/whorulesamerica/power/local.html#economy (retrieved June 2, 2008).

————. 2005c. San Francisco is different: Progressive activists and neighbor-
    hoods have had a big impact. http://www.whorulesamerica.net (retrieved
    June 2, 2008).

————. 2006a. Wealth, income, and power. http://www.whorulesamerica.net (re-
    trieved August 22, 2007).

————. 2006b. *Who rules America? Power, politics, and social change.* 5th ed. New
    York: McGraw-Hill.

Dreier, Peter, John Mollenkopf, and Todd Swanstrom. 2004. *Place matters: Metropol-
    itics for the twenty-first century.* 2nd ed. Lawrence: University Press of Kansas.

Eakins, David. 1966. The development of corporate liberal policy research in the
    United States, 1885–1965. PhD diss., University of Wisconsin, Madison.

————. 1969. Business planners and America's postwar expansion. In *Corpora-
    tions and the Cold War,* ed. David Horowitz, 143–171. New York: Monthly
    Review Press.

Earle, Tim. 1997. *How chiefs come to power: The political economy in prehistory.*
    Stanford, CA: Stanford University Press.

Egan, Timothy. 2005. Ruling sets off tug of war over private property. *New York
    Times,* July 30. http://www.nytimes.com/2005/07/30/national/30property.html
    (retrieved August 10, 2007).

Elkin, Stephen. 1985. Twentieth century urban regimes. *Journal of Urban Affairs*
    7:11–28.

————. 1987. *City and regime in the American republic.* Chicago: University of
    Chicago Press.

Elson, Diane. 2000. Socializing markets, not market socialism. In *The socialist reg-
    ister 2000: Necessary and unnecessary utopias,* ed. Leo Panitch and Colin Leys,
    67–86. London: Merlin.

Feagin, Joe R., and Robert Parker. 1990. *Building American cities: The urban real
    estate game.* Englewood Cliffs, NJ: Prentice-Hall.

Fehliman, Clinton E. 1947. The economic history of Santa Cruz County, Califor-
    nia: 1850–1947. Santa Cruz: University of California, Santa Cruz.

Fisher, Larry. 1982. Housing horrors. *Santa Cruz Express,* February 11, 8–10.

Flacks, Richard. 1971. *Youth and social change.* Chicago: Rand McNally.

————. 1977. Notes on the Hayden campaign. *Socialist Revolution* 7:59–78.

————. 1988. *Making history: The radical tradition in American life.* New York:
    Columbia University Press.

————. 1995. Think globally, act politically: Some notes toward new movement
    strategy. In *Cultural politics and social movements,* ed. Marcy Darnovsky,
    Barbara Epstein, and Richard Flacks, 251–263. Philadelphia: Temple Uni-
    versity Press.

————. 2005. The question of relevance in social movement studies. In *Rhyming
    hope and history: Activists, academics, and social movement scholarship,* ed.

David Croteau, William Hoynes, and Charlotte Ryan, 3–19. Minneapolis: University of Minnesota Press.

Fosler, R. Scott, and Renee A. Berger. ed. 1982. *Public-private partnerships in American cities.* Lexington, MA: Lexington Books.

Friedland, William, and Michael Rotkin. 2003. Academic activists: Community Studies at the University of California, Santa Cruz. In *Community and the world: Participating in social change,* ed. Torry D. Dickinson, 41–62. New York: Nova Science. (Also available in PDF form under the "History and Philosophy of Community Studies" link on the left side of the home page for the Community Studies Program at http://communitystudies.ucsc.edu [Retrieved June 2, 2008.])

Frug, Gerald. 1999. *City making: Building community without building walls.* Princeton, NJ: Princeton University Press.

Funicello, Teresa. 1993. *Tyranny of kindness: Dismantling the welfare system to end poverty in America.* New York: Atlantic Monthly Press.

Gale, Richard 1986. Social movements and the state: The environmental movement, countermovement, and government agencies. *Sociological Perspectives* 29:202–240.

Gaventa, John. 1980. *Power and powerlessness: Quiescence and rebellion in an Appalachian valley.* Chicago: University of Illinois Press.

Gendron, Richard. 1996. Arts and craft: Implementing an arts-based development strategy in a "controlled growth" county. *Sociological Perspectives* 39:539–555.

———. 1998. The fault lines of power: The political economy of redevelopment in a progressive city after a natural disaster. PhD diss., University of California, Santa Cruz.

———. 2006. Forging collective capacity for urban redevelopment: "Power to," "power over," or both? *City and Community* 5:5–22.

Gilderbloom, John I. 2008. *Invisible city: Poverty, housing, and new urbanism.* Austin: University of Texas Press.

Glickman, Paul. 1979. The buying of Santa Cruz, or, the 1977–1978 recall of Santa Cruz County Supervisors Phil Baldwin and Ed Boravatz: An historical analysis. Santa Cruz: University of California, Santa Cruz.

Goodall, Leonard. 1968. *The American metropolis.* Indianapolis: Merrill.

Gorz, André. 1967. *Strategy for labor: A radical proposal.* Translated by Martin A. Nicolaus and Victoria Ortiz. Boston: Beacon Press.

Gotham, Kevin Fox. 2002. *Race, real estate, and uneven development.* Albany: State University of New York Press.

Gottdiener, Mark. 1987. *The decline of urban politics: Political theory and the crisis of the local state.* Newbury Park, CA: Sage.

Gregor, Thomas. 1985. *Anxious pleasures: The sexual lives of an Amazonian people.* Chicago: University of Chicago Press.

Guthrie, Douglas, and Michael McQuarrie. 2005. Privatization and low-income housing in the United States since 1986. In *Research in Political Sociology: Politics, Class, and the Corporation*, ed. Harland Prechel, 14:15–51. Oxford: Elsevier Ltd.

Hahnel, Robin. 2005. *Economic justice and democracy: From competition to cooperation.* New York: Routledge.

Hamman, Rick. 1980/2002. *California Central Coast railways.* Repr. Santa Cruz: Otter B. Books.

Hartman, Chester. 2002. *City for sale: The transformation of San Francisco.* Berkeley: University of California Press.

Hartman, Chester, and Gregory Squires. ed. 2006. *There is no such thing as a natural disaster: Race, class, and Hurricane Katrina.* New York: Routledge.

Harvey, David. 1973. *Social justice and the city.* Baltimore: Johns Hopkins University Press.

———. 1976. Labor, capital and class struggle around the built environment in advanced capitalist countries. *Politics and Society* 6:265–295.

———. 1981. The urban process under capitalism: A framework for analysis. In *Urbanization and urban planning in capitalist society,* ed. Michael Dear and Allen J. Scott, 91–121. New York: Metheun.

———. 1982. *The limits of capital.* Chicago: University of Chicago Press.

———. 1985. *Consciousness and the urban experience: Studies in the history and theory of capitalist urbanization.* Oxford: Basil Blackwell.

Hays, Samuel. 1964. The politics of reform in the Progressive Era. *Pacific Northwest Review* 55:157–169.

Hess, Gary R. 1998. *Vietnam and the United States: Origins and legacy of war.* New York: Twayne Publishers.

Hinman, Keith. 1976. Redwood stands and booster 'vans: An economic history of Santa Cruz and its environs, 1870–1930. Santa Cruz: University of California, Santa Cruz.

Hoffman, William. 1976. Democratic response of urban governments: Empirical test with simple spatial models. *Policy and Politics* 4 (4): 51–74.

Humphrey, Craig R., Rodney A. Erickson, and Edward J. Ottensmeyer. 1989. Industrial development organizations and the local dependence hypothesis. *Policy Studies Journal* 17:624–642.

Hunter, Floyd. 1953. *Community power structure: A study of decision makers.* Chapel Hill: University of North Carolina Press.

Hutchinson, William H. 1972. *California: Two centuries of man, land, and growth in the Golden State.* San Francisco: Canfield Press.

Hyde, Harold, and Randall Jarrell. 2002. Harold A. Hyde: Recollections of Santa Cruz County. Santa Cruz: University of California, Santa Cruz.

Imbroscio, David. 2004. The imperative of economics in urban political analysis: A reply to Clarence Stone. *Journal of Urban Affairs* 26:21–26.

Jacobs, Jane. 1961. *The death and life of great American cities.* New York: Vintage Books.

Jezierski, Louise. 1990. Neighborhoods and public-private partnerships in Pittsburgh. *Urban Affairs Review* 26:217–249.

Johnson, Bob. 1982a. 1982: First shot for new coalition. *Santa Cruz Express,* December 30, 8.

———. 1982b. Right gets together. *Santa Cruz Express,* August 5, 8.

———. 1983a. City council sweepstakes. Santa Cruz Express, October 13, 10.

———. 1983b. High priced heat in city council race. *Santa Cruz Express,* November 3, 15–17.

———. 1983c. 1982: Rebuilding the Right. *Santa Cruz Express,* January 13, 8.

———. 1994. School of hard knocks. *Metro Santa Cruz,* October 6–12, 10–12.

Jones, Bryan. 1989. Why weakness is a strength: Some thoughts on the current state of urban analysis. *Urban Affairs Quarterly* 25:30–40.

Jones, Bryan, and Lynn Bachelor. 1984. Local policy discretion and the corporate surplus. In *Urban economic development,* ed. Richard Bingham and John Blair, 245–267. Newbury Park, CA: Sage.

Jones, Donna. 2000a. Cabrillo College opens. In *Santa Cruz County: A century,* ed. Don Miller, 35. Santa Cruz: Santa Cruz Sentinel.

———. 2000b. The fight for Lighthouse Field launched a political career. In *Santa Cruz County: A century,* ed. Don Miller, 47. Santa Cruz: Santa Cruz Sentinel.

———. 2000c. Regents take a shine to Santa Cruz after tour of land. In *Santa Cruz County: A century,* ed. Don Miller, 44. Santa Cruz: Santa Cruz Sentinel.

Kantor, Paul. 1995. *The dependent city revisited: The political economy of urban development and social policy.* Boulder: Westview Press.

Kantor, Paul, and Stephen M. David. 1988. *The dependent city: The changing political economy of urban America.* Glenview, IL: Scott, Foresman.

Kantor, Paul, Hank V. Savitch, and Serena Vicari Haddock. 1997. The political economy of urban regimes: A comparative perspective. *Urban Affairs Review* 32:348–377.

Krugman, Paul. 1994. *Peddling prosperity: Economic sense and nonsense in the age of diminished expectations.* New York: Norton.

Kuttner, Robert. 1997. *Everything for sale: The virtues and limits of markets.* New York: Knopf.

Lee, Paul A. 1992. *The quality of mercy: Homelessness in Santa Cruz, 1985–1992.* Santa Cruz: Platonic Academy Press.

Lefebvre, Henri. 1970. *La revolution urbaine.* Paris: Gallimard.

Leonhardt, David. 2007. A word of advice during a housing slump: Rent. *New York Times,* April 11, A1, C8.

Liebow, Elliot. 1993. *Tell them who I am: The lives of homeless women.* New York: Free Press.

Lindblom, Charles. 2000. *The market system: What it is, how it works, and what to make of it.* New Haven, CT: Yale University Press.

Lipset, Seymour Martin. 1963. *The first new nation: The United States in historical and comparative perspective.* New York: Basic Books.

Logan, John, and Harvey Molotch. 1987. *Urban fortunes: The political economy of place.* Berkeley: University of California Press.

———. 2007. *Urban fortunes: The political economy of place.* 2nd ed. Berkeley: University of California Press.

Logan, John, Rachel Whaley, and Kyle Crowder. 1997. The character and consequences of growth regimes. *Urban Affairs Review* 32:603–630.

Lydon, Sandy. 1985. *Chinese gold: The Chinese in the Monterey Bay region.* Capitola, CA: Capitola Book Company.

———. 1998. All that glitters. In *The Society of California Pioneers of Santa Cruz County,* ed. Stanley D. Stevens, 6–12. Santa Cruz: Museum of Art & History.

Lydon, Sandy, and Carolyn Swift. 1978. *Soquel Landing to Capitola-by-the-Sea.* Cupertino, CA: California History Center.

Lyndon/Buchanan Associates. 1990. Urban design plan phase 1: Recommendations for recovery plan. Berkeley: Lyndon/Buchanan Associates.

MacGregor, Bruce. 2003. *The birth of California narrow gauge: A regional study of the technology of Thomas and Martin Carter.* Stanford, CA: Stanford University Press.

Mann, Michael. 1986a. A crisis in stratification theory? Persons, households/families/lineages, genders, classes, and nations. In *Gender and stratification,* ed. Rosemary Crompton and Michael Mann, 42–56. Cambridge, UK: Polity Press.

———. 1986b. *The sources of social power: A history of power from the beginning to A.D. 1760.* Vol. 1. New York: Cambridge University Press.

———. 1993. *The sources of social power: The rise of classes and nation-states, 1760–1914.* Vol. 2. New York: Cambridge University Press.

Marouli, Christina. 1995. Women resisting (in) the city: Struggles, gender, class and space in Athens. *International Journal of Urban and Regional Research* 19:534–548.

Marshall, Carolyn. 2007. As college grows, a city is asking, 'who will pay?' *New York Times,* January 19, A12.

Massey, Douglas. 2005. *Return of the "L" word: A liberal vision for the new century.* Princeton, NJ: Princeton University Press.

McAdam, Doug. 1988. *Freedom summer.* New York: Oxford University Press.

McCord, Shanna. 2007a. For 100 years, relationship between city and Boardwalk has seen its ups and downs. *Santa Cruz Sentinel,* May 6, A-1.

———. 2007b. Santa Cruz may have option to buy Lighthouse Field. *Santa Cruz Sentinel,* August 7, A-1.

McFadden, Daniel. 1981. The importance of home-base support. *New Directions for Institutional Advancement* 12:35–47.

McMillan, John. 2002. *Reinventing the bazaar: A natural history of markets.* New York: W. W. Norton.

Mills, C. Wright. 1956. *The power elite.* New York: Oxford University Press.

Moberg, David. 1983. Surf City socialism. *In These Times,* January 26–February 1, 11–13, 22.

Molotch, Harvey. 1970. Oil in Santa Barbara and power in America. *Sociological Inquiry* 40:131–144.

———. 1972. *Managed integration: Dilemmas of doing good in the city.* Berkeley: University of California Press.

———. 1976. The city as a growth machine. *American Journal of Sociology* 82:309–330.

———. 1988. Strategies and constraints of growth elites. In *Business elites and urban development: Case studies and critical perspectives,* ed. Scott Cummings, 25–47. Albany: State University of New York Press.

———. 1999. Growth machine links: Up, down, and across. In *The urban growth machine: Critical perspectives, two decades later,* ed. Andrew E. G. Jonas and David Wilson, 247–265. Albany: State University of New York Press.

———. 2004. Spilling out (again). In *Enriching the sociological imagination: How radical sociology changed the discipline,* ed. Rhonda F. Levine, 87–90. Boston: Brill.

Molotch, Harvey, and Marilyn Lester. 2004. Accidents, scandals, and routines: Resources for insurgent methodology. In *Enriching the sociological imagination: How radical sociology changed the discipline,* ed. Rhonda F. Levine, 91–104. Boston: Brill.

Mumford, Lewis. 1961. *The city in history: Its origins, its transformations, and its prospects.* New York: Harcourt.

Norris, Floyd. 2007. The long life span of a housing downturn. *New York Times,* June 2, B3.

Nudelman/Hovee. 1992. Santa Cruz Factory Outlet Center opportunity evaluation. Portland, OR: Nudelman/Hovee—A Consulting Partnership.

Olin, L. G. 1967. Development and promotion of Santa Cruz tourism. Master's thesis, San Jose State University, San Jose, CA.

Orlando, Alverda. 1994. Davenport and its cement plant: The early years 1903–1910. *Santa Cruz County History Journal* 1:49–60.

Pateman, Carole. 1970. *Participation and democratic theory.* Cambridge, UK: Cambridge University Press.

Perry, Frank. 2007. *Lime kiln legacies: The history of the lime industry in Santa Cruz County.* Santa Cruz: Museum of Art & History.

Peterson, Paul. 1981. *City limits.* Chicago: University of Chicago Press.

Piven, Frances Fox. 2007. *Challenging authority: How ordinary people change America.* Lanham, MD: Rowman and Littlefield.

Piven, Frances Fox, and Richard A. Cloward. 1982. *The new class war: Reagan's attack on the welfare state and its consequences.* New York: Pantheon Books.

Porter, Ed. 2005. Coast hotel reflections. *Metroactive,* March 9. http://www .metroactive.com/papers/cruz/03.09.05/coast-0510.html (retrieved June 23, 2007).

Pring, George W., and Penelope Canan. 1996. *SLAPPs: Getting sued for speaking out.* Philadelphia: Temple University Press.

Rae, Douglas. 1971. *The political consequences of electoral laws.* New Haven, CT: Yale University Press.

Rast, Joel. 1999. *Remaking Chicago: The political origins of urban industrial change.* DeKalb: Northern Illinois University Press.

Reader, Phil. 1998. The "missing" pioneers. In *The Society of California Pioneers of Santa Cruz County,* ed. Stanley D. Stevens, 12–20. Santa Cruz: Museum of Art & History.

Renner, Tari, and Victor DeSantis. 1994. Contemporary patterns and trends in municipal government structures. In *The Municipal Yearbook 1993,* 57–69. Washington, DC: International City Managers Association.

Roberts, Alasdair. 1994. Demonstrating neutrality: The Rockefeller philanthropies and the evolution of public administration, 1927–1936. *Public Administration Review* 54 (3): 221–228.

Robertson, Kent A. 1990. The status of the pedestrian mall in American downtowns. *Urban Affairs Review* 26:250–273.

Rosato, Michaelangelo. 1990. Downtown should be designed for people. *Santa Cruz Sentinel,* December 9, A-19.

Rosenstone, Steven J., Roy L. Behr, and Edward H. Lazarus. 1996. *Third parties in America: Citizen response to major party failure.* 2nd ed. Princeton, NJ: Princeton University Press.

Rosenthal, Rob. 1994. *Homeless in paradise: A map of the terrain.* Philadelphia: Temple University Press.

Rotkin, Michael E. 1991. Class, populism, and progressive politics: Santa Cruz, California, 1970–1982. PhD diss., University of California, Santa Cruz.

———. 2005. We need to replace the old Dream Inn. *Metroactive,* March 9. http://www.metroactive.com/papers/cruz/03.09.05/coast-0510.html (retrieved June 23, 2007).

Sanday, Peggy. 1990. *Fraternity gang rape: Sex, brotherhood, and privilege on campus.* New York: New York University Press.

Sanders, Heywood. 1987. The politics of development in middle-sized cities: Getting from New Haven to Kalamazoo. In *The politics of urban development,* ed. Clarence Stone and Heywood Sanders, 182–199. Lawrence: University Press of Kansas.

Santa Cruz Redevelopment Agency. n.d. History of the Redevelopment Agency. http://www.ci.santa-cruz.ca.us/ra.

Schiesl, Martin J. 1977. *The politics of efficiency: Municipal administration and reform in America, 1800–1920.* Berkeley: University of California Press.

Schirmer, Robin. 1987. Tourism: Blight or blessing? *The Sun,* August 20, 16–17.

Schramm, Richard. 1987. Local, regional, and national strategies. In *Beyond the market and the state: New directions in community development,* ed. Severyn Bruyn and James Meehan, 152–170. Philadelphia: Temple University Press.

Schriftgiesser, Karl. 1960. *Business comes of age: The story of the Committee for Economic Development and its impact upon the economic policies of the United States, 1942–1960.* New York: Harper and Row.

Schwadron, Terry, and Paul Richter. 1984. *California and the American tax revolt: Proposition 13 five years later.* Berkeley: University of California Press.

Shaw, Randy. 1999. *Reclaiming America: Nike, clean air, and the new national activism.* Berkeley: University of California Press.

Shearer, Derek. 1982. How the progressives won in Santa Monica. *Social Policy* 12:7–14.

Shiller, Robert J. 2005. *Irrational exuberance.* 2nd ed. Princeton, NJ: Princeton University Press.

Smeeding, Timothy. 2008. Poorer by comparison: Poverty, work, and public policy in comparative perspective. *Pathways* 1:3–5.

Smith, Michael P. 1988. *City, state, and market: The political economy of urban society.* New York: Basil Blackwell.

Spain, Daphne. 1992. *Gendered spaces.* Chapel Hill: University of North Carolina Press.

Squires, Gregory, ed. 1989. *Unequal partnerships: The political economy of urban redevelopment in post-war America.* New Brunswick, NJ: Rutgers University Press.

Stewart, Frank. 1950. *A half century of municipal reform: The history of the National Municipal League.* Berkeley: University of California Press.

Stone, Clarence N. 1976. *Economic growth and neighborhood discontent: System bias in the urban renewal program of Atlanta.* Chapel Hill: University of North Carolina Press.

———. 1989. *Regime politics: Governing Atlanta, 1946–1988.* Lawrence: University of Kansas Press.

———. 1993. Urban regimes and the capacity to govern: A political economy approach. *Journal of Urban Affairs* 15:1–28.

———. 2005a. Looking back to look forward: Reflections on urban regime analysis. *Urban Affairs Review* 40:309–341.

———. 2005b. Rethinking the policy-politics connection. *Policy Studies* 26:241–260.

———. 2006. Power, reform, and urban regime analysis. *City and Community* 5:23–38.

Stone, Clarence N., and Heywood Sanders. 1987. Reexamining a classic case of development politics: New Haven, Connecticut. In *The politics of urban development,* ed. Clarence Stone and Heywood Sanders, 159–181. Lawrence: University Press of Kansas.

Story, Louise. 2008. No lull in mortgage pitches. *New York Times,* February 18, C-1.

Swanstrom, Todd. 1985. *The crisis of growth politics: Cleveland, Kucinich, and the challenge of urban populism.* Philadelphia: Temple University Press.

Szasz, Andrew. 1994. *EcoPopulism: Toxic waste and the movement for environmental justice.* Minneapolis: University of Minnesota Press.

Thompson, Jonathan. 2007. Progressive innovation in the 1970s United States: Madison, WI, and the Conference on Alternative State and Local Public Policies. *Progressive Planning* 170:23–25.

Tiebout, Charles. 1956. A pure theory of local expenditures. *Journal of Political Economy* 64:416–424.

U.S. Bureau of the Census. 1972, 1977, 1983. County and city data book. Washington, DC: U.S. Government Printing Office.

———. 1993. Population and housing characteristics for census tracts and block numbering areas, Santa Cruz, CA PMSA. CPH-3–294D. Washington, DC: U.S. Government Printing Office.

Venkatesh, Sudhir. 2006. *Off the books: The underground economy of the urban poor.* Cambridge, MA: Harvard University Press.

Vermosky, George [aka Nancy Matlock]. 1981a. Rx for victory. *Santa Cruz Express,* October 1, 8.

———. 1981b. Solid roots and local snoots. *Santa Cruz Express,* October 29, 6.

Vision Santa Cruz. n.d. Articles of incorporation. Santa Cruz: Vision Santa Cruz.

Vision Santa Cruz Board of Directors. 1990. Meeting minutes. May 21.

Wagner, David. 1993. *Checkerboard square: Culture and resistance in a homeless community.* Boulder: Westview Press.

Warner, Kee, and Harvey Molotch. 1995. Power to build: How development persists despite local controls. *Urban Affairs Review* 30:378–406.

———. 2000. *Building rules: How local controls shape community environments and economies.* Boulder: Westview Press.

Weber, Max. 1904/1958. *The Protestant ethic and the spirit of capitalism.* Repr. New York: Charles Scribner.

Weinstein, James. 1962. Organized business and the commission and manager movements. *Journal of Southern History* 28:166–182.

———. 1967. *The decline of socialism in America, 1912–1925.* New York: Monthly Review Press.

Whalen, Jack, and Richard Flacks. 1989. *Beyond the barricades: The sixties generation grows up.* Philadelphia: Temple University Press.

Whitt, J. Allen. 1982. *Urban elites and mass transportation.* Princeton, NJ: Princeton University Press.

Whyte, William H. 1988. *The city: Rediscovering the center.* New York: Doubleday.

Williams, Sidney, and Corwin Mocine. 1963a. *Downtown Santa Cruz sketch plan.* San Francisco: Williams and Mocine: City and Regional Planning.

————. 1963b. *General plan for future development.* San Francisco: Williams and Mocine: City and Regional Planning.

Wills, Catherine. 1981. Allusions of grandeur: Restoring the Santa Cruz Boardwalk. Master's thesis, University of California, Berkeley.

Wisconsin Historical Society. 2007. Milwaukee sewer socialism. In *Turning points in Wisconsin history.* http://www.wisconsinhistory.org/turningpoints/tp-043/ ?action=more_essay (retrieved June 2, 2008).

Wolff, Edward. 2000. Recent trends in wealth ownership, 1983–1998. Cambridge, MA: Jerome Levy Economics Institute.

————. 2004. Changes in household wealth in the 1980s and 1990s in the U.S. Working Paper No. 407, Jerome Levy Economics Institute, Bard College. http://www.levy.org (retrieved June 2, 2008).

Woodside, William. 1986. The future of public-private partnerships. In *Public-private partnerships: Improving urban life,* ed. Perry Davis, 150–154. New York: Academy of Political Science.

Wright, Phillip, and Jon Gundersgaard. 1976. The temperate Progressives of Santa Cruz, 1906–1916. In *Businessmen and municipal reform: A study of ideals and practice in San Jose and Santa Cruz, 1896–1916,* ed. David Eakins, 18–19. San Jose: Sourisseau Academy for California State and Local History.

Wright, Stephen C. 2001. Strategic collective action: Social psychology and social change. In *Blackwell handbook of social psychology: Intergroup processes,* ed. Rupert Brown and Samuel Gaertner, 409–430. Malden, MA: Blackwell.

Zald, Mayer, and Bert Useem. 1987. Movement and countermovement interactions: Mobilization, tactics, and state involvement. In *Social movements in an organizational society,* ed. Mayer Zald and John McCarthy, 247–272. New Brunswick, NJ: Transaction Books.

Zeitlin, Maurice. 1983. The American crisis: An analysis and modest proposal. In *The future of American democracy: Views from the Left,* ed. Mark Kann, 116–136. Philadelphia: Temple University Press.

Zweigenhaft, Richard, and G. William Domhoff. 2003. *Blacks in the white elite: Will the progress continue?* Lanham, MD: Rowman and Littlefield.

INDEX